Mindfulness and Its Discontents

Mindfulness and Its Discontents

Education, Self, and Social Transformation

DAVID FORBES

FERNWOOD PUBLISHING
HALIFAX & WINNIPEG

Editing: Jenn Harris
Cover design: Tania Craan
Printed and bound in Canada

Published by Fernwood Publishing
32 Oceanvista Lane, Black Point, Nova Scotia, B0J 1B0
and 748 Broadway Avenue, Winnipeg, Manitoba, R3G 0X3
www.fernwoodpublishing.ca

Fernwood Publishing Company Limited gratefully acknowledges the financial support of the Government of Canada, the Canada Council for the Arts, the Manitoba Department of Culture, Heritage and Tourism under the Manitoba Publishers Marketing Assistance Program and the Province of Manitoba, through the Book Publishing Tax Credit, for our publishing program. We are pleased to work in partnership with the Province of Nova Scotia to develop and promote our creative industries for the benefit of all Nova Scotians.

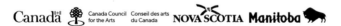

Library and Archives Canada Cataloguing in Publication

Title: Mindfulness and its discontents : education, self, and social transformation / David Forbes.
Names: Forbes, David, 1949- author.
Description: Includes bibliographical references and index.
Identifiers: Canadiana (print) 20190062347 | Canadiana (ebook) 20190062398 | ISBN 9781773631165 (softcover) | ISBN 9781773631189 (EPUB) | ISBN 9781773631172 (Kindle)
Subjects: LCSH: Mindfulness (Psychology) | LCSH: Self-realization. | LCSH: Education—Psychological aspects. | LCSH: Neoliberalism.
Classification: LCC BF637.M56 F67 2019 | DDC 158.1/3—dc23

Contents

Acknowledgements

Grateful thanks to colleagues from far and wide who resist the hype and see both the perils and promise of mindfulness as a social practice; they have provided valuable ideas and encouragement along the way: Manu Bazzano, Beth Berila, Jenn Cannon, John Downing, Kristina Eichel, Paula Haddock, Kevin Healey, Funie Hsu, Ilmari Kortelainen, Rachel Lilley, Ram Mahalingham, Nomi Naeem, Deborah Orr, Steven Stanley, Julia Wahl, Zack Walsh, Jeff Wilson. Special thanks to my fellow mindful crank and friend, Ron Purser, who has helped steer me on course in the "incorrect" direction.

Much appreciation for the support of my colleagues at Brooklyn College: Geri DeLuca, Linda Louis, Karel Rose, Deb Shanley, Peter Taubman, and Barbara Winslow; William Helmreich at City College; and in the CUNY Graduate Center Urban Education Doctoral program, Kostas Alexakos, Gillian Bayne, Christine Saieh — and Ken Tobin, whose support has been invaluable. Thank you to my students at both Brooklyn and the Grad Center who ground me and run with ideas in surprising and creative ways.

Members of my Brooklyn KM sangha kept me on the right emotional path during challenging times; gratitude to Stephanie Golden, Frannie Hoff, and Amy Selzer.

I am most fortunate to have worked with Candida Hadley, a gentle, skilful, and wise editor, at Fernwood Publishing. Jenn Harris is an extraordinary copyeditor and I feel very lucky to have had the benefit of her sure-handed expertise.

Family members Vicki Forbes and Richard Friesner, thank you for being there for me. And to Iris Lopez, to whom I dedicate this book, love always and forever, I'm beyond grateful for your love and support.

Non/Song of My Non/Self

> A child should be allowed to take as long as she needs for knowing everything about herself, which is the same as learning to be herself. Even twenty-five years if necessary, or even forever. And it wouldn't matter if doing things got delayed, because nothing is really important but being oneself. (Riding 1993: 15)

Since I was a child, I wanted to not just know and be myself, but to step outside and transcend myself. Who was I really? What did it mean when grown-ups told me to just be myself? Even when feeling conflicted and inauthentic, wasn't I still always myself? Later I pondered the question taken up by philosophers — what is the nature of the self? And by Buddhists — is there even a solid, unchanging self? The self I presented in everyday life often felt like a restrictive mask, one that I and others were supposed to wear and that few noticed and spoke (up) about. I was bothered by living in a consumerist society — being expected to have the right clothes and material goods — and couldn't help but see beneath and beyond the conventional surface of things. Was there something hidden about one's self? On our bookshelf at home was a first edition of *The Little Prince*, and like many children and adults I was drawn to its famous line: "It is only with the heart that one can see rightly; what is essential is invisible to the eye." For many of us the book stands as a critique of a careless, frenetic planet of "grown-ups" who overvalue and try to control matters of unimportance, in need instead of full, heart-seeing presence, whether for a friend, a sunset, or a single rose....

At the same time, I sensed that here, in this time and place into which I was born, this historical, contingent, messy, glorious world, lay all the possible and actual ways I could create and live a transcendent life with others. I saw this as a sensuous, spiritual, and active way to be. One of my literary heroes, Tom Joad in *The Grapes of Wrath,* took to heart what Casy the preacher told him: "Maybe … a fella ain't got a soul of his own, but on'y a piece of a big one" (Steinbeck 1977: 463). That big soul is all of human nature; Casy saw it as love itself. Tom Joad began to realize he was inseparable from others; he was able to let go of simply thinking about himself and his family and became dedicated to fighting for a decent and just world for all.

While I grew up with and continue to have many advantages of which I keep becoming more aware, through disposition and an upbringing in a progressive, internationalist, anti-racist household I developed a strong sense of social justice and empathy for the underdog. I have always felt that we must make the Earth a place that belongs to everyone — because it does; that mean and selfish people need to be stopped; that deluded ones (sometimes myself included) need to be educated; and that human-ity and the universe are made meaningful by some kind of absolute love that can't often be seen but is nonetheless right here with us. It was like the chicken soup Bessie Glass served her daughter Franny during her spiritual breakdown in J.D. Salinger's story about the Zen-inspired Glass siblings. Franny's exasperated (and exasperating) brother Zooey asked her, "How in *hell* are you going to recognize a legitimate holy man when you see one if you don't even know a cup of consecrated chicken soup when it's right in front of your nose?" (1961: 195). Virginia Woolf (1985: 72) wrote of the hidden yet self-evident design that links us and that we ourselves create: "Behind the cotton wool is hidden a pattern; that we — I mean all human beings — are connected with this; that the whole world is a work of art; that we are parts of the work of art … we are the words; we are the music; we are the thing itself."

As in Allen Ginsburg's *Howl,* I wanted to envision and bring forth the world as "Holy! … Everything is Holy!" I was drawn to Walt Whitman's *Song of Myself* and other ambitious Whitmanesque writings infused with cosmic consciousness that strive to evoke the mystical, hidden sacredness of prophetic love within an embodied, diverse, and democratic everyday life. These included Hart Crane's *The Bridge,* James Joyce's *Ulysses,* Ross Lockridge Jr.'s novel, *Raintree County,* Frans Masereel's wordless books, and William Blake's poem (and the English song), "Jerusalem": I will not cease from mental fight, till we have built Jerusalem *here*. Garcia Lorca, in "Ode to Walt Whitman" (1955: 119), asked, "Ah, filthy New York, / New York of cables and death. / What angel do you carry, concealed in your cheek?" — and I still want to know. I became intrigued with contemplative practices like Zen, which I felt could help me see the sacred within the ordinary world and realize that the self co-arises with everything else.

The counterculture — the anti-war, civil rights, feminist, and other progressive and resistance movements — felt Whitmanesque too. They provided expansive spaces for many of us that seemed sacred and prophetic in their own right, ones in which we believed we could create heaven on earth, a democratic fellowship of love, sensuality, social justice, and goodness for everyone. Martha Nussbaum (2003: 656–57) has since expressed for me what the Whitman tradition offers, a sensuous "new cosmology" that stands over "the cosmologies created by philosophical and religious systems; the finite moral individual, democratic citizen, equal to and among others, who contains the world within himself [sic] by virtue of his resourceful imagination and his sympathetic love."

Included in this cosmology is lightheartedness and humour; despite my seriousness there were enough times I could share in the sound of subversive laughter as a form of dissent from the lunacies of the day. Along with other smart-aleck Jewish boys, I was drawn to progressive satire that poked fun at the hypocrisies and absurdities of a self-centred, consumerist, racist, and militarist society and that hinted at a better one, often with moral outrage — *Mad* magazine, *Catch-22*, Lenny Bruce, Dick Gregory, *Dr. Strangelove*, Tom Lehrer, Jules Feiffer, Jean Shepherd, the Fugs, Frank Zappa. Even the humourless little prince was supposed to laugh; he gave his cosmic laughter as a gift to the narrator, who would hear it whenever he looked up at the stars. Years later, critical of the psychiatric industry's tendency to dismiss and pathologize people who question everyday life and struggle for authenticity, I wrote a satirical piece diagnosing the little prince as a paranoid misfit (Forbes 1987).

Like many others drawn to psychology and counselling, I studied and entered these fields because I wanted to help others heal, grow, and figure things out — while doing the same for myself. Along with these, critical thinking, seeing through bullshit, questioning — like Marx and the

Freudian left — a self-centred, alienating, capitalist society, and uncovering the hidden workings below the surface are still things I value.

At a later point in my life, though, my thinking hit a brick wall; I couldn't reason my way out of some of my own dilemmas. I discovered mindfulness as a helpful path in therapy and through the portal of some Buddhist teachings. There are various schools within Buddhism, and it changes as it encounters different societies and cultures, in particular the West. I've found, though, that they share a wisdom and moral framework intended to alleviate our basic unhappiness — the suffering that stems from thinking that we must cling to the idea of a solid, unchanging, isolated self. Overall, it's also a practice for developing one's mind, and a way of living in which we have compassion for and realize our interconnectedness with all beings and things.

With respect to mindfulness, its original place in Buddhism is that it is just one of eight paths toward helping us become free from self-attachment. The paths include ethical precepts that address proper conduct, such as non-violence, respectful speech, and making an honourable living based on universal love and compassion. In this context, mindfulness is a practice in which we remember or recall that we are not separate, unchanging selves but are undivided from each other. I was drawn to the particular mindful practice of insight (vipassana) meditation that originates in the Theravada tradition while also finding resonance with various aspects of Zen and Tibetan Buddhism.

Scientist Jon Kabat-Zinn extracted mindfulness from its place in the eightfold path of Buddhism and popularized it in the West. His secular definition has become the gold standard in therapy, medicine, education, and his own program, Mindfulness-Based Stress Reduction (MBSR): "paying attention in a particular way; on purpose, in the present moment, and non-judgmentally" (Mindfulnet.org. n.d.).

I found this definition unsatisfying: technical, vapid, devoid of any moral basis or wisdom, and lacking any critical social context, analysis, and direction. Consequently, because it has no moral or value-based foundation, I've seen that people can and do employ secular mindfulness in self-serving ways that reinforce a self-centred social system. Bhikkhu Bodhi (2011), a Buddhist scholar, makes this point when he says that the word *mindfulness* "has become so vague and elastic that it serves as a cipher into which we can read virtually anything we want."

I sought a deeper and broader sense of mindfulness. When I saw that mindfulness — a contemplative, non-conceptual endeavour, as I understood it — could both include and transcend critical thinking and contribute to an advanced stage of consciousness connected to everyone, I took to practising it. I watched my mind with both dispassion and compassion. After a while, I could begin to see thought patterns come and go. I became less attached to them; my sense of self expanded and evolved and I began to further question the existence of a private self, separate from others. Beyond practising mindfulness as a therapeutic aid I sought to see the hidden, mystical qualities of the world to which all the great wisdom traditions allude, which are bound up with universal compassion and a purpose greater than private gain, self-gratification, and ego attachment. In Buddhism one of the greatest ways to embody these qualities, even prior to being an awakened Buddha, is to become a bodhisattva, to commit to helping all sentient beings become free from delusion and suffering — all the while not investing any ego in the outcome. One hell of a challenge — one that appealed to my inner Catcher in the Rye, wanting to help kids (and everyone) from falling over the cliff.

For similar reasons I was drawn, too, to the Abrahamic prophetic traditions, the Judaic, Christian, and Islamic prophets' anger at selfishness, greed, and indifference toward others, and their demand to enter into history and actively speak out and turn toward social justice and universal love. Like those Buddhist monks who come down from a mountain monastery to offer wisdom to laypeople, prophets did not retreat into monastic life but took a universal moral stance that was of their time and society. They warned folks that if they continue to just think of themselves, turn away from caring about the needy, and lose their moral sense of universal purpose, then in the near future there will be negative consequences for everyone. The world is not finished, they proclaimed, it is not perfect as it is, but requires that humankind contribute to make it a loving home for all people.

An inspiring prophetic-flavoured piece for me was Clifford Odets' Marxist, Depression-era play *Awake and Sing!*, in which he brings to bear on members of a working-class Jewish family the prophet Isaiah's call to awaken from the deadness of their materialist addiction. The grandfather tells his grandson, "Boychick, wake up! Be something! Make your life something good … take the world in your two hands and make it like new. Go out and fight so life shouldn't be printed on dollar bills" (Odets 1979: 48).

Is this prophetic call to awaken from selfishness and greed, to let go of your attachment to your ego, to recognize our inseparability, much different than that of the Buddha ("one who is awake"), or of that mensch, Jesus (the small self has to die)? Distinctions granted, at their root, are a bodhisattva, a Marxist, and a mensch all that dissimilar and can we not draw parallels? There's a three-guys-walk-into-a-bar joke in there somewhere, I know. Another wake-up call: although co-opted as a generic Internet meme and by corporations as a way to entice millennials to buy stuff (Quart 2017), activist African-Americans coined the watchword phrase "stay woke" to caution others to remain aware of how the mainstream media lies or covers up stories about police brutality and other racial and social injustices — to be awake to what's going on. Dick Gregory, in an Instagram post some months before he died in 2017, posted, "To the young folks of all ethnicities I say #staywoke not as a catchphrase but as a lifestyle" (Megh Wright 2017).

What, then, links mindfulness with the prophetic? The prophetic is the demand that mindfulness itself wake up from its individualistic, self-absorbed approach and, as with Buddhism and the prophetic traditions, on emergent ground, embody a moral, social, universal, transformative stance and action in society for the sake of all beings.

My own thinking took a quantum leap when I came across the work of Ken Wilber and his Integral take on all things (2000, 2006, 2016). For years in my personal and professional life, I couldn't help but see how various aspects of any problem were interconnected and was never happy just attributing any one of them to be "the cause" — whether psychological, medical, spiritual, political, or cultural. This was and remains the fragmented tendency of specialized professional and academic fields; there are always missing pieces and frequent disinterest in trying to see the bigger picture, and it led me on a restless quest to put things together.

So it was gratifying to find a personal home in an Integral perspective, a meta-theory that sees itself as *post*-postmodern, not relativistic: while all perspectives may have partial truths, some are more true than others

(Wilber 2005). Integral insists on taking into account all the pieces of a puzzle or phenomenon from as many perspectives as possible, and to make explicit from which of those places we are seeing or speaking about something. These include conscious personal experience, models of self-development, science, culture, and social structures and systems. There are four basic perspectives to consider. One is from the "I," subjective, or first-person point of view: mine — what I feel, think, believe, and value. Another viewpoint is "It," an objective or a third-person one — what others observe about me or another from the outside, sometimes using scientific methods. A third is from the perspective of "We," as intersubjective, or second-person — how people, you and I and/or others, make and share meaning together, as in groups and cultures. The last one is interobjective or third-person plural, "Its" — seeing things from the standpoint of systems and structures such as societies, organizations, and natural and physical environments.

Through an Integral approach, I also became more attuned to developmental thinking and growth. It articulated my suspicion that reaching the experience of an awakened state through meditation is not enough. We also need to consider developmental stages of self-growth that frame this experience and all of our worldviews. We interpret the meaning of our states of consciousness through the filter of our stage of self-development. Developmental stages, along with the first-, second-, and third-person perspectives, is the second important Integral tool I use to gauge the perspective, or framework, from which I and others perceive and think about things. I will refer to some developmental models — in particular, those of Susanne Cook-Greuter, Robert Kegan, and Ken Wilber. All share the basic hierarchical order of egocentric, conventional, post-conventional, and integral levels of self-development.

From an early, egocentric perspective, a person can only see things from their own viewpoint: it's all about me. Someone who moves on to a conventional framework can now follow social rules, and identifies with and is loyal to their group, from which they value approval — *we* are right versus those "others." In the next, post-conventional stage, a person is autonomous; they can think for themselves beyond social norms and take the good of others beyond their group into account.

A still later stage is Integral, or universal; people at this stage come to see and understand the relative merits of all previous worldviews. They no longer identify their worldview with any one perspective, nor do they become attached to it. Instead, they identify with the well-being of all. At each stage, a person can take more perspectives from earlier ones into account; at the most evolved stage people experience complexity and freedom in terms of fluidity and can move between various viewpoints, states, and stages themselves.

I find developmental thinking useful since it can account for both secular and religious experiences, beliefs, and moral values. At the Integral stage of moral development, people recognize that they share underlying commonalities while they still see and appreciate unique differences. They can hold to a universal morality without having to identify with a particular religious tradition or set of principles. Ethics are built into and are an inextricable aspect of these later orders of consciousness; in those stages, ethics are no longer an external set of rules or values. A person at that last stage could be spiritual and/or religious, or not; it's the stage, the framework of consciousness, that is operative, not the particular religious or moral belief system.

So while Integral meta-theory questions attachment to just one viewpoint, it does so with the intent to develop, evolve, and awaken for everyone the greater meaning of the universe. While my approach to mindfulness is Buddhist-inspired, I am not an adherent of one kind of religious or spiritual belief, nor do I privilege subjective experience over all other perspectives. I seek to de-identify with systems of religions, beliefs, and thoughts themselves (isms), and I share some affinity with the vision of interspirituality (Johnson and Ord 2013). My aim is to reach that later, more encompassing, transcendent stage of self-development and with others experience the fluid, open, universal context of everyday living relations — well, when I'm not cussing out corporatized politicians on TV or just looking for a good taco truck in Brooklyn.

I use the Integral meta-model in critical, socially transformative ways (Patten and Morelli n.d.). I share an outlook with critical psychology, an approach that questions much of mainstream psychology itself (Parker 1999; Rose 1998). Critical psychology regards individuals as social rather than private, self-contained, and self-centred beings. It sees personal distress not as a privatized matter but as an aspect of troublesome social relations and forces. It argues that the idea of a solid, unchanging "self" is a social construct. It is critical of how various practices of self-regulation developed by the field of psychology operate to maintain the interests of those in power within neoliberal capitalism. And it sees people not as neutral, static objects of study but as dynamic, changing beings who engage in progressive, liberating, and mutually benefiting activities.

Overall, for me it has to be the whole embodied shmear — education and critical thinking; therapy and personal development; meaningful, expansive relationships; contemplative practice and awakening; and social analysis and action toward community and justice for everyone. And of course, good art, music, food, friendship, sex, and love....

Looking back, I would like to have practised a mindfulness inspired by wisdom traditions as a part of my own youthful growing up. As a counsellor educator, I began to share mindfulness with working-class urban youth and those who counsel and teach them, working to place it within their everyday lives, which were often marked by anger, fear, sadness, and pain (Forbes 2004). I was not content to see mindfulness as just a personal act performed inside one's head but rather as an overall practice that could help us reflect on, challenge, and change not just ourselves but the relationships, communities, and unjust social organizations of which we are a part.

In tracing the path of my interest in mindfulness, I admit to loosely following a trajectory that Jeff Wilson, in his thorough and insightful book, *Mindful America,* has identified in the lives of many mindfulness practitioners: "personal transformation, the desire to share with others, and the search for a better America." However, more like Wilson himself, and unlike many mindfulness boosters who, as he points out, think that "mindfulness is written into the teleological evolution of the human race" and will "save America" — it's become a civil religion, he says — I have needed to step back and examine mindfulness itself, how it is practised and employed within this society (2014: 177–79).

While I considered mindfulness in part to be a potential radical tool for liberation along with other activities — seeing how one's thoughts are conditioned by dominant messages from society, gaining insight into and letting go of self-centred patterns, even the self itself — I found that it had become not just secularized but profaned; not just unmoored from Buddhism but severed from any foundational moral worldview and enactment of wisdom, ethics, and social justice. I saw that there are well-intentioned people who are attached to their belief in mindfulness as much as to any belief system or practice, who don't think, let alone in critical terms, about its higher moral purposes and about the notion of the self, and who use it for self-aggrandizement and/or don't think to question the troublesome societal status quo, of which the self is a part, and change it for the better. These proponents, often with evangelical zeal, believe that if you just practise mindfulness you will become more caring and will even come to know how to act with skill in a caring way. They believe that if each of us just practises it, the world — with its various complex, stubborn, unjust social systems and institutions — will then change and turn into a more kind and compassionate place. The believers seldom acknowledge there is little to show for meditation's actual effects in education and therapy; strong objective evidence is lacking (Davis 2015; Horgan 2015). More to the point, Wilson (2014) showed that most mindfulness proponents, who are white and middle class, hold to an individualistic approach that maintains their privileged position, and through personal change alone are content to promote mindful capitalism and mindful consumerism. Sociologist Jaime Kucinskas (2018) further showed how the elite of the mindfulness movement, as a movement of individual change, became linked with a group of capitalist elites. In line with neoliberalism — the still-dominant system and belief that the market solves all problems, and that individuals by themselves can and should meet all their needs there — mindfulness has marketed itself and has become its own brand. Mindfulness, when it is unaware of its own social context, reinforces neoliberalism.

There is a need to critically contemplate the social forms taken by mindfulness itself. My colleagues and I have criticized — and have been criticized for doing so — "McMindfulness," the particular way mindfulness has become a self-serving, privatized, individualized, neoliberal practice that ignores social and cultural contexts, and thereby reinforces harmful, inequitable, and greed-promoting structures and institutions — which in turn contribute to the stress from which so many seek relief through mindfulness in the first place.

But social criticism in its own right can and should be defended; it can be turned on its head as a positive force. Following philosopher Michel Foucault, critique is not just to say things are not right, but to undercut what is considered self-evident and show that it no longer has to be accepted as such (Ng and Purser 2016). Social critique is valuable as a way to question conventional ideologies, beliefs, and practices. It can dislodge ordinary notions and create a space to consider how things in concrete ways could and should be more just and universal.

Criticism itself, then, is an active, a creative, and a constructive process:

> A critique … calls on both knowledge and perceptions to be able to differentiate, judge and navigate a concrete situation. To critique is not simply to equate expressions of distaste or to point derisively at something one dislikes. Creative critique is *Möglichkeitssinn* (a German word for the skilled sense to find and shape meaningful opportunities).… Critique gets activated by the phenomenon that needs critique. (Larsen 2014: 174; original italics)

Mindfulness requires an accompanying structural, cultural, moral, and developmental analysis. Others and I propose an evolving, critical and social mindfulness, one that converts critique into a constructive practice that is inseparable from embodied social activity and history (see Stanley, Edwards, Ibinarriaga-Soltero, and Krause 2018). Mindfulness becomes a conscious, liberating act that dismantles attachments to conditioned patterns of dominant beliefs. It opens up possibilities for change toward more evolved and mutually fulfilling relationships. Although critics are not required to come up with proper, predetermined alternatives on the spot, as some demand of us, I will suggest some future directions in the last section. To be clear: this is not a dismissal of secular mindfulness itself, nor is it an insistence that we return to Buddhist mindfulness *per se*; rather, it is a critique of how educators and others employ it, often unintentionally, in ways that reinforce a neoliberal system of self-centredness (see Arthington 2016). The aim is to encourage mindfulness educators to think critically about their practice, to transform it and take a more radical, informed, universal perspective.

Is this a jeremiad, an angry kvetch that just points a finger at people's moral failures? While it is fuelled by anger at injustice and takes a universal, democratic stance, I don't claim to speak for or from any ultimate source of authority and try to avoid self-righteousness. The prophetic tradition, though, calls for speaking and acting on what is wrong and what needs to be made right in a particular time and place, and this is one of those instances. In a prophetic voice, Reverend William Barber says that those who fight by themselves for an inclusive society need to come together and "shock the heart" of the U.S. with an "army of moral defibrillators" (Wootson Jr. 2017); perhaps this book can join the current.

I engage here in critical, moral, constructive thinking about mindfulness itself and its relationship to education, to the self, and to social transformation. The book is fuelled by the argument that we should practise mindfulness as a personally and socially transformative activity as we engage in and create our own history. It is not a Cartesian reflection of the private mental processes of an isolated or alienated individual out for personal gain or happiness, separated from one's body, nature, culture, and society. I reject the Cartesian assumption of a mind–body split that undergirds much of the way proponents present mindfulness today. Nor do I accept the belief of many mindfulness educators that we each already know what is best for us, and that if each person just practises mindfulness the world will become a peaceful, happy place for all. These beliefs ironically reinforce the values and social structure of an individualistic, alienating society. They have led proponents to use mindfulness as an instrument to gain self-centred skills in stress reduction, self-promotion, self-enhancement, hedonic happiness, and corporate profits and productivity over the common good. By encouraging people to look solely to themselves and to look within, in alignment with neoliberal values, they have allowed mindfulness to contribute to a therapeutic adjustment toward an unhealthy society within schools, corporations, the workplace, the military, and elsewhere.

Instead, mindfulness needs to be an inseparable aspect of an embodied social process that includes and transcends the self by letting go of our attachment to it; that critiques the neoliberal, corporate-based status quo — and the way it uses mindfulness — in order to create a moral, democratic life that is developmentally fulfilling for each person, sentient being, the Earth, and the universe itself.

Section I

Our Mindful Problem

1

A Fateful Deal

Not long ago, Jon Kabat-Zinn sought universal peace and love. He discovered the dharma, wise Buddhist teachings aimed at ending human suffering, which he felt rang true. Kabat-Zinn wanted to secularize, or popularize, the dharma, to make the teachings accessible to many people. He wanted to be the one to bring the dharma to the West.

What is the dharma? It includes the practice of mindfulness; the study of the insubstantial nature of the self and the impermanence and interdependence of all things, or groundlessness; the moral demand to live an ethical and compassionate life in which one helps free all suffering beings; and the quest to let go of self-attachment and to awaken to realize the non-duality of the universe.

The West, via capitalism, its dominant economic system (so far), generates a certain kind of suffering. It creates hungry selves who are never satisfied with their personal brand and who always feel insecure. It then tortures them to search without end for a better brand for their non-existent selves and more stuff for their unattainable security.

Asian immigrants to North America have been practising Buddhism since they began arriving in larger numbers in the nineteenth century (Hsu 2017), and the Beat writers popularized Zen in the 1950s. Yet there was limited mainstream interest in Buddhism, let alone in "mindfulness," in the United States until the 1970s, when Kabat-Zinn and others popularized it (Wilson 2014: 13–42). In the late nineteenth/early twentieth century, Burmese monk Ledi Sayadaw helped to reinvent the Theravada tradition and make mindfulness meditation accessible to laypeople. He simplified the practice as a way to preserve Buddhism from British colonialism and started a lineage that influenced Kabat-Zinn and his peers, who simplified it further.

Kabat-Zinn's effort to bring the dharma to the West in simplified form was a big deal. The result, however, was that the meaning of the dharma was sacrificed. And the West got to keep things as they are: lots of hungry selves in search of better brands and more stuff for their unattainable security.

Kabat-Zinn knew that in the West people only accept things if they are stamped with the secular authority of science and medicine. He knew that he wasn't going to succeed if he talked in terms of a foreign religion, or any religion for that matter. He also knew that people in the West want to feel good, get ahead, and get a better brand. They like to see themselves as customers in charge of what they consume. They want to be able to purchase a spiritual product or commodity if they feel like it. And they want it now. Jeff Wilson says that they want the meditation practice "on demand, to provide them with health, and peace, and calmness. But they don't want the supposed downsides of religion, such as dogmas, rules, being beholden to others, power differentials, belief in things that don't exist, and all this" (Schulson 2016).

So, in order to secularize the dharma and make it accessible to the West, Kabat-Zinn threw most of it out. He converted and simplified the language. He took one of its pieces, mindfulness, that he believed would help the West, and made it his cornerstone. Kabat-Zinn placed it into a Western medical and therapeutic model and called it Mindfulness-Based Stress Reduction (MBSR). He promoted the model as a technique to reduce stress, improve health, and strengthen one's personal brand. To give it authority he provided scientific research that claimed it "worked." Toward what? Reducing stress, feeling better. Buddhism was psychologized and medicalized; it went from a practice for awakening to the insights of the dharma to a science-based coping method to deal with personal stress (Cohen 2010). Of course, many people ate it up. After all, almost everyone is under stress and wants to chill. Everyone wants a quick technology backed up by science that helps them feel good and improve their personal brand. The technology of mindfulness was born. It became a success, more popular than free kale, quinoa, and kombucha at a hipster health fair.

Kabat-Zinn believed that he had captured the essence of the Eastern teachings, mindfulness as an accessible technology. He jettisoned the religious baggage of Buddhism — the stuff about karma and hungry ghosts, but also the body of ethics and wisdom in which mindfulness is embedded. He cut out the insights about the nature of the self and the deeper causes of suffering. He secularized mindfulness and made it a service. Jeff Wilson (2014) says, "The secularization is explicitly designed to make [mindfulness] more marketable. One secularizes in order to better commodify, such that one can more effectively market to a wide range of people, or simply a not-yet-served niche of people." So, mindfulness was not just brought to the West, it reinforced the neoliberal market values of the West. It became a marketable commodity itself that helps you destress — so you can return to more stressful striving. You can then improve your personal brand and become a more marketable commodity yourself.

For Kabat-Zinn, mindfulness was no longer about the Buddhist dharma. He was right. For Kabat-Zinn and his disciples, mindfulness "is not about Buddhism, but about *paying attention*" (Szalavitz 2012, italics added). Is MBSR the dharma then? Does it include moral guidelines and wisdom about the nature of things? Does eating ZenSoy pudding give you enlightenment?

Paying attention is something fundamental and significant; what we choose to focus on is an intimate practice that says who we are, what we value, even love. Attention is a part of our ability to develop important attachments with children and to cultivate empathy, friendship, and intimacy (Nixon 2018; Taffel 2014). Author and linguistic scholar Aviya Kushner finds that in Hebrew, Aramaic, and Arabic, to pay attention generally translates as to "set your heart upon" (Kushner 2018).

However, today attention itself has become "both a scarce resource and a commodity" (O'Donnell 2016: 31). We can't discuss attention without reference to society, and to the attention economy. This refers to the way Silicon Valley corporations such as Google, Facebook, Apple, Spotify, and others vie to capture our attention and loyalty through "invasive screen-based technologies" and social media (Doran 2018a; O'Donnell 2016: 34). These corporations are driven to hold our attention in addictive ways for as long as possible in order to increase their revenues by selling profitable ads. But this aggravates our lack of autonomy, passivity, and impoverished social interactions; in families, the fragmented attention of parents creates insecure attachments with many children that contributes to childhood and adolescent anxiety and depression (Nixon 2018; Taffel 2014).

In critical social terms, then, we could choose to see the inseparability of the individual and society, and the way society commodifies our attention. We could reflect on and practise mindful attention as a way to identify, critique, and resist the attention economy and those who profit from capturing our attention. In schools, attention becomes a question of student conformity and social control. When so much of schooling invokes boredom against which many children rebel by becoming inattentive, we can see why schools want to employ mindfulness as a way to get them to pay attention. Rather than understanding the experience of bored children and advocating for them against the school system, psychotherapist Bruce Levine (2013) points out that mental health professionals have a fundamental bias "for interpreting inattention and noncompliance as a mental disorder." But none of these issues is relevant to Kabat-Zinn's vague, neutral notion of attention; nobody is interested in going there.

Or, at a more profound level, we can consider that mindfulness as attention means to become aware of the groundlessness of all existence — non-dwelling awareness itself, the absolute — and practise mindfulness as a way to attend to this deeper meaning. No interest here, either, though — since there's no longer any wisdom tradition to explain what this means, no distinction is made between attention to everyday stuff and this deeper state of awareness.

So without taking a stand on the meaning of attention, whether in critical, socially engaged terms or in a fundamental (ontological) sense, mindfulness becomes a scientific technique for paying attention in the relative everyday world. It is now available to all and suitable for any purpose. Contrary to the dharma, it helps you enhance your self, not let go of it. You can pay attention to anything your ego wants. Paying attention becomes the proverbial hammer in search of things to bang. Mindfulness, paying attention, is now a tool to reduce stress in order to better your personal brand. Kabat-Zinn leaves questions of ethics to the quality of the training and background of each individual MBSR instructor. Since no belief system is necessary to ground ethics, he thinks that it is "the personal responsibility of each person engaging in this work to attend with care and intentionality to how we are actually living our lives, both personally and professionally, in terms of ethical behavior" (2011: 294). It follows, too, that there's no need to stand against a troublesome attention economy that captures and exploits our attention as consumers for marketable, profitable purposes.

This is technical neutrality, which amounts to moral and social relativism. Neuroscientist Tracy Dennis, the lead researcher on a mindfulness project designed to help troubled high school students better regulate their attention and emotions, sums it up like this:

> At its core, I believe that mindfulness is a technology of consciousness. The power and efficacy of this technology are due to its ability to shift our perception of ourselves and others. This shift in perception in turn shapes how we regulate our emotions in response to what happens in our minds and in the world. (The Congressman: Brainwave 2013)

As a result, MBSR, unlike Buddhism or any profound tradition, lacks a moral foundation. Its technical, neutral definition, lack of principles, and absence of any critical insight into social context opens up mindfulness to a host of self-centred and greed-driven uses. There's mindful social marketing. Mindful profits. Even mindful soldiers who practise mindfulness before they are deployed to go out and shoot people (Stanley 2014). In the aforementioned project with troubled teens, whom the mindfulness researchers told to meditate to regulate themselves, the onus was on the students to make any changes in their lives. The researchers set out to show that the neuroscience of mindfulness would alter the students' minds and lead to positive emotions (Changing Minds at Concord High School n.d.). This medicalized, individualist approach blocks out critical thinking about negative emotions. It skips over asking why the students even have them. It remains oblivious to the idea that socially organized alternatives to school alienation are possible — for example, if students, adults, and the school community came together to critically, mindfully discuss, oppose, and transform inequitable power structures and school policies in order to establish more meaningful and fulfilling activities.

As these things go, Kabat-Zinn was not quite satisfied with the deal he'd made with the West. He wanted to have it all. He missed some of that old-time religion. So he pulled a neat trick and went further. He whitewashed the dharma and appropriated its original meaning: he declared that his brand of scientific mindfulness is "not different in any essential way from Buddhadharma" and called it the "universal dharma" (2011: 296). MBSR, he said, is a new lineage (Bazzano 2015). The dharma doesn't belong to Buddhism, he claimed; it is timeless human nature. Kabat-Zinn took over the meaning of the dharma, colonized it, stripped it of its history and cultural tradition, declared it to be in the public domain — and claimed to know how to teach it. In this way he got to have it both ways. He got to keep the link with the exotic East and its spiritual caché without the mystifying baggage of religion. He got to keep both science and the dharma, or so he believed. MBSR is now declared a scientific technology derived from human nature, the universal dharma. People were impressed with that.

Let's look first at the contradiction of claiming that mindfulness is the universal dharma. It's natural, proponents claim; it's scientific, everybody has mindfulness inside. "Buddhism holds no exclusive claim to it," Saki Santorelli says; "Mindfulness is awareness itself — the knowing capacity that we consider the central feature of our humanness." He also says that "mindfulness is a technology — an elegant means of investigating what it means to be alive" (2016: 66–67). There's that fall back on a scientific, neutral technology, toward supposed universal human values. You have the opportunity to "see things as they are, unclouded by the usual filters of conditioning and culture." You now are better able to make "wise and appropriate choices." Pay attention and you will naturally think and do the right thing. The source of wisdom is found inside of you, in a timeless, culture-free zone, removed from things like, say, having a privileged background or favourable life conditions. So what are those wise and appropriate choices, and who says they are? Humanness ... what it means to be alive ... things as they are. Mindfulness becomes naturalized, de-contextualized: it's human essence.

Do these sound satisfying to you? What do they mean in everyday terms? Nobody talks about that. That's because there are no ethics and wise viewpoint to frame the intention or object of the awareness in the actual world. Nothing is left that resembles the original dharma, or for that matter, any other moral worldview. It's all just "universal" human nature, and also just a "technology." Not only is that not dharma, that's not science. It's more like faith — faith that attention leads to kindness, compassion, and wise or appropriate choices, whatever those mean, in actual, everyday neoliberal society. It's faith that there are things "just as they are" you can see with the aid of mindfulness, unfiltered by our everyday meanings and culture. But how can you "see things as they are" beyond the "filters of culture" if you, like everyone else, are born into a culture that filters meaning? You can do so only if you're a true believer.

The belief in mindfulness as something universal leads Kabat-Zinn to squirm whenever he's confronted with actual "things as they are" — like racial injustice and white privilege. To choose to see everything in a haze of universality is to gloss over actual differences in social context. He would rather speak in nice, fuzzy abstractions about humanity. In a dialogue with Angela Davis, Kabat-Zinn frames his statements about ending social injustice in vague, globalized terms that float above distinctions about race and privilege. He says that mindfulness is a "transformative practice" that is capable of moving society in a more 'human" way and "that we need something that speaks to all humanity." Angela Davis is skeptical that mindfulness can assist in the necessary structural transformations of racist society; she asks him to explain who "we" are, since she finds it "difficult to say 'our' actions"; Kabat-Zinn laughs and says, "yeah … that may be my white privilege? I don't know?" (Spirit Rock Meditation Center 2015).

Mindfulness, he says elsewhere,

> is a way of being. I have a lot of faith that if people just learn how to be in the present through simple mindfulness meditation, then the practice does the work of transformation and healing. We do not need to do it for them. People are so creative and intrinsically intelligent that given a chance, they perceive the truth within their own experience. "When I get attached to something, I suffer," they realize, "and when I don't get attached, I don't." (Boyce 2016)

There's that clear affirmation of faith: by just learning how to "be in the present," the "practice does the work." It comes wrapped in a moral void, a vague "way of being" that's left up to each individual, who will find their own truth.

Because MBSR tries to have it both ways — it's secular science, it's universal Buddhist — some defenders tip to the Buddhist side. One MBSR trainer, posting on a Facebook mindfulness site, affirms his faith and sees MBIS [Mindfulness-Based Interventions] as radically transformed Buddhist practices. He believes that by observing the habitual reactivity of the mind we can recognize the way to be free from that reactivity, and then respond from that place of freedom: in other words, he says, MBIS are the Four Noble Truths. The Four Noble Truths! This sleight-of-hand reduces the Buddhist dharma, a 2,500-year old doctrine, practice, and ethics intended to end basic suffering, to the technology of observing and changing your habits through attention. That's like saying the CliffsNotes for Hamlet are the same as the original Shakespeare, just radically transformed.

To claim MBSR is the universal dharma — well, of course people began to talk. Some members of other religions, some who thought it worth keeping the separation of church and state, saw MBIS as a way to smuggle in a religious tradition, like the Trojan Horse. In fact some of Kabat-Zinn's followers themselves are glad to embrace "stealth Buddhism" — heck, let's bring in the Trojan Horse — to schools, the military, and corporations. They think that by doing so, by introducing what they think is the dharma, these institutions and society as a whole will become nicer places with better people. Not only is there no evidence that this works; it's unethical to call something the dharma when it isn't, and it's unethical to not tell people up front that what you are teaching them is nevertheless from a certain religion (Brown 2016; 2014b).

It's not surprising, then, that wanting to have MBSR both ways has come back to bite Kabat-Zinn and his proponents. In 2016, a parent brought suit against a public school district that was teaching an MBSR-based program. A legal consultant firm argued that the program, despite its attempts to cast itself in secular terms, was still Buddhist (National Center for Law and Policy 2016).

To sum up Kabat-Zinn's contradiction that mindfulness is not Buddhist but at the same time is Buddhist: he says that mindfulness "is not about Buddhism, it's about paying attention." But he also says: mindfulness itself is "the universal dharma" — that is, the teachings of the Buddha. With respect to ethics, British psychologists William Van Gordon and Mark D. Griffiths, in noting Kabat-Zinn's ambiguity about whether MBSR is

Buddhist, point out that mindfulness in Buddhism "is practised in the context of a comprehensive set of guiding ethical and spiritual principles" whereas in MBSR, ethics are embodied solely in the Hippocratic oath (Van Gordon and Griffiths 2015). To add to the confusion, just because you declare something as true does not make it so: claiming that his version of mindfulness is the universal dharma does not make it a fact.

In wanting it both ways — it's not about Buddhism, it's the universal dharma — mindfulness ends up neither fish nor fowl. As a result, it gets it in the neck from both sides. To Buddhists it is a watered-down, secular program that lacks depth of meaning; to secularists it is too religious, too Buddhist. To claim that MBSR is Buddhist and then ban it from schools is a supreme irony. When MBSR tries to smuggle in what it thinks is the dharma, it first deludes itself — the claim that MBSR is the universal dharma is not true. Then it gets caught doing something it hasn't done — by the secularists who object to it smuggling in what they (and some of the MBSR folks) think is actual Buddhism.

But mindfulness programs are not Buddhism. They do not have Buddhism's profound practice of examining the nature of the self and of moral values, of studying and doing what is right, and of looking at what wisdom means in the fullest sense of non-duality. Unlike Buddhism it does not bring the self into question; it has no moral worldview; and it is not a soteriology — a way out of human suffering — just a way to help the self cope and adjust.

For example, MBSR introduces the famous raisin exercise as a way to demonstrate being in the "here and now" through mindfulness. Instead of mindlessly popping a raisin in your mouth, you are asked to mind-fully employ your five senses in a slow, deliberate way to focus on and experience the raisin. You feel its texture between your fingers; smell the raisin; listen to the sound as you hold it up to your ear and squeeze it; then experience the various taste sensations from placing it in your mouth, chewing it deliberately, and finally swallowing it. In this way you come to know the sensations of the raisin in the present.

While being in the present can relieve you of some troublesome thinking, with the raisin exercise you gain no self-transformation, no insight into the fundamental nature of the self and the deeper cause of your suffering in everyday life. Suffering, Buddhists say, has to do with the temporality of change, and with trying to cling to a self that lacks a permanent and separate identity; it's something to face, not something from which to escape (Purser 2015; Heffernan 2015).

Of course, neither is there interest in forming any insight into the social nature of the raisin: reflecting on the farm workers' lives and the work conditions of those who grew and harvested the raisin as part of corporate agribusiness. Nor of meditating on how truckers transported the raisin from the fields, or considering the practices of the corporate advertisers and supermarkets that profit from the sale of the raisin. This mindfulness is an individualized, privatized endeavour. It is not equipped with a conceptual framework that can lift the veil of mystification about the social conditions under which the raisin got there, no attention toward seeing past the delusion of the raisin as a commodified entity abstracted from its interlocking social context.

Sure enough, though, the secularists who object to MBSR on religious grounds have a point — after all, Kabat-Zinn and his supporters call it the universal dharma. A kind of Buddhism Lite, it ends up as a technology of attention that might get you to relax … and simply adjust to conventional roles, be nice (compassionate), and make socially approved choices.

In that one case, school administrators banned mindfulness from the school day because it is supposedly Buddhist. However, if mindfulness programs in the schools were Buddhist, or at least took a strong moral stand, they might oppose much of the work of public schools themselves. They might instead promote emotional insight, meaningful learning, and kindness rather than allowing and encouraging inequality, stressful competitive individualism, and the self-regulation that keeps things in place for those in power.

In the deal over mindfulness, the capitalist West is winning. As it stands, mindfulness ends up reproducing the very things that drive people to seek relief — but it helps people to better adjust to those things. When Kabat-Zinn defined mindfulness as a technology of attention free of a moral understanding of social context, it served to strengthen rather than challenge the greedy neoliberal mentality of self-promotion and corporate productivity. When he declared mindfulness to be the universal dharma, he both gutted the dharma's meaning of ego dis-attachment and exposed mindfulness to the charge of smuggling religion into public schools. The

West gets to keep running its endless, competitive game of self-satisfaction and security-seeking without having to give up its core beliefs.

Of course, there are people who like mindfulness the way it is. It appeals to those who need to de-stress from the exhaustive, relentless pursuit of their personal brand and unattainable security — so they can better resume the exhaustive, relentless pursuit of their personal brand and unattainable security. Nothing in mindfulness questions and resists the individualistic, commodified status quo. Nothing in it leads in practical terms toward a transformative, evolved society or planet. It lacks a meaningful framework that links the personal with the social; it is an orphan in search of a moral worldview.

Both gambits — mindfulness as science and mindfulness as universal dharma — are two sides of the same bent coin. As it stands, mindfulness is neither. At best, it's a new hybrid practice, some of which some people find to be instrumental in psychotherapy, self-help, regulating behaviour, and medical treatment.

The issue is not about secular versus religious practices. The issues are: what kind of society and individuals do we want? What kind of education and children do we want? What kinds of values do we stand for? If we want personal and creative consciousness to evolve and if we want to practise universal care, can we embed mindfulness within a more meaningful vision and framework?

2

McMindfulness and Neoliberalism: A Prophetic Critique

On the Internet is an image of Ronald McDonald, the McDonald's fast food icon, seated in a lotus position. A number of Thai Buddhists see this as disrespectful to the Buddha (Coconuts Bangkok 2012). Others are rightly critical of the colonialist and harmful cultural appropriation of Buddhism by the West, and the lack of regard for Asian Buddhism in the U.S. and Canada (Hsu 2017). Engaged Buddhists and I are critical of McMindfulness, which this image can represent. Meanwhile, Jon Kabat-Zinn altogether denies that McMindfulness exists (Shonin 2015).

McMindfulness

The technical, neutral definition of mindfulness and its relativist lack of a moral foundation has opened up secular mindfulness to a host of dubious uses, which are now called out by its critics as McMindfulness (Purser and Loy 2013; Hyland 2017). McMindfulness occurs when mindfulness is used, with intention or unwittingly, for self-serving and ego-enhancing purposes that run counter to both Buddhist and Abrahamic prophetic teachings to let go of ego attachment and enact skilful compassion for everyone. Instead of relinquishing the ego, McMindfulness promotes self-aggrandizement; its therapeutic function is to comfort, numb, adjust, and accommodate the self within a neoliberal, corporatized, militarized, individualistic society based on private gain.

While the term *McMindfulness* had been used before, Ron Purser's and David Loy's article, "Beyond McMindfulness," published online in 2013 (July 1), caused a defensive stir. The authors argued that a "stripped-down, secularized technique" of mindfulness not just fails to aid in awakening people and organizations from "the unwholesome roots of greed, ill will and delusion, it is usually being refashioned into a banal, therapeutic, self-help technique that can actually reinforce those roots." McMindfulness aims to reduce private individual stress and does not admit to any interest in the social causes of stress. In corporations, "mindfulness training has wide appeal because it has become a trendy method for subduing employee unrest, promoting a tacit acceptance of the status quo, and as an instrumental tool for keeping attention focused on institutional goals." Mindfulness, they argued, needs to reclaim an ethical framework that goes beyond privatized adjustment to a society based on market capitalism that contributes to stress and other sources of unhappiness.

McMindfulness practices psychologize and medicalize social problems. Rather than a way to attain awakening toward universal love, it becomes a means of self-regulation and personal emotional control. McMindfulness is blind to neoliberalism's present moral, political, and cultural context. As a result, it does not grasp that an individualistic, therapized, and commodified society is itself a major generator of social suffering and distress. Instead, the best it can then do, ironically, is to offer to sell us back an individualistic, commodified "cure" — mindfulness — to reduce that distress. Meditation apps monetize mindfulness: Headspace's revenue is estimated at $50 million a year and the company is valued at $250 million (Barclay 2017). These enterprises cater to Big Business, with which they have a long history (Wieczner 2016; Goldberg 2015). Silicon Valley has a ball producing profitable, hi-tech, marketable mindfulness apps as "brain hacks" despite an utter lack of evidence that they are helpful (Ehrenreich 2015). In New York, for-profit meditation studios like MNDFL and Inscape have sprung up and are booming.

Neoliberalism

McMindfulness reinforces neoliberalism, still the predominant ideology and policy today. (Giroux 2014a; McGuigan 2014). Neoliberalism is an ideology and political rationality that promotes individual competition for and the purchasing of all of one's needs through the market — which, through austerity policy, replaces the structures and even the concepts of social institutions and the public good. British writer and activist George Monbiot (2016: 66) defines it thus:

> Neoliberalism sees competition as the defining characteristic of human relations. It redefines citizens as consumers, whose democratic choices are best exercised by buying and selling, a process that rewards merit and punishes inefficiency. It maintains that "the market" delivers benefits that could never be achieved by planning.

This ideology promotes a privatized, individualistic, market-based worldview and structure. Its ideology posits that stress, lack of attention, and reactivity are problems that lie within the individual, not society, societal institutions, or social relations. The individual alone is responsible for overcoming these presumed deficits and competing with others. This promotion of competition, upon which capitalism depends, is also a way to keep people divided and under control, by opposing each other. In neoliberalism, one must become a perpetual self-entrepreneur and consumer of choice. As a result, those constricted by the increasing lack of social mobility foist much blame upon themselves and others.

Neoliberalism denies that societal structures and institutions exist — in Margaret Thatcher's words, "there is no such thing as society." Neoliberals claim that austerity is necessary; those who are well off receive tax cuts that reduce social spending while the rest of us are told to do more with less. From this standpoint, therapeutic mindfulness fits in well with the neoliberal agenda. It serves as a preventative cost-cutting measure (less remedial therapy needed, more self-regulation), which makes it popular with health care providers — for example, the National Health Service in the United Kingdom (Mindful Nation UK 2015).

The denial of society has troubling implications for seeing and opposing social inequities such as racism; neoliberalism dismisses racism as a social, structural, and institutional injustice, and in obscuring its systemic nature, it thereby weakens the need to fight it. In claiming that everything is a matter of individualized choice, neoliberals believe that each individual is responsible for their own success and failure (Davis 2013; Robbins 2004). They dismiss any talk of structural inequality as political correctness. Although racial neoliberalism and unequal structural power relations still exist, they disappear as topics from public discourse and policy (Enck-Wanzer 2011). The individualistic focus of neoliberalism and the negation of society contributes to a therapeutic culture, a turning inward and away from societal relations, in which the solution to problems is to adjust, manage, and market the self; social problems become psychologized (Illouz 2008; Rakow 2013).

McMindfulness and Neoliberalism

By negating and downplaying actual social and political contexts and focusing on the individual — or, more so, the individual's brain — McMindfulness interventions ignore seeing our inseparability from all others. They ignore seeing our inseparability from inequitable cultural patterns and social structures that affect and constitute our relations, and thereby ourselves. McMindfulness thus forfeits the moral demand that follows this insight: to challenge social inequities and enact universal compassion, service, and social justice in all forms of human endeavour. Without a critical account of the social context of neoliberal individualism, mindfulness as a self-focused practice and discourse minimizes social critique and change, and contributes to keeping existing social injustices and inequitable power structures intact. With regard to those who write about mindful politics, Jeff Wilson (2014: 185) noted, "Most mindfulness authors pin their hopes on a mindful capitalism as sufficient to bring about the kinder, wiser society they envision." There is nothing revolutionary about the so-called Mindful Revolution. Chris Goto-Jones (2013) says, "The revolution doesn't require any particular change in values or economic systems…. For a revolution this movement shows remarkable conservatism. The leading voices make no demands on followers. They need not become activists or participate in political struggle." The change is through individual psychology alone.

Much of secular mindfulness is about helping one become a happy self, individualistically; it's about improving *my* happiness, well-being, and productivity with minimal time and effort. In some ways it is like a McDonald's happy meal — mass advertised to "work" and mass produced; empty, calorific comfort food that's convenient, quick, affordable, and maybe even addictive. This is related to what some corporate boosters call "spiritual capitalism" — an oxymoron: spirituality in the form of mindfulness gets co-opted and reduced to being another commodity for sale, and a profitable one at that (Beres n.d.).

Spiritual capitalism proponents see all corporations as being services through which they enhance personal meaning and ethics, and treat everyone with love and compassion — a better way of doing business in order to increase profits. However, the records of many predatory banks, oil companies, and brokerage firms and their executives suggest a powerful interest in something other than spirituality. The lack of any moral transformation of consciousness further undercuts any claim to spiritual values.

Therapist Jeremy Safran (2014) says, "It's the marketing of mindfulness practice as a commodity that is sold like any other commodity in our brand culture, a brand that promises to deliver … McMindfulness is the marketing of a constructed dream; an idealized lifestyle; an identity makeover." Jeff Wilson (2014) says that entrepreneurs link new branded forms of mindfulness with "health, eco-friendly values, and private spirituality." Like any marketable product, mindfulness needs to continually expand into new niches — for example, to schools, in which some mindfulness educators seek to help teachers and students adjust to stress and distractions through copyrighted programs. A Happy Meal is aimed at children and generally now includes a marketing tie-in to a TV show, film, or toy line (Corcoran 2017). Because mindfulness itself cannot be a branded product, Wilson notes, its promoters need to sell peripheral products that are supposed to enhance it. Besides mindfulness apps and meditation studios, other marketable products include the Mindful Mom Bracelet, Be Mindful Card Deck for Teens, the Mindfulness Thumball, Take a Mindful Minute Rug for classrooms, and Mindful Minerals (whose ad appears on the website and catalogue, "Time for Me" [2019]).

Neoliberalism, Mindfulness, and the Self

Socially engaged mindfulness practitioners have forged a critique of the now-widespread use of mindfulness by corporations, whose bottom line interest is company profits. Scholars Ron Purser and Edwin Ng (2015) point out that when workplaces employ mindfulness it often becomes a way to blame individuals for their own stress. This ignores the social and economic conditions that contribute to toxic work environments; their critique centres on how corporate mindfulness programs assume "the self-governing logic of neoliberal individual autonomy," the myth that individuals can just choose stress or wellness, misery or happiness. Neoliberal ideology demands that each private person be responsible for their well-being and free of any dependency on public institutions, which are to be phased out. Each of us should meet all our needs through self-help products and marketing strategies for success that involve self-discipline and competitiveness.

This critique of mindfulness as an unreflective practice is centred on Michel Foucault's (1991) notion of governmentality, which takes a particular form within neoliberal societies. Governmentality is the need to have people govern or regulate themselves in accordance with the dominant power structure, as a form of internalized social control. It is not just a coercive practice by the state but includes various types of knowledge, expertise, and practices that arise to guide people's voluntary conduct: "Under the conditions of neoliberal capitalism, the logics of governmentality are imbued with the moral rhetoric of 'free choice' and are geared towards self-optimizing, consumerist and entrepreneurial ends" (Ng and Purser 2016). An aspect of governmentality that Foucault (1988) considered was the use of technologies of the self. Individuals learn to apply technologies for self-care, such as those focusing on health and self-esteem, which, when internalized, render people more governable within the power structure. Through technologies of the self, according to the principles of neoliberalism, individuals (rather than the state) become more responsible for their own well-being through self-care, meeting their needs through marketplace purchases.

A desirable feature of a corporatized society, and within this later era of cognitive capitalism (one that values knowledge and depends on cognitive labour; see Moulier-Boutang 2012), is the neoliberal self (Honey 2014). The neoliberal self employs self-help practices or technologies that yield subjects who see themselves as responsible for their own social welfare and well-being. In cognitive capitalism, a boss's direct order no longer subjects workers to discipline; people under individual contracts condition themselves to adopt self-discipline and self-control. Without a critical perspective on such values and aims, mindfulness as governmentality then becomes a technology of the self, an autonomous or entrepreneurial, self-regulating subject that reinforces neoliberalism (Arthington 2016; Doran 2018a; Reveley 2015; Saari 2017).

Neoliberalism, Mindfulness, and Education

Neoliberal education beliefs and policies dominate public schools, something that mindfulness educators seldom bother to realize, let alone address. Because mindfulness is a technology of the self without a moral foundation, many mindfulness programs in schools are compatible with endorsing and encouraging students and teachers to adhere to neoliberal values and practices. Students get the message that is it important and necessary to compete against others for a successful route through school and college or university, and that they should value self-centred and self-promotional skills while learning how to get along and collaborate with others, a skill valued by corporations. Through mindfulness, students and teachers learn to become self-sufficient and self-regulating. They learn to look within rather than critically questioning school relation-ships, values, and policies. They are rewarded for focusing on what the school curriculum wants, and for adopting positive, compliant attitudes and behaviours; these are instrumental dispositions useful for success in a competitive economy.

Mindfulness educators believe with evangelical zeal that mindfulness can help solve global problems and that each single person can accomplish this. A leading mindfulness educator claims there's a "mindful revolution"; he says that it begins within each of us and can then "transform the entire world" (Rechtschaffen 2014: 10). The widespread myth that social and institutional change occurs just by each person paying more attention to their experience in the moment, devoid of social context and critique, underlies a number of school-based mindfulness programs. It makes them a strong fit for individualistic neoliberal market values and goals.

The neoliberal educational reform movement, under which mindful school programs often unwittingly operate, seeks to limit the quality of public education itself. It attacks and defunds public schools, instead favouring and funding private, market-based charter schools and subsidizing textbook publishing corporations. Neoliberal policies scapegoat and humiliate public school teachers (Denby 2016a); they strip them of job protections and collective bargaining rights as they dismantle and weaken teachers' unions. They adopt and demand a market-based accountability system borrowed from the private sector. This means they de-professionalize and deskill teachers by making their jobs dependent on the success of their students ("value-added assessment"), micromanaging teaching, reducing pedagogy to routinized methods, and pinning student performance nationally to funding sources by employing outcomes-based criteria to test scores. In low-income areas, high-stakes test measurements become the stressful criteria by which schools are determined to succeed or close; some of those schools tend to operate like prisons, treating students as objects of surveillance and control (Giroux 2014a). While advancing such neoliberal policies is not the ostensible reason well-intentioned mindfulness educators teach it in schools, it is too often the unintended consequence.

Prophetic Critique

Challenging McMindfulness involves a prophetic critique (Woods Jr. and Healey 2013) — herein, I will enjoin and apply three perspectives that are useful in understanding the problem. For Robert H. Woods Jr. and Kevin Healey, professors of media ethics, this critique first includes moral values from religious traditions, such as the demand for universal justice and the denunciation of selfishness. Members of the liberation theology movement in Latin America, along with other progressive religious activists like Reverend William Barber in North Carolina, uphold these values. Second, it employs critical theory to challenge inequitable forms of power in society, in particular neoliberalism and capitalism. Third, it invokes the importance of self- and cultural development, calling for our highest personal growth, our universal human capability that draws from and reaches toward advanced stages and modes of imagination and compassion. A prophetic critique opposes dominant cultural narratives and value structures that are reactionary and morally regressive.

Challenging McMindfulness, then, is a prophetic critique of greed, ill will, and delusion in concrete, historical terms at both personal and societal levels. It is a call for all of us to realize and enact the non-duality and inseparability of all aspects of life. Critics of McMindfulness insist that the personal and the social are indivisible, and that mindfulness should contribute to both full development and universal social justice in all areas of life. A prophetic critique shares with the Buddhist intent of mindfulness the demand to remember to let go of attachment to our ego and to realize our interconnectedness.

Unless mindfulness consciously opposes neoliberal values and structures, it aligns with neoliberalism — and becomes employed for self-serving and ego-enhancing purposes that run counter to both Buddhist and Abrahamic moral teachings. A prophetic critique calls out competitive individualism, commodification, materialist greed, and the maintenance of the status quo of power and privilege that benefits the few.

Educators such as David Purpel value the prophetic in schools. He says (2010: 13) that "an education that speaks in a prophetic voice responds not to the possibility of becoming rich and famous but to the possibility of becoming loving and just." Curriculum theorist Duane Huebner also endorses prophetic qualities in education: to reject instrumentalism, affirm the imagination, go beyond parochial understandings, and speak out in public for all children and youth (Smith 2014: 198).

Prophetic critique is Integral in that it combines traditional approaches from the East (contemplative Buddhist practices) as well as from the Abrahamic prophetic tradition of social justice from the West. Buddhist scholar and social activist David Loy (2013) says that contemporary Buddhism must focus not just on individual suffering but also on its unjust institutional causes. David Brazier (2002), a Buddhist priest, psychothera-pist, and writer, argues that the Buddha was strident in his criticism of the religious, social, and personal mores of the day. Feminist Buddhist scholar Rita Gross (1993) writes in a "prophetic voice" and declares the need for Buddhism to develop its prophetic commitment to justice and equality. While aware of the Biblical prophets' misogyny, she sees it as reflecting a cultural bias, not their core vision, and advocates for a post-patriarchal Buddhism that addresses both existential and social suffering (Strain 2018). Even many Buddhist sanghas (communities), without an awareness of structural poverty, racism, and gender and sexual inequality, are neoliberal; they favour personal practice over collective liberation, and focus on achieving individual enlightenment rather than seeing its inseparability from social justice, social institutions, and systemic forces that shape people's lives (Bartone 2015).

The larger point is that an Integral approach does not just rely on canonical texts or traditions; it includes and transcends traditional perspectives — both Buddhist and Abrahamic, and both inner, personal contemplative practices and outer social action to overcome suffering. It further makes use of science, social theory, cultural critique, and critical analysis of dominant ideologies with an eye toward developing more liberating practices and consciousness for all. "The prophetic consciousness," David Purpel (2010: 10) writes, "is one in which the material and the spiritual are not separate categories but vital and interacting dimensions of human existence."

A prophetic critique demands that as part of our personal mindful practice, and in all areas of human endeavour, we envision and enact a society with others that promotes optimal human development, intrinsic love and relationships, joy, wise compassion, democratic social justice, and universal care. Such a practice in turn often requires of us a level of painful awareness, or mindfulness, of fear, sadness, cruelty, and injustices, not just in society and with others but in our own hearts, and an ability to be with, witness, and face these together with compassion and love.

3

The Minefulness Industrial Complex: The Happy Self

It's not about you. (The Ancient One to Dr. Strange)

McMindfulness relies on, reinforces, and generally turns a blind eye to our narcissistic culture and neoliberal system. It thereby contributes to that culture and system itself, which we can dub the Minefulness Industrial Complex (Wallis 2014; he uses "minefulness" and attributes the term to Richard Payne). It is not mindfulness *per se* that is the problem, but how often people convert it to a profitable commodity and practice within a culture that promises self-centred results by peddling personal happiness as a commodity. Psychologist Thomas Joiner (2017a, 2017b) writes:

> Mindfulness has become pernicious, diluted and distorted by the prevailing narcissism of our time. The problem has somewhat less to do with how it's practiced and more to do with how it's promoted … all the while, [people] are tediously, nonjudgmentally and in the most extreme cases monstrously focused entirely on themselves. That is troublesome for mental health practice and for our larger culture.

Which self wants to be de-stressed and happy? Mine! The Minefulness Industrial Complex wants to help your self be happy, promote your personal brand — and, of course, make and take some bucks (yours and mine) along the way. The simple premise is that by practising mindfulness, by being more mindful, you will be happy, regardless of what thoughts and feelings you have, or what you do in the world.

What is this self about? It's the same solitary, separate, disconnected self that Buddha says is not a solid, isolated entity. It's the self that Jesus says needs to die to be born anew within a larger, loving whole. It's the self you need to lose, says Gandhi, in service to others. And it's the object of worship in the "deadening cult of the self," says journalist Chris Hedges (2015), that lies at the heart of the capitalist system and that must rely on relentless selfishness to survive. Mindfulness *per se* has abandoned any clear commitment to slaying the selfish self, whether ontological or social; it is indifferent to the nature and hierarchy of self-development that at the highest rung overthrows attachment to the self. It has no explicit interest in critically analyzing the capitalist social structure, culture, or ideology that frames the meaning of the self. It is silent about the detailed problems of the world and how to address these issues with others. In this way, mindfulness itself is mindless.

Let's start with some (mindless) no-brainers. Of course you're stressed out — who isn't? Of course you want to be happy and successful. The question is, what does that mean? Maybe this is "you": You don't want to have to think about unpleasant things out there like climate change, income disparities, racism, and power. You want to avoid or at least minimize dealing with unpleasant people on the subway or freeway, your loud neighbour, or your irritating in-law. And if you do have to face them, you want to not let them get to you and calmly go about your life. You want you and your kids to succeed in school, career-wise, and in personal relationships. Sure, you always want to feel secure and have lots of nice things, and when it's time to go, you want to die rich with a lot of stuff, even if you're miserable. Personal success and security is happiness.

Whether or not that's you, there's another kind of happiness worth examining.

We can first look at two basic meanings of being happy and see which one fits best with mindfulness as practised today. The first kind of happiness is hedonic. In a hedonic life, you want to feel good and be positive; collect as many sensuous pleasures as possible to enhance self-gratification. You do whatever it takes to de-stress yourself — collect and buy things, chill out with music or sports, keep the focus on your sensations. After all, work sucks for most people (um, why is that, mindfulness promoters? Do we just need more mindful capitalism?), so it feels fair and fine to compensate with self-pleasure (Keohane 2015).

That's the neoliberal deal: lousy, meaningless work you're still supposed to feel good about in exchange for a 55" flat-screen TV and video games for the kids. Hedonic happiness, of course, aligns with corporatized workplace and consumer values and actions. Some corporations, like T-Mobile, were keen on mandatory employee happiness — employers were forcing workers to be cheery at all times — until the National Labor Relations Board ruled against it; and companies that want employees to be happy on their own do so not out of kindness but to improve productivity and profits (Rodriguez 2016). The problem, says psychologist Svend Brinkmann, is when happiness becomes required. Performance reviews stipulate positive growth at the expense of tackling difficulties; demanding expressions of happiness is "almost totalitarian," he notes, and "thought control" (Goldhill 2017; Brinkmann 2017).

On the consumer side, corporations and the media want you to seek hedonic happiness so you'll buy more stuff. You know that the advertising industry spends billions to get you to buy things you don't need, to get you to feel you are lacking something, to feel you are incomplete without it. They know that even when you buy something, you'll end up feeling disgruntled or unfulfilled and that, with the aid of built-in obsolescence, you will need to return for the next fix, the latest model, and bigger, better add-ons and apps. A corporate consultant argues for ways mindfulness can help market products for women: "Understanding why mindfulness matters and how women are embracing it in their everyday lives will lead to a better and more authentic connection between your brand and your target consumer" (Kim 2015).

Hedonism is also about propping up the self so that people will buy *you* as a commodity; in the psychology of neoliberalism, you come to want to promote your identity, your own personal brand, what one writer calls voluntary self-commodification (Millward-Hopkins 2017). Some public school teachers even create their own brand, and ethically suspect Silicon Valley corporations are happy to accommodate them — as long as the teachers market their products too (Singer 2017). To have a personal brand is the epitome of succeeding in a mineful culture. It's an elusive, endless chase to arrive at a point of completeness through trying to promote and gratify the self, since seeking unattainable lasting happiness itself is a source of stress. So you don't escape the stress in this way, you just compound it.

The other kind of happiness is eudaemonic (Aristotle) — using your highest skills in the service of helping others realize a more decent life, something larger than your own self or ego. At a later stage of human development, beyond the egocentric and conventional ones, you might come to see that everyone's happiness is intertwined with your own — it's not either/or. At an evolved point you realize that your small self is part of a much larger whole and you no longer distinguish between self and others. Happiness means pursuing a meaningful life, which leads to a deeper kind of fulfilment. The pursuit of pleasure does not always lead to life satisfaction, but the pursuit of a meaningful life can. Eudaemonic life is not always pleasant and happy. For example, Gandhi and Martin Luther King Jr. did not have carefree lives in the hedonic sense. Minefulness culture makes no such distinction between hedonic and eudaemonic well-being.

Philosopher Alain Badiou draws a similar line, although here he employs "happiness" as the favoured term, over "satisfaction," akin to hedonic, conventional pleasure: fitting into what the world says you should be striving for. For Badiou, happiness challenges the status quo, and is eudaemonic. Satisfaction, on the other hand, is a "restricted figure of subjectivity":

> Happiness is fundamentally egalitarian, integrating the question of the other, whereas satisfaction, linked to the selfishness of survival, knows nothing of equality. And satisfaction is not dependent on the encounter or the decision. It occurs when we find a good place in this world — a good job, a beautiful car, nice holidays abroad. Satisfaction is the consumption of things that we fought to obtain. After all, we try to occupy a suitable place in the world such as it is, precisely in order to be able to enjoy its perks. So satisfaction is a restricted figure of subjectivity, as compared to happiness — it is the figure of success according to the world's norms. (Davidson 2015)

The minefulness industry favours hedonic satisfaction over eudaemonic happiness. It fits into the broader culture of self-promotion and consumer capitalism. It's all about my personal quest for happiness through focusing on my personal responsibility for my attitudes about and conditions of my life. It treats me as if I live just in my head. It's as if the rest of the messy world, and my larger relations with it and with others, are separable from my life. In this way it reproduces the self-centredness of conventional, narcissistic society without naming and challenging it. It doesn't take a stand for eudaemonic action. It focuses on me and my satisfaction.

Social critics implicate minefulness culture in what they call the *Wellness Syndrome* (Cederström and Spicer 2015), the *Happiness Industry* (Davies 2015), *Happiness as Enterprise* (Binkley 2014), and as an aspect of our *Desperately Seeking Self-Improvement* (Cederström and Spicer 2017), *Bright-Sided* thinking (Ehrenreich 2010), and our *Pursuit of Happiness* that is creating *America the Anxious* (Whippman 2017) — so, are you *Happier?* (Horowitz 2017). These critics aim at the heart of the neoliberal agenda. The government and corporations take great interest in the notion that each individual can and should work on and be responsible for their own well-being and happiness. Doing so takes the heat off the government and corporations — indeed, society itself: they don't have to take responsibility for the conditions that contribute to stress, illness, and unhappiness. Your own success and failure fall back on you alone, and you learn to monitor and regulate yourself accordingly. Business professors Carl Cederström and André Spicer show how the push for well-being wins out over political demands:

> The just redistribution of material resources (through "social welfare"), the recognition of previously maligned identities (through "identity politics") and the representation of political voices (through "democratization") have now become replaced by a new ambition: personal rehabilitation. Here, the unemployed are not provided with an income, they get life coaching. Discriminated groups don't get opportunities to celebrate their identities; they get an exercise plan. Citizens don't get the opportunity to influence decisions that affect their lives; they get a mindfulness session. (2015: 133–34; see also Holloway 2015)

Journalist Ruth Whippman (2016) points out that mindfulness has become our preferred solution to difficult problems:

> This is a kind of neo-liberalism of the emotions, in which happiness is seen not as a response to our circumstances but as a result of our own individual mental effort, a reward for the deserving. The problem is not your sky-high rent or meager paycheck, your cheating spouse or unfair boss or teetering pile of dirty dishes. The problem is you.

Mindfulness is one means of furthering this self-blame. Workers who feel good, healthy, and responsible for anything that happens to them, who regulate their own stress and unhappy emotions, are good for business and productivity. They save money by cutting the exorbitant health-care costs needed to treat symptoms resulting from stress. Students, too, can regulate themselves, their difficult feelings of anger, their frustrations and sadness, with mindfulness practices. They then turn their gaze inward onto their own attitudes and drives, adjust to the present order of things such as competing with others, and leave the school power structure and social barriers untouched.

Positivity should not become a requisite, says Brinkmann (2017) — we need to remain firm and resist the self-improvement fad that can lead to harm when other feelings are suppressed. The belief that anyone can and should make themself feel happy implies that unhappy people are to blame for their own conditions.

Badiou sees the link between seeking personal happiness (eudaemonia) and changing the world toward more universal goodness. He says we shouldn't settle on satisfaction and that we have the right to insist on real happiness: "There is a moment where you need the desire to change the world in order to save the figure of humanity within you, rather than giving in to the injunction to accept the impossibility of happiness" (Davidson 2015).

When asked if you can help change the world when you are happy, Badiou replies:

> Yes! That is, in staying faithful to the idea of being happy, and defending the fact that happiness does not look like satisfaction.

The world's masters do not like change, so if you choose to maintain, against winds and tides, that something else is possible, then they will use all means at hand in order to tell you that you are wrong. (Davidson 2015)

Real happiness in Badiou's sense is a political act; it goes against the powerful, who like things as they are. Minefulness proponents believe that practising mindfulness will lead straight to eudaemonia or Badiou's happiness. They talk a good game about compassion, which they argue is akin to eudaemonia and real happiness. They believe that the personal practice of mindfulness leads to compassion for others. That would indeed be a game-changer. Imagine, they say, if everyone meditates, we would have a compassionate society. Really? This belief lacks social and political analysis and prefers just to keep things on the level of the abstracted, privatized, competitive individual.

Mindfulness proponents don't see compassion as a social, relational quality but as a personal, individual act. There is no sense or understanding of the interrelated nature of society itself, of public life and the public good, as anything other than a bunch of atomized individuals meditating inside their heads. This is how the neoliberal agenda colonizes happiness and self-care. Without an explicit stance on actual social injustices, without challenging real barriers that prevent people from living in an actual compassionate society instead of a competitive one based on profit, without criticizing the callous individualism of the market, mindfulness by itself does not change the world. Mindfulness just as easily leads to hedonism, satisfaction, and self-aggrandizement. It just as easily leads to minefulness.

We need to realize and understand in critical ways the actual forms of the world. We then can decide together to enact ways to be happy in the greatest sense, in the service of ourselves and others, in resistance to the dominant structures and ideas of a racist, neoliberal society, and as a way to create and live in the kind of decent, just world we desire. Buddhist teacher Stephen Batchelor (1998: 99) says, "The more we become conscious of the mysterious unfolding of life, the clearer it becomes that its purpose is not to fulfil the expectations of our ego."

It's Not About You

"It's not about you" is a homily with wise potential. In a Google image search, though, the phrase seems to mean that by thinking about your customers and not yourself, you can gain better marketing savvy and financial success in business (but you need to buy the book linked to the image), or that you should just be thinking about Jesus or God and not yourself. In another cultural appropriation of Buddhism, Marvel Comics' (and movie character) Dr. Strange, a privileged, narcissistic white guy, undergoes a painful learning process. He travels to Tibet and in the end lets go of his selfish ego and takes action on behalf of the greater good of the universe, of which he realizes he is a part. The Ancient One, a stereotypical Tibetan monk with superpowers (transformed into a Celtic female guru in the film in order not to offend China over crediting Tibet), helps him work it out and tells him, "It's not about you." Like Dr. Strange — though without having to schlep to Tibet and undergo a painful training regimen, just to yield to some shallow, simplistic, and ignorant tropes taken from Asian traditions drummed up by Hollywood — we hope that in a deeper sense we, too, can come to learn that "it's not about me."

4

Seeing Things "As They Are": Relative and Absolute

> A Zen metaphor warns us not to take the finger pointing at the moon for the moon itself, but "the moon itself" is also not the moon. (Loy 2010: 7)

When it comes to mindfulness, it is important to consider the meaning of the relative and the absolute, and the relationship between them. Manu Bazzano (2017: 147), a Zen teacher and psychotherapist, distinguishes the two: The "'relative' indicates our ordinary perception of a separate, self-existing 'I' relating to a world 'out there,' whereas in the absolute dimension, as the word itself suggests, the self is dissolved and the experience of the world regains a natural fluidity." Dawn Haney (2016) of the Buddhist Peace Fellowship says the Buddha "taught about two truths, ultimate and relative reality. He didn't say that ultimate reality was the real truth and relative reality was the fake truth — they both are true." What is difficult to perceive is that both realities are not the same and yet co-exist, and there is a dialectical relation between them. What makes it even more difficult is that the absolute itself is hard to see.

There is also a dialectical connection between ways to get to see the absolute. In many wisdom traditions, there are two paths to the absolute; one says, "Wake up, like this, and once you do you will see it right here and now!" The other says, "Not so fast, you need to spend much time and follow these instructions, rituals, and practices: climb this ladder like this, and maybe then you will get to see it."

The Immanent Relative Everyday

Let's first look at the relative world; secular mindfulness advocates don't have a strong grip here. Consider, for example, the need for some white meditators to help dismantle racism. Some think denial of race, or colour-blindness, is the right way to go: hey, we're all one, why make distinctions? While that may be true at bottom, in the absolute sense, Haney (2016) says, "We demand that Black Lives Matter, because in the relative reality, they don't. If we want all lives to matter, it's time we started making sure that black lives matter."

In the relative world it is inadequate to say that mindfulness or contemplation allows us to see things "as they are"; this might make more sense when we speak of the absolute. But in relative terms, things "as they are" have an implicit meaning from a particular perspective, which needs to be made clear through language, analysis, and dialogue. In Zen there's the well-known saying: the finger is not the moon. That is, the finger at best is a metaphor, like language, or a map, or a sign, that points to the direct experience of seeing the moon; it cannot substitute for directly seeing (from a first-person perspective) the moon "as it is."

Loy's quote at the beginning of this chapter takes this a critical step further. He suggests that even getting past the pointed finger to the direct perception of what one thinks of or understands as the "moon" is not a given — even "the moon" is not the moon. In the relative, everyday world it is still a concept understood within a shared cultural context. We contextualize or frame the meaning of "the moon" through our understanding and interpretations that we share and create together. Any one of a number of perspectives frame what we see. These depend on our cognitive, emotional, cultural, societal, and historical time and place. So, when you see the "moon" directly, "as it is," you may regard it as an astronomical body and object of scientific study that controls the tides; a celestial god or entity who smiles down on us and controls our fate; the universal representation of the feminine; an immediate perception of an indelible lost love; or a poetic "ghostly galleon tossed upon cloudy seas."

But wait — isn't that first factual, scientific definition really "the moon as it is"? Shouldn't we just go with the third-person perspective, the scientific, objective description as the only "real" way to see things as they are?

Then again, why should the objective, scientific, definition of "the moon" always be the preferred, default meaning? If we think in terms of first-, second-, and third-person perspectives, we can see that the materialist, rational, objective scientific paradigm (third-person perspective) dominates much of our everyday thinking in what we regard as truth.

This first shows us the importance of perspectives, the need to consider from what viewpoint something gets defined as "the way it is." The case of the moon also shows us that the scientific method — a third-person, objective perspective — has won out in the world over superstition, beliefs, and poetry; it gets to define the way things are. But while the scientific, materialist paradigm has contributed to humankind's advancement with regard to what is true, its dominance in the relative world also has had negative consequences. First, it has squelched the legitimacy of the interior as a source of knowledge, the ability to see the world in imaginative, mysterious ways. In Wilber's terms, the world has become disenchanted, a "flatland" — the universe is just material and objective processes with no consciousness, no values, meaning, or depth, and in the face of the dominant third-person perspective, he says, we struggle to re-enchant the world as best we can (Wilber 1998). Another important point is that in everyday life, apart from science, those in power too often define "the way things are" and whose viewpoint becomes the way we see reality. In Marxist terms, this is hegemonic ideology — the view of those who rule through power becomes the acceptable cultural norm through which the rest of us see, value, and understand things.

All of this is not to say we should idealize and return to pre-scientific magical and mythical thinking, or that we should put scientific study on a relativistic par with poetry or pre-scientific beliefs, or that whoever has power gets to define the truth, as if all views are equally valid. It tells us instead that it is important to account for the kinds of perspectives with which we see the world and to evaluate which ones are best suited for which conditions and experiences.

The belief that one sees things directly as they are (third-person, objective perspective), without accounting for the cultural context of how we construct and interpret those things (second-person perspective), is what Wilber (2006) calls the "myth of the given": reality is directly perceived in just one way, shared and agreed by everyone. It is the myth that one's present worldview (or that of the mindfulness teacher or therapist, or yours and theirs together, or that of the dominant social order) is the one valid, objective, unquestioned framework.

Yet we construct much of the relative world through interpretable frameworks of shared — but often not explicit — meanings, as in the prior examples of how various people literally see/interpret the meaning of "the moon," or that thing up there. So we need to discuss, interpret, act on, and/but also bring objective inquiry and scientific method (third-person perspective) to bear on what we see. The myth of the given is rampant in mindfulness. There is no critical analysis in mindfulness of the arguable, troublesome, changeable, social, and relational nature of stress, feelings, and experiences from different people's viewpoints. For mindfulness, the myth of the given keeps neoliberal thinking and inequitable social structures as they are — uncontested, lurking in the background, unacknowledged — a mythic given, not as something that is impermanent and that people can and should change.

This doesn't mean we should just deconstruct everything into arbitrary social configurations the way relativists and some postmodernists do. That's the other untrue extreme: there is no objective truth, there is no physical entity that we call the moon, everything is relative, it's what we feel or think or name, and can be assigned any meaning in personal terms any time — as if narratives via language, beliefs, and all subjectivity determine objective reality.

Rather, it's important to make perspectives explicit in developmental, cultural, and social terms, asking "where do you stand?" There still is a perspective of truth — truth itself is an absolute, within a relational (not relative) context. So if someone says there *is* no truth or there *are* no facts, listen closely: that is still an absolute claim about what the speaker believes *is* true as absolute fact, a performative contradiction. A Trump surrogate says, "There's no longer such thing as fact, because anything is true if enough people believe it" (Holmes 2016), and another calls for "alternative facts" (Graham 2017). In this way they reinforce a dangerous trend, furthered by the way corporatized interests in profits have changed and manipulated much of the media — that there is nothing but the cocoon-world of subjective beliefs and feelings; that the number of hits, "likes," and sales on social media count more than the factual truth. The statement that there is no truth itself is uttered as an absolute fact, something the speaker believes exists as truth, which undercuts the argument.

Mindfulness teachers and advocates in education are seldom interested in critically exploring "the way things are" in ways that require social, cultural, political, and developmental interpretation and analysis; they are even less interested in critically questioning and resisting the dominant worldviews that frame "the way things are" and in asking where one *should* otherwise stand. Instead they believe that mindfulness will yield a direct perception of reality — often their own unexamined version, and/or of those in power who reinforce conventional beliefs — and that a mindful person will just come to wiser and more compassionate insights and even more skilful ways to enact them. Kabat-Zinn (2006), among many mindfulness practitioners, believes that practising mindfulness itself can lead in direct ways to a moral life; education researcher Terry Hyland (2015) says this evokes the same uneasiness we feel in the face of the Socratic claim that the truly wise person will never act in an evil way. Buddhist wisdom and practice, as Buddhist educator Judith Simmer-Brown (1987) points out, at least assumes responsibility for disrupting patterns of relative truth that cause suffering and confusion.

The Transcendent Absolute Universal

"The biggest meta-stories are mostly religious: God, Brahman, the Tao. Such stories try to point at something that transcends stories. Yet a meta-story cannot get outside itself to explain the relationship between stories and that-which-is-outside-stories" (Loy 2010: 7).

Meta-stories serve as the finger pointing to the ultimate absolute. We would all love to get a perspective on all perspectives, to be all-seeing and all-knowing — to find the meta-story on the human story and its relationship to the absolute. But as Loy notes in the preceding quote, a meta-story can't get beyond itself to do so; it's still a story involving words. "To say that we can say nothing about nirvana is to say something about nirvana" (2010: 8). He reminds us of philosopher Ludwig Wittgenstein's statement: if we can't speak about it, we must be silent. The experience of the universal ground, or groundlessness, of being, formlessness, non-duality, awareness or consciousness itself, is a particular phenomenon that we can experience but cannot express, just point to at best with metaphors. In an absolute sense the experience may not be describable through language at all. In Judaism, God's relative names can be spoken but the one absolute, true name cannot. During some practices of meditation and at other times, we can catch glimpses of the absolute, pure awareness itself. In this space are no distinctions, no categories or even words that divide the world into dualities. This is the absolute being, not the relative doing. Theologian and philosopher Paul Tillich (1967: 82) describes this absolute being as the basis of truth, because it is the "transcendence of subject and object…. And it is identical with the Holy, the ground of everything that has being." He says the Absolute is not an absolute being, which is a contradiction; it is Being-Itself, and is beyond thinking and talking about. We are all united in the absolute, which is above and inclusive of both the Other and me. In Buddhism, relative factors "are seen from within a vast perspective of unconditional mind that pervades everything, a liberative perspective that is foundational to Buddhism" (Sherrell and Simmer-Brown 2017: 87).

The Sufi poet Rumi's popular stanza is one description of the relationship between relative perspectives and the absolute:

> Out beyond ideas of wrongdoing and rightdoing,
> there is a field. I'll meet you there.
> When the soul lies down in that grass
> the world is too full to talk about. (Barks 1995: 36)

Your perspective is always within a relative, everyday social context, wrong and right, and yet also always stands in relation to an ineffable absolute field "beyond," which is "too full" (or too empty) to say anything about. Within contemplative traditions, there are at least two co-arising "selves" — a relative and an absolute; a temporal, finite and an infinite, transcendent, unqualifiable self, I-amness or awareness itself. Some meditators and mystics reach a state where they experience a union with the absolute or the infinite. The relative, everyday self is the form taken by the infinite ("empty") self (or as Wilber says, it is the world we experience when we step out of meditating). Tillich (1967: 109) calls this union *agape*, the Greek word for love as the highest, absolute moral principle, "the 'star' above the chaos of relativism." Separating the absolute and the relative, as is common in the secular mindfulness movement, is, in Buddhist terms, a "violation of the truth of each of them" (Sherrell and Simmer-Brown 2017: 87). The absolute and the relative are inseparable and co-arise — they are right here together; or, as the Buddhist Heart Sutra says, form is emptiness, emptiness is form, and to split them off from each other weakens each of their qualities and fails to do them justice.

Not content just to separate them, secular mindfulness advocates also conflate and thereby confuse the relative and the absolute. On one hand, they claim that there is an objective absolute reality — "the way things are." They then fail to address the actual historical world of the relative everyday. So, some practices invoke "things as they are" in absolute terms that override the relative social world: Be with what is; be, not do; engage in radical acceptance; be in the present, be in the here and now. On top of ignoring social reality, they then speak of the absolute itself in inadequate, vague, and empty ways, more mystifying than mystical.

In the counselling field, this conflation is called spiritual bypassing: a person ignores taking on the actual social realm of experience in concrete terms and just describes things they believe occur in absolute spiritual ones. Psychotherapist John Welwood, who coined the term, says:

> We often use the goal of awakening or liberation to rationalize what I call premature transcendence: trying to rise above the raw and messy side of our humanness before we have fully faced and made peace with it. And then we tend to use absolute truth to disparage or dismiss relative human needs, feelings, psychological problems, relational difficulties, and developmental deficits. (2011; see also Masters n.d.; and Sherrell and Simmer-Brown 2017)

To the extent secular mindfulness avoids or denies actual social conditions and practical issues, and instead speaks in spiritual generalities, it is a form of spiritual bypassing. It offers an abstracted and impoverished worldview that says little about the everyday world. Besides Kabat-Zinn's response to Angela Davis, some white people will apply spiritual techniques and language to avoid or deny difficult discussions about racism or to gloss over a racist comment. They will refer instead to how we all create our struggles with "our negative thinking, energy or low vibrations," and claim that we're really all spiritual "love and light" (Williams 2017). Other examples are people who never get angry, who insist on always being nice and positive, or who avoid discussing difficult choices and abrogate responsibility for concrete problems in specific terms, all in the name of spiritual values, or letting God handle things.

One of the clearest and most blatant instances of spiritual bypassing occurred during a Wisdom 2.0 Conference in San Francisco in 2014. At the start of a panel on Google's corporate mindfulness program, a local group called Heart of the City took the stage with a megaphone and a banner that read "Eviction Free San Francisco." The protesters wanted Google to pay for their harmful impact on housing and public infrastructure and to fund affordable housing. The conference organizers and Google representatives forced the protesters off the stage — the video shows this — then held a two-minute meditation session and went on as if nothing had happened. For the conference participants, their meditation was more important than addressing the real-world issue before them in the so-called here and now. They valued absolute spirituality rising above any conflict or discomfort in the actual, relative world that would disrupt their own corporatized spiritual moment. This display of Google's tone-deaf, dismissive condescension — we can let others have their point of view as long as we don't take it seriously and let it impact our own inner peace and wise viewpoint — was praised by the Wisdom 2.0 organizers (Purser and Forbes 2014; Ream 2014; Wallis 2014).

The other side of spiritual bypassing is a kind of material bypass: deeper, spiritual meanings of terms like mindfulness and attention get sacrificed, watered down, and reduced to relative, mundane terms. MBSR's now-standard definition of mindfulness as "paying attention" means noticing things in the everyday relative world. To equate paying attention in MBSR's terms with dharmic enlightenment or the end of existential suffering is a reductive parody of contemplative traditions and meanings.

With much of secular mindfulness, we are served a calorific plate of pseudo-objectivity, covered by a thin sauce of pseudo-spirituality, and are left ill-nourished.

Integral: Working the Dialectical Border

Paul Tillich says that we stand in a dialectical relationship between the relative and the absolute. Integral as a meta-perspective expresses this dialectical relationship to the extent it has relative dimensions and points to the absolute. With a meta-Integral framework, we first can focus on the relative cultural contexts and implicit perspectives of contemplative practices themselves. We do this by examining the subjective, developmental, cultural, objective, and social structural contexts of contemplative approaches. In this way, we can add an "Integral address" to contemplative and holistic education practices, to make the perspectives explicit and illuminate the implicit cultural and developmental worldviews of mindfulness educators that underlie contemplative education in the relative world. We can then move from metaphysics (unexamined beliefs) to post-metaphysics — the identification and location of a perspective, even of one that understands, perceives, and points to the absolute.

But Integral as a meta-theory in the relative sense is a map, not the territory; it is not an enclosed, rational, total system that describes and contains the absolute. It is a metaphorical finger pointing to the ineffable mystery of human consciousness, the ground, or groundlessness, of being — which envelops us in love — as we ourselves through history seek to overcome ego-attached delusion and meanness, and create new forms of such love (Integral as absolute). In relative terms (and early Wittgenstein's), we employ Integral meta-theory as a ladder; once used, we kick it away. But even Wittgenstein (1980: 7e) had a dialectical relationship with his ladder. He later said that we are already here and have no need of a ladder. If the only way to get to where we want to go can be reached by a ladder, he says, "I would give up trying to get there. For the place I really have to get to is a place I must already be at now." In the absolute sense, then, we don't need a ladder, we are already present with the ineffable groundlessness of being.

We can use the relative ladder of self-development to arrive at the most advanced and inclusive developmental stage or order. If we get there, we can then say, along with developmental psychologist Susanne Cook-Greuter (2013: 87), that "consciousness or rational awareness is no longer perceived as a shackle, but as just another phenomenon that assumes foreground or background status depending on one's momentary attention." The hierarchical model of developmental growth has become a ladder we no longer need in order to arrive somewhere but can use or discard at will. Imagine that you are so well evolved, so well attuned to the fluidity of all things, that you can switch back and forth with ease between the relative and the absolute, between the small self and the big, universal self, or the groundlessness of all being. Similarly, Manu Bazzano (2017: 148) describes a basic tenet in Zen teachings that the relative and the absolute "are inseparable and the practitioner's task is to learn how to move fluidly between the two without getting stuck anywhere but committing him/herself to ontological *ambiguity*" (original italics). About Zen, he says: "By embracing both the relative and the absolute, a fluidity is created that injects a sense of mystery and poetry in the everyday whilst at the same time bringing down to earth any fleeting experience of the sublime."

Along with the practice of meditation, an understanding of the relative and absolute sense of time can help us reach this fluidity. Ron Purser (2015), following thirteenth-century Zen master Dogen, regards two levels of time — the absolute and the relative. He takes apart the myth of the present moment when it's presented in secular, relative terms — for example, when mindfulness is used as a therapeutic practice and we are told to notice the present moment. By getting you to notice and be in the present, it can alleviate surface suffering — you can know the moment — but it provides no foundational (ontological) wisdom or insight into the deeper nature of suffering at an absolute level. What is more, it reinforces the private self and the separation of the self from the rest of the world. In conventional relative terms, time, as a series of moments, is experienced as split from the self; the "present moment" is something you try to capture. You are positioned as an active agent, one who is here, while the present is there. The emphasis is on measuring your success by checking your progress within a mode of self-surveillance. In this way the self is even strengthened, as are conventional dichotomies; the self takes a position separate from and outside the flow of time, which is seen as lying on a horizontal dimension, moving along from past to present to future.

There's another take on time: absolute time, based on Dogen's notion of a vertical dimension, or time-being. In this sense, time is always present; you are time. This is an absolute present, or presence, unified with all moments. Dogen said: "In essence, all things in the entire world are linked with one another as moments. Because all moments are the time-being, they are your time-being" (Purser 2015: 685). Zen meditative practice is not about a witnessing self that tries to achieve a present moment in the outside world; rather, in the vertical or absolute sense, the world out there and a witnessing self drop away; in this way, one experiences a non-going and non-happening, a non-striving. Perhaps you can see further how much secular mindfulness conflates the absolute and the relative, and fails to distinguish them let alone consider their interrelatedness, thereby failing to do justice to both.

We still require language to point to the open and unpredictable unfolding experience of the absolute and its relationship to the relative. Meditation does not uncover the structural qualities of social life, which is where some social scientific, empirical perspectives are useful: the need for both inner and outer. Yet when it comes to expressing the absolute, art, music, and poetry — using words or other forms of symbolic expression as metaphors that point beyond themselves — are often as truthful, or more so, than social science. Zen koans likewise twist, topple, and dismantle linear and rational language and thought to help us reach the ineffable realm of experience of the absolute in everyday life beyond language. With regard to music, here's an apt description by a movie critic of the relationship between the absolute and the relative, the holy and the everyday, in the songs and singing of Hank Williams and the special resonance he had with his fans. His voice

> has a singular sound, and it carries a specific American history and way of feeling and being that finds the holy not only in the Bible, but also in a lonesome whippoorwill, a midnight train and ordinary life and people. When Williams sang to his audiences, they knew that he heard them, too. (Dargis 2016)

This is beyond structure, beyond an enclosed system or idea captured by language; it is one form of an embodied fluidity between the relative and absolute. Are there others?

5

Mind, Self, and Transformation

We all experience personal consciousness. We refer to this as the "mind" or "interiority" or the "self." These terms are metaphors; the mind does not exist by itself in nature as some private, inaccessible sphere apart from human activity. The mind and the self are social constructs we have been conditioned to regard as entities that exist "inside" ourselves, independent of the social world. The flip side of this dualist myth is the strict belief in materialism — the idea that consciousness itself indeed cannot "exist" since only things that are observable and measurable can exist, and that consciousness therefore must be reducible to the material brain.

When we speak of the mind, we are referring to qualities found within activities of everyday life. So when we say something is a trait or quality of the individual mind, that quality is inseparable from actual social existence, the societal and historical world that people co-create and mediate. When we speak of being more conscious, or mindful, having higher intentions, displaying more advanced states of mind, being able to see in more insightful or imaginative ways, or just feeling perplexed, stifled, ecstatic: these are expressed, enacted, referenced, and understood in the social world, in the *qualities* of one's actions embedded within a constellation of relationships that frame their meaning. Marx's famous description of our unique capacity for imagination, the quality that places us above other living beings, is at the same time an inseparable aspect of human life and activity:

> A spider conducts operations that resemble those of a weaver, and a bee puts to shame many an architect in the construction of her cells. But what distinguishes the worst architect from the

best of bees is this, that the architect raises his [sic] structure in imagination before he erects it in reality. (1967: 178)

Yet these "mental qualities" or "states of mind" are not just social constructions brought into existence by language or discourse — as clinical psychologist David Smail (2012) noted, language is not generative of reality itself. There is still embodied conscious awareness that language does not create, but arises from human needs and values. Smail (2012: 91) says, "Reality is sensed in embodied experience before it is articulated in words — that is to say, it is rooted in our subjectivity"; however, we live in a social world, "and what we say needs always to be checked against other kinds of evidence, including where necessary every other possible intimation we may have of our living existence in material reality."

Social actions within that material reality in turn occur in historical, socially organized cultures and structures of power that people create, shape, and mediate to meet their needs for a better life. These actions are not mere neutral or relative responses to stimuli but are purposive, what developmental psychologist Anna Stetsenko (2015: 102, 113) describes as people taking a Transformative Activist Stance (TAS), in which "producing knowledge is always an act of creating reality and inventing the future." People are not just situated in and shaped by the world and need to adapt to it, she points out, but rather, we co-create our own development and the social world. This approach is a "deliberate, goal-directed, and purposeful transformation of the world based in a commitment to social change" and is therefore "the foundation of human development, encompassing processes of being, doing, and knowing." Truth is not relative, she says, it is partisan; "robust and concrete" within a particular historical time, "as defined by its specific predicaments that are determined ... by concrete sociocultural and political-economical conditions." These embodied conditions and people's activities constitute the "fabric of human development and the world itself."

We can argue that human consciousness itself is purposive and directed at creating a better future. Badiou (2009) argues that consciousness exists not in neurons but only in the symbolic social interaction of many individuals who are socially engaged in seeking truth. This notion of truth is the opposite of the neoliberal belief in privatization that says atomized individuals can and should create and be solely responsible for their individual selves, or their own truth, apart from the material and social world. Instead, it accounts for historical conditions and depends on our social actions together toward the betterment of all of us as social beings. At a deeper level, it says that reality does not become real until we experience and enact it as social beings. Again, however, this is not to say that thinking something makes it so, or that there is no material world.

Philosopher and feminist theorist Elizabeth Grosz points out that one reason we cannot fully see ourselves, to understand our own consciousness, is that it is "always larger and more comprehensive than our understanding of it" (Grosz and Bell 2017). This is akin to the Zen phrase that the mind is like the eye that sees but cannot see itself. We don't get to see the processes by which the mind works or to realize that the self is not an actual entity but an organizing process. Buddhist meditation and applying observations to one's and others' self-developmental structures are ways to approach the nature of the self, or awareness or consciousness, as an object of contemplation or study, from outside of our own perceptions. Some argue that a particular use of psychedelic drugs in therapy also enables us to dissolve our model of the self, which they see as a "cognitive strategy" to see things anew (Gerrans and Letheby 2017).

We can further suggest that there is an implicit moral direction in self-processes. Grosz (in Grosz and Bell 2017) sees consciousness itself as having a built-in moral or ethical value and proposes that the immaterial qualities of the world, what she calls incorporeality, "are the directions or orientations to which things tend, their future movements." Following the Stoics, she sees ethics as one of these immaterial conditions — not in the traditional sense of separate, judgmental rules that govern life from the outside, but as present in all life itself and that directs our lives. "The incorporeal is thus a name for the direction immanent in our actions, the direction to the future in which we may overcome ourselves, become more than ourselves."

For Buddhists as well, ethics are not an objective set of precepts outside of experience. Rather, ethics can be understood as an interdependent phenomenon inseparable from the aim to end unhappiness for the good of all. This is not meant in the sense of a hedonistic, individualized, therapeutic reduction of discomfort but as a way to relieve the fundamental human problem of suffering (dukkha) — clinging to the myth of a solid self and failing to realize our inseparability from the needs of all others.

The belief in the privatization of the self, the private mind, can be further contextualized and critiqued from this view that consciousness is inseparable from human social activity and that it is directed toward truth and an ethical life. Neoliberal society endorses and accelerates privatization. Smail wrote: "Nothing could suit corporate plutocracy more than for people to believe that the real satisfactions of life stem ultimately from the cultivation of privacy: that subjective well-being ... is a matter of 'personal growth' *from the inside*" (2012: 95, original italics).

The construct of a self that needs shoring up is inadequate in the first place. Subjectivity — consciousness — occurs first without the construct of a self: a self arises *because* we have consciousness. We need to strengthen subjectivity and rescue it from the neoliberal myth that a private, separate self exists and is altogether responsible for its own well-being, and that it can ground its happiness and security in money, the marketplace, and things external to it. This means letting go of the myth of the autonomous, isolated, privatized self that by itself can create its own success and instead acknowledging and further enacting our social interdependence together at a deeper level.

Secular mindfulness tends to reinforce the myth of the private self. It maintains a duality between the self and the object it observes, the mind. Kabat-Zinn refers to it as an object of investigation that can be full or empty of thoughts. A witness still sees an object, the "mind," while the moral value content of the "mind" is of no interest (Stanley and Longden 2016). Religious studies professor David McMahan (2016) links this approach with a dualistic way of knowing that comes from a tradition of scientific objectivity; the point is, this is not the only way to know something. At a conference on Buddhism and neuroscience, he spoke on how mindfulness is created to resemble the kind of neutrality to which a secular, scientific gaze rooted in European Enlightenment epistemology aspires, one that values objectivity, individual autonomy, and personal choice.

To see ourselves not as isolated, private selves but as social beings is to begin to decentre the self. Buddhist perspectives take this further and serve as a countervailing force to neoliberalism, to attachment to a self that is concerned with money and material goods, and even to language itself, since language divides the self from others and creates other dualisms. When Dogen was able to let go of the construct of the self he came to see that "mind is no other than mountains and rivers and the great wide earth, the sun and the moon and the stars" (Kapleau 1989: 205).

Once we see that meaning depends on relational contexts, there is no longer an inside and an outside. Meditators come to know that in breath awareness there is no simple boundary between inside and outside and that language marks this distinction. If we seek to avoid lapsing into Cartesian private selfhood through language that maintains borders between self and the material world, we can consider the Buddhist notion of emptiness, no-thing-ness, or groundlessness. Emptiness is not a confining totality of "oneness," nor is it nihilism. It means that no being has an intrinsic essence or meaning but co-arises with everything else. Bazzano (2017: 72) cites Huineng, an early figure in Chinese Buddhism, while saying that to affirm our resistance to being defined by Cartesian duality and divisive language lets us become a person who "does not abide either inside or outside; he (sic) is free to come and go." John Lennon had a more lighthearted take on this profound notion: "Your inside is out and your outside is in, and your outside is in and your inside is out, so come on!" Psychologist Steven Stanley (2012: 636) writes:

> The breath itself is a selfless phenomena; neither mine or not mine. The breathing process exists at the intersection between all that is identified as "me" and all that is not "me." The sensations of the breathing at the nostrils, for example, are at the boundary between what we call "inside" and what we call "outside." But this is an artefact of language; really there is no simple separation.

This kind of advanced insight sparks the sustainability movement; at a more evolved stage of awareness, like Dogen, we become aware that the Earth is indeed our self, our body. Of course, this doesn't mean that people can only work to save the environment if they reach a more evolved stage; or unlike what spiritual writer Eckhart Tolle and others believe, that when many people's minds are unpolluted from being in a meditative state that environmental problems will magically then disappear (see Scofield 2012).

Where is the self, then? Where is the mind of the self? Loy (2010: 87) says, "The fruit of the Buddhist path is a freedom serene and empowered because [it is] not preoccupied with securing a self that cannot be secured." Recognizing we are not grounded allows us to feel the ground of being itself:

> If we can open up to that ungroundedness at our core, if we can let go and yield to it, then we find that it's the source of our creativity and our spirituality, that at the very core of our being there's something else there, something formless that can not be grasped, something that transcends the self and yet is the ground of the self. (Loy 2005)

When we are able to let go of the construction of the self, when we let the ego go — or, as a famous Jewish prophet once said, the small self must die in order to be reborn as part of a larger universal love that never dies — then "mind" becomes full, or free. It is non-dual, and the division between self and the world dissolves. It becomes a non-dwelling mind that, Loy suggests, sticks nowhere and is free everywhere.

Here again, in developmental terms, is an evolved order at a later stage in which one can move with fluidity between the relative and the absolute and not identify with either. To bring it back to the dialectic between the absolute and relative worlds, resolving that best occurs through our purposive social activity. Loy (2005) says, "The world is perfect just as it is now, and yet it also calls desperately for radical action. That paradox can't be resolved in an intellectual or rational way, but it can be resolved in our practice, in how we actually live our lives."

It is living that experience with fluidity that enables us to not be fixed on either of those two perspectives. We may awaken to realizing our inseparability with the universe as our body, and to see the cosmos — of which we are a part — as a living, self-organizing quality. We may then together create, enact, and embody a caring, just universe. This is a significant advance over the Cartesian and neoliberal myth that mindfulness is about the individual privately attaining well-being, happiness, or compassion as self-enhancing attributes. It overcomes thinking that one must adjust to and reproduce the status quo and instead stands for "changing the entirety of how one lives one's life," and living it in an ethically responsive way (Stanley 2012: 635).

Mindfulness as often performed in secular settings still operates within the Cartesian framework and reinforces the private self as something apart from the world. From an evolving approach, mindfulness meditation is no longer a private, self-centred activity apart from everything else. Along with other endeavours, it is a radical, socially engaged, transformative practice.

Section II

Critical Studies in Social Mindfulness

6

Smile, Anger, Judgment

Anatomy of a Smile

Thich Nhat Hanh (1992: 6–8) suggests we smile when we wake up and go about our day as a way to affirm our awareness and determination to live in peace. He also says, "The source of a true smile is an awakened mind." Nhat Hanh is describing two smiles. One is in relative terms, the other is in the absolute sense. For the first type, he says we should wake up in the morning and smile all day to express our intention to be aware and live in peace. Although smiling on purpose would not be a "true smile," it is nevertheless a signal of intent and a desire to live in peace. He then adds the second kind, a true smile that will naturally arise when one is already awake. The problem is, despite our intentions, since we're living in the relative world, a smile is not always a simple matter.

"Oh, come on," you say, "are you such a New York grump that you're going to deconstruct a request for a simple smile, and pick on that nice guy, Thich Nhat Hanh?"

No, on what he says.

For intentional smiling, if you want to smile in order to say yes to your commitment to live in peace, that's fine. Just know this: in the relative world, a smile is not an abstract entity but an action that gets interpreted depending on context: the meanings, perspectives, and worldviews of the person doing the smiling and of those who see it. The smile of Alice's Cheshire cat just hangs in the air; its body disappears. Disembodied, no context. Mona Lisa's smile is mysterious and ambiguous; we don't know why she's looking like that. What's up with her? Those are not everyday occurrences. Wilber (2006: 298–99) points out that Nhat Hanh too often avoids actual intersubjectivity — in this case, what an awakened mind in the form of a smile *looks like* between people in the relative everyday world of North America in the twenty-first century. It's not a given.

Some days I don't feel like smiling and neither do you. If I'm feeling pissed or just "meh," but walk around smiling in order to "affirm awareness and determination to live in peace," it will look and feel forced and phony. As Hamlet says, "one may smile, and smile, and be a villain."

In class my students and I discussed the idea of smiling in the morning and during the day to see if they could apply what Nhat Hanh says to life in Brooklyn. We looked at stages of self-development, cultural context, behaviour and physiology, and the structure of power, including gender.

Developmental stages are relevant here. For someone at an earlier stage of self-development who does not grasp Nhat Hanh's higher intention, a smile can mean different things. For an egocentric person, smiling can be manipulative and used for personal gain. A person at a conventional level may see smiling as a way to please others and get along with them. We need to distinguish these.

Culture and power: smiling can be an indication of deference and lower status. Some people with less power need to smile more than others — some people with lower class status, some girls and women. If you are a woman, can you just decide to smile? Within almost all societies girls are still socialized to smile more than boys. When a woman in a subordinate position of power smiles, it can make her seem even more subordinate (Drummond 2012). On the other side, one study showed that when the male instructor smiled, even while giving a sexist statement, women tended to adopt a more submissive posture; since women are more inclined to rely on body language, they may see the interaction as more friendly (de Lemus, Spears, and Moya 2012).

Gender is an issue of power and women in particular are often in a bind. When they smile in public, some men see them as available and give them unwanted attention. When they don't smile, some men on the street they don't even know will tell them that they should smile and may even harass them. Many women have good reason to be angry about that and fight back, and other men need to step in and speak up when that occurs.

Some feminists embrace what's known as "resting bitch face" (RBF), a natural tendency for some people that appears as anger to others when the face is at rest. One feminist woman of colour, Jennifer Fumiko Cahill (2018), with tongue somewhat in cheek, takes a mindful attitude. "Instead of fighting my bitchface," she says, "I choose to live my authentic facial truth, to be fully present in my scowl and to inhabit it mindfully." She tells other women with RBF, "Join me and embrace your stern faces, deploying them as a reminder to all who dare look upon them that we have not cosigned this bullshit, we are not OK."

Again, RBF is an issue more for women and not for men — at least not by that name: "When a man looks stern, or serious, or grumpy, it's simply the default," says Rachel Simmons, an author and leadership consultant at Smith College. "We don't inherently judge the moodiness of a male face. But as women, we are almost expected to put on a smile. So if we don't, it's deemed 'bitchy'" (Bennett 2015).

Here at first we see a discrepancy between inner and outer: I don't feel angry but my face is read as angry by others. Doesn't that show there are private thoughts that are at odds with the outer social world? Yes, but again it is resolved through social discourse and by making injustices known. We can reference, investigate, and explain this phenomenon through social interchange — mindfully, if you like: by identifying and speaking about it and about one's feelings, we come to know the nature of this experience as a social phenomenon in need of greater awareness that can lead to better, mutually satisfying social relations. In cases of greater and more significant conflict between inner feelings and outer appearance, we rely and insist on honest relationships with others. For example, we may speak with caring friends and/or with counsellors and therapists, as well as through genuine and skilful political dialogue and action, to help us resolve the discrepancies — to bring our inner experience and outer, observed behaviour into better alignment.

More women are in jobs that require emotional labour — and this includes having to smile, which they experience as alienating. Sociologist Arlie Hochschild (2012: 8) worked with flight attendants, who considered their smiles as part of their work. They often spoke of their smiles as "being *on* them but not *of* them. They were seen as an extension of the makeup, the uniform, the recorded music, the soothing pastel colors of the airplane décor, and, which taken together, orchestrated the mood of the passengers." Svend Brinkmann makes a similar point — when positivity is forced on workers, feelings tend to become commodities; this leads to the workers becoming alienated from their own experience (Goldhill 2017). Hiding feelings and smiles, on the other hand, can be an expression of power. Police virtually never smile, to show they are in control and mean business.

Some wealthy white women who meditate can afford to smile. A number of media representations of meditators are coded in terms of inequities of gender, race, and class, although again it is women who smile and who promote mindfulness. Three *Time* covers on mindfulness show sexualized figures of young, white, slim, able-bodied women, each of whom look to be from a privileged social class background (Mitchell 2014). The world recedes and the focus becomes one of tranquil, inner peace, in private retreat from social realities and that complex, outside world.

On the streets or in the subway in New York we regard a person who goes around smiling with wariness. What's going on with this dude? One apologist for a privatized, individualist mindfulness devoid of social context suggests ways to be "mindful in the subway" (Gelles 2017). This includes turning "your lips up into a half-smile," and working your way around the subway car, offering a "gaze of warmth and kindness" toward everyone you see. If you've performed this and have managed to avoid people moving away from you for your odd behaviour, you can now advance to practising mindfulness on the rest of your trip. Be mindful (and smile) after you've paid the fare increase, waited for the delayed train, squeezed into the crowded car, dodged the homeless panhandler, and cursed out the MTA and the governor for defunding public transportation (Purser and Forbes 2017).

Yet in the rest of the U.S., compared to Europe — and New York — there's more smiling … some of which one critical blogger considers "fake desperate smiles" that "only just tell me that *more* suffering is being created with every flash of the teeth" (Haque 2016). Unlike Nhat Hanh, she distinguishes too much smiling as coming from the predominant "myth of positivity" and sees emotional honesty and acceptance as a more advanced viewpoint. Young people in America, Haque says, should be able to express their anger and challenge the ideology, shared by mindfulness proponents, that says if you're in pain there must be something wrong not with society but with you. Smile if you feel like it and/or if your intentions are good, but be aware of the insidious cultural domination of positivity and don't feel compelled to do so.

A smile is also a behaviour, an exercise not always linked to one's feelings; you can move your mouth upwards with or without a higher intention. It has neurological correlates — the behaviour alone can lead to more serotonin production and muscle relaxation. You might even feel happier, more relaxed, and so you smile to change your mood. As a deliberate strategy, consider the songs that tell you to smile though your heart is aching, and that whenever you feel afraid, whistle a happy tune. Okay, good advice, but none of this leads to a more evolved state of awareness or more skilful or moral action. Those require making explicit a meaningful worldview and intention that you endorse and practise.

After some discussion, the class locates Nhat Hanh's position. We consider states of awareness and stages of development. His second smile arises from at least a high state of consciousness, one in which as he says you can experience the awakened mind that sees the absolute. The problem is he neglects the relative world. Because Nhat Hanh does not also take up the concrete realities and concerns of smiling or not smiling every day in actual situations, we argue that he is not expressing a later stage of universal consciousness. He couches his advice to readers in the language of the spiritual and the absolute — spiritual bypass. It evades actual everyday realities and a critical perspective on what social injustices are occurring.

Nhat Hanh holds to the absolutist myth that meditating the right way leads to good outcomes. He has said, for example, that as long as business leaders practise "true" or right mindfulness and do not have selfish reasons, it doesn't matter if the original intention stems from more efficiency or profits — the practice will change their perspective on life since it naturally develops the desire to end others' suffering (Confino 2014).

The belief here is that well-intentioned mindfulness *by itself* will lead to good results in business. This is naïve enough, but it further ignores the actual corporate structures and capitalist world in which, in order to remain in business, efficiency in the service of profits and the need to satisfy shareholders must take precedence over the well-being of both employees and citizens.

Edward Ryan (2017), a Yale clinical psychologist and long-time meditator, questions whether smiling means being enlightened:

> Have you ever noticed how much smiling there is in American Buddhist circles? Almost every photograph of a meditation teacher or a psychotherapist who integrates Buddhist mindfulness into her or his clinical practice is characterized by an enormous beaming smile. Sometimes I have thought it may be a form of advertisement. Sometimes the smiling even seems competitive: "See how happy I am!" Am I mistaken to think that the implication is that these superlative smilers are enlightened, and that enlightenment naturally leads to blissful happiness? Not to be cranky — I enjoy smiling, both my own and others — but always smiling? And smiling so intensely? What is all the smiling about? I do not think it can be enlightenment.

Go ahead and meditate to become awakened, live in peace, and smile if you choose, or just let it happen. But distinguish that from positive psychology; activist Laurie Penny (2016), says, "When you're washed up and burned out from putting your body on the line to fight the state, it's especially galling to be told to share a smile and eat more whole grains." See yourself as a social being in a particular place in the social world marked by power inequities, understand why many people can't or won't smile, and with others help create actual conditions that can lead to peace, justice, and full awakening (and genuine smiles) for everyone. In this sense, any good self-care, even in the form of a smile, can be part of — but not a substitute for — conscious resistance with others to injustice and a conscious act to prefigure a better world.

Prophetic Anger

> The women watched the men, watched to see whether the break had come at last. The women stood silently and watched. And where a number of men gathered together, the fear went from their faces, and anger took its place. And the women sighed with relief, for they knew it was all right — the break had not come;

and the break would never come as long as fear could turn to wrath. (Steinbeck 1977: 480)

In *The Grapes of Wrath,* the men had just learned there would be no work for three months; they were living in a migrant tent camp during days of relentless rain, their family members sick and dying, their children getting shot at as they were forced to steal food. In an earlier scene, the men were being thrown off their land by the banks, had their houses bulldozed, and were on the verge of hopelessness and despair. In each case, Steinbeck describes how the women watched the men's faces to see if they would break — give up. But each time, when the men came together something happened: their fear turned to anger. The women saw that this was a positive thing because then the men became "whole." For these men and women at such a time and place, anger was not a problem. On the contrary, the men's anger was a healthy sign of their strength and determination to stand up and fight *together* for themselves and their families against injustice.

Some mindfulness folks regard anger as a negative occurrence that just seems to arise without understandable cause. Often they talk about it as a privatized, internal, individual response, a free-floating feeling that is disconnected from why people are angry within the context of their actual lives. Mindfulness proponents seldom situate anger within a social situation, let alone as something shared with others like the men in the story. Contrary to the belief that all feelings like anger are private and internal, however, our task involves more than connecting the inner with the outer. It is to see the inner and the outer as indivisible. Feelings like anger are embodied qualities of people's actual everyday lives and relationships that we need to see in moral terms based on their experience.

Ezra Bayda (2010), a Zen teacher, is someone who treats anger as an abstracted, internal, negative phenomenon, one to be worked on and dissolved. Don't express the anger when it arises, he suggests, so that you can feel the physical energy of anger in order to find its problematic emotional roots. "This can be particularly difficult when the anger is strong, when we really want to hold on to the defensive strategies of blaming and self-justifying to avoid feeling the pain underneath." Why do this? Well, he says, this allows us to see into its roots. "And when we see it right as it arises, we learn to see how it is rooted in fear."

For Bayda, anger is not a legitimate response in its own right, it is always going to lead to blame and self-righteousness. More so, he reverses the experience of the men in *The Grapes of Wrath*. What's under the anger, he thinks, is fear, and that's what has to be felt and acknowledged: you're afraid. But for the men it's the opposite; they become whole when the fear turned to anger. It's the anger itself, as a collective, embodied response, that animates and inspires the men and gives them and the women hope that they will figure something out. Steinbeck himself sees anger in a positive light, when it's employed for, not against, something, as a "symbol of thought and evaluation and reaction: without it what have we got?" (DeMott n.d.).

For Thich Nhat Hanh (2002: 126), too, anger is a problem. "When we get angry we suffer." Nhat Hanh sees anger as negative energy, and mindfulness is positive. He sees anger as an added source of pain and not the best response to people's situations. Anger, he says, needs to be turned into the energy of understanding and compassion. We should act on the basis of compassion, not anger, he says. This is because "human beings are not our enemy.... We cannot take sides" (2002: 128, 131). This approach differs from Steinbeck's men — who needed to take sides — and from some who fight for social justice. It differs from Jesus's teaching to love your enemies. Jesus too emphasized our love for everyone, what Nhat Hanh considers our compassion, which is true on the absolute plane. At the same time, Jesus does not shy away from the relative world, calling people who are greedy, hurtful, and unjust toward us and others our enemies, against whom we must take sides, albeit with compassion and love.

When is anger a problem and for whom? Social context matters; anger is not a free-floating "negative emotion" that can never have a legitimate or justifiable cause. Social-emotional learning (SEL) school programs, often combined with mindfulness, abstract anger from its social context and see it as something that "visits" us, or as a "normal" response to generalized events such as frustration, stress, or disappointment. Those who wish to maintain their power see anger as undesirable and disruptive; anger management is often a popular strategy in schools employed by those in power as a therapeutic method to pacify students.

SEL teaches students individualistic skills to regulate feelings and improve relationships. The organization most closely associated with it, the Collaborative for Academic, Social, and Emotional Learning (CASEL) (2018b), defines it as

> the process through which children and adults acquire and effectively apply the knowledge, attitudes, and skills necessary to understand and manage emotions, set and achieve positive goals, feel and show empathy for others, establish and maintain positive relationships, and make responsible decisions.

We need to look at issues of racism, privilege, and power, and ask, along with Vicki Zakrzewski (2016), education director at the Greater Good Science Center at UC Berkeley, if SEL is "to be used as a band-aid for fitting the student into a particular academic mold determined by the dominant culture? Or can it help educators and schools understand and prevent the violence children experience when their authentic selves, cultural identities, and experiences are not acknowledged?" Zakrzewski cites trauma expert Kenneth Hardy, who points out that for students who face racism, self-management becomes conflated with anger management; when self-management is prescribed for many youth of colour who suffer from the "race-related trauma of rage," it fails to address the "hidden wound of racial oppression." This, Zakrzewski says, "can play out in the classroom when teachers use SEL as classroom management — getting the students to be quiet and compliant, rather than acknowledging and discussing the harsh realities they face in the world."

Some SEL anger management programs apply mindfulness techniques. In one study, mindfulness educators used it to help students calm down so they could better take a test. One student who practised it said, "I get mad easily and [mindfulness] helped me calm down. On the test, I got mad at some questions and got out of concentration. [Focusing on my breath] got me back on track. I just let the monkeys go" (Goodman and Greenland 2009: 418, original brackets).

Being calm for a good purpose is fine. But we need to ask, why did the questions get him mad? What about the test itself? When is his anger about questions and about the pressures of a high-stakes test legitimate and justified? What pressures is the student feeling and what are their sources? Is this issue ever even addressed? That is, when is mindfulness used to adjust students to unhealthy, unjust situations like high-stakes tests by mitigating their anger instead of legitimating it and correcting the unjust sources of the anger?

Instead of using mindfulness to adjust students to fear-inducing high-stakes tests, educators instead should link the embodied expression of anger with the actual conditions of the students' lives, help them make the connections, and demystify the privatized experience and place it within a moral social context. They then can find ways to abolish harmful standardized tests and create meaningful forms of education together.

Mindfulness can benefit from a prophetic stance, a quality of the Abrahamic traditions. Theologian Abraham Heschel (1975), describing the Old Testament prophets, says that such an approach stands for moral universalism. It is critical and discerning, and can be wrathful; at the same time, it is motivated by concern over injustice and holds out the possibility for redemptive inclusivity, respect, and mutuality — that is, loving justice, or compassion.

Some within the Buddhist tradition also employ anger, along with compassion, toward social justice. The Dalai Lama says that intention is important; you can best direct anger at the actions of another and out of genuine concern, and not at the other person themselves. In an interview, he said that "the deep motivation is compassion, but it takes anger as the means to accomplish its ends" (Ueda 2013; see also Tricycle 2012, interview with John Makransky). Overall, professor James Reveley (2016) affirms, in school-based mindfulness programs, righteous anger is needed for students to resist neoliberalism.

Wrathful compassion doesn't always need to be identified as such, as a conscious moral awareness that takes the Other into account; sometimes it appears as plain anger against social injustice. As with the men in *The Grapes of Wrath*, we have to read into the anger and see the implicit moral outrage against the injustices that require it; compassion for the landowners, corrupt police, and bankers who were harming their families did not figure into the men's response, nor did it need to. In *The Last Angry Man* by Gerald Green (1956), the doctor, Samuel Abelman, dedicated himself to helping the people in his poor Brooklyn neighbourhood and was, even in self-defeating ways, often angry. A response of anger appears strange when everyone else just accepts what's wrong as part of what they see as the way things are. As one character described the doctor's irascible integrity, though: unlike others, he was angry at the everyday meanness and fraud he encountered, whether from individuals or corporations.

Some mindfulness practitioners treat anger as an absolute negative and destructive quality; yes, anger can be a problem for both the angry person and the object of the person's wrath, depending on the reason. Yet anger by itself is not the problem. Rather, it depends on whether the anger is for the good of self and all others, and the extent of ego attachment. Contrary to positive psychology, there is nothing intrinsically negative about any emotion, including anger.

Another way to think about it is to ask yourself how much of your own ego is invested in the anger: is the anger vengeful, based on self-righteousness and self-entitlement, attached to your own self-image, privilege, or hurt pride, or is it directed toward unjust actions based on love and that should be opposed with skill? Some men who feel entitled to keep their patriarchal privilege and power over women feel threatened by the #MeToo movement against sexual harassment and by women fighting back against restrictions on reproductive rights; they have reacted with harsh rage that sometimes leads to violence, fuelled by their desire to maintain their supremacy in a self-serving way. Underneath, they are afraid of losing their own power.

We can see anger not as a private matter but as an embodied way of knowing that is embedded in our existing social relations. Buddhist David Brazier says that feelings such as anger give us information about our involvement in the world and what the world requires. Feminist philosopher Jen McWeeny (2010) argues that instead of seeing oppressed women's anger as irrational and hypersensitive, acknowledge that anger is a clear and justified response to institutional oppressions. The anger is knowledge that embodies the sense that one has been wronged; it affirms self-worth and self-agency, and this knowing is liberating. In light of the #MeToo movement in response to sexual harassment, women's anger is justified, and more women are affirming their right to feel and express their anger in the face of those who carry out and/or who are complicit in this injustice (Jamison 2018).

African-Americans, too, sometimes are accused of being too angry and loud. In some Buddhist meditation groups as well as in educational settings, certain cultural patterns of emotional expression of some black people are judged in negative terms as being outside white norms; in meditation groups, this escapes the net of traditional mindfulness. Similar to the #MeToo argument, anger is often justified given people's experiences of institutional and personal racism, and its expression can be self-affirming. What is more, it calls into question the implicit cultural norm of white people's ways of behaving as the one acceptable way to express oneself and illuminates the significant differences in the experiences of each group (Sherrell and Simmer-Brown 2017). For African-American women in particular, Audre Lorde (1997: 280) wrote, anger, which she distinguishes from hatred, is an appropriate reaction to racist attitudes, and when "expressed and translated into action in the service of our vision and our future is a liberating and strengthening act of clarification."

Contemplative social activist James Rowe (2015) says that skilful oppositional thinking, including anger, among socially engaged contemplative communities is crucial to social change; contemplatives need to deploy oppositional approaches to, for example, toxic fossil fuel companies, while being aware of relative and absolute truths. Yes, we are all interconnected in an absolute sense, but in relative terms we also are required to oppose those who seek to harm ourselves, others, and the Earth. That practice, Rowe argued, can lead to collective liberation. Political psychologist Nicholas Faulkner (2013) sees "compassionate anger" as valuable in political ways since it is triggered by seeing injustices done to many people, not just ourselves.

The issue of compassionate anger brings us back to the question of our highest intention regarding our anger. In the U.S., many people suffer from despair and are angry living in an impersonal society and economic system that favours a few and thwarts the so-called American Dream. Raw, unreflective anger can turn against oneself, as with some instances of depression or substance abuse; or against others, as with the rise of hate groups and the murderous mass gun shootings by white males. In a supportive review of three feminist books on American women's anger, author Rebecca Solnit (2018) cites a fable that illustrates the Buddhist value of universal compassion and love. She quotes the co-founder of

Black Lives Matter, Alicia Garza, who, in one of the books, asks:

> The question for us is: Are we prepared to try and be the first movement in history that learns how to work through that anger? To not get rid of it, not suppress it, but learn how to get through it together for the sake of what is on the other side?

This is an astute account of a mindful, well-developed approach: stay with the anger and work through it with others for a greater purpose. Solnit (2018) shows that for two of the book authors, "what is on the other side" is compassion and love, and notes that "most great activists ... are motivated by love, first of all."

As a society, can we connect our feelings of anger with an informed critical awareness of our own social existence as it is marked by inequitable and unjust conditions? Can we together engage in mindful, righteous anger that is motivated by love, and that helps us all to heal, grow, and transform ourselves?

Judgment: The Death of Bin Laden

On May 2, 2011, U.S. military forces hunted down and killed Osama bin Laden, the mastermind of the attack on the United States on September 11, 2001. Among the various responses from religious, spiritual, and mindfulness leaders and teachers was one printed in the *Huffington Post* as "Osama Bin Laden Dead: A Mindful Response" (Goldstein 2011). Elisha Goldstein, a psychologist, mindfulness teacher, and author of numerous books on mindfulness, saw crowds of animated people "screaming and jumping around in jubilation over the death of a man ... it seemed like I was watching some kind of dark comedy. I thought, 'What is the difference between what I am seeing on the video and a crowd standing by and cheering while some enemy is getting stoned to death in front of us?'" He says it was "a good moment for America" but then questions the responses: "was it a moment for cheering, laughing and jubilation?" His answer would seem to be "no" and implies that there are better ways to respond. He is disinterested in understanding anything about those who cheered and sees no difference between their reaction and some vicious torturing of an enemy.

Like many mindfulness teachers, Goldstein skips any recognition, let alone analysis, of facts about the events or the celebrants, making the usual leap into an absolute realm, one of his own choosing. The question is, he asks, "what will it take for us to recognize that we are all connected to one another? Causing pain to another group of people is a strange place to derive happiness from. It seems to be a false happiness; at the root it's really anger or fear." This of course is no longer mindfulness, which is supposed to be non-judgmental and compassionate; the author negatively judges the crowd's happy response as inappropriate and inauthentic, claiming instead to know the real source of their feelings — anger or fear.

Goldstein smuggles in his own individualistic beliefs and calls it mindfulness. He asks, then answers his own question, what is the best mindful prescription? As usual, the solution is to go within, change one's individual self. He seems to believe this will radiate outward to the world and cause less war. The author denies this is a "Pollyanna notion" and that there is indeed war, pain, and trauma. Yet, he says, we need to take a good look at the wars raging inside us in response to "our own personal traumas in life." This is a "very simple path," he says, although "not at all easy." Even bin Laden was not at peace within himself, the author surmises, which led to his misguided delusions that murdering thousands was the right path. The author ends with a hope that we free ourselves from mistaken reactions to the wars within and help guide everyone toward empathy, compassion, and peace "within ourselves and the world."

Goldstein asserts that this is a "mindful response." Yet he does not step back and consider his own point of view, his disapproval about the cheering people and judgment about their real motivations, his overriding their experience in favour of looking within and insistence that we are all connected to each other. What makes his opinion and judgment count as mindful? Are there not other ways to look at what happened, and other ways to respond to bin Laden's death and those happy folks?

From the framework of certain self-development models and their respective stages — for example, Cook-Greuter's Individualist (2013); Forman's Relativistic-Sensitive (2010); and Wilber's Green (2016) — the author's response in this case appears to be lined up at a post-conventional stage that shares similar characteristics. According to these developmental models, someone at this level tends to feel that we are all connected and should have compassion for everyone — except for those who don't feel that way themselves, like those who feel vengeful or glad about bin Laden's death. The author doesn't display any connection with or compassion for them. Another marker of this way of thinking is the notion that everyone must accept everyone else and not judge others — except for those who disagree with this very position of mine (ours): we judge and do not accept those misguided folks, since *they* are so judgmental and unaccepting. We should all see ourselves as interconnected and should agree on things — and if you don't agree with me that we all are interconnected and should agree on things, then you are wrong.

Let's contrast this take on bin Laden's death with the response of another author, Corey deVos (2011), who identifies as an Integral thinker:

> Because the psychological and cultural injuries Osama bin Laden inflicted upon the world were so great, so-called "symbolic victories" like this one (pyrrhic or otherwise) end up having a powerful impact all the way up and down the developmental spiral. Events like these cut through us all, and tend to "light up" different aspects of different people in different ways ... we should ... allow the full spectrum of emotion to arise ... and try to refrain from casting judgment upon others' reactions just because they are not responding the way we would like or expected them to.... The full gamut of ego-centric, ethno-centric, world-centric, and Kosmo-centric reactions ... should all be invited to the table, even as we aspire to widen our circle of care and move toward something much deeper and wider and better within ourselves.

DeVos says that one of the key elements of Integral consciousness is the ability "to hold and handle paradox without the need to 'choose sides' and reduce the rich complexities and contradictions of reality to one side or another of a simple binary. This capacity or paradox becomes vital in times like these."

DeVos understands that such an unusual and emotional event brings out various qualities among people. Let's acknowledge the full range of feelings without judging them, he says. While deVos also includes values of compassion and interconnectedness that mindfulness proponents endorse, he goes further by applying them to those whom Goldstein criticized. He adds two significant pieces: he considers the self-development stage of the celebrants and encourages their growth. Let's look, he says, at the celebrants' worldviews and their various responses, which arise from these. DeVos is aware of developmental stages and holds them from an encompassing, Integral perspective of awareness. This differs from Goldstein's own level of development, in which he identifies with his own worldview. Like others at the Individualistic/Relativistic/Green stage, he does not recognize how his own perspective — all must agree, and if you don't agree with me, you're wrong — is paradoxical and problematic. As an Integralist, DeVos, on the other hand, sees that the cheering crowds display a conventional worldview. People at a conventional level of self-development identify with the norms and values of their own group, and consider those outside the group to be the Other. The demonstrators displayed this perspective in that they took pride in the action of their country over an enemy who harmed us. DeVos then encourages us to not just rest in the acceptance of this standpoint but also to expand our understanding and compassion toward more people and to grow beyond ourselves in both depth and breadth. He applies this practice to those with various responses to bin Laden's death. Goldstein, however, unaware of developmental frameworks that would define the limits of the cheering crowds (conventional) as well as of his own position (relativist), flies his particular judgmental perspective under the flag of mindfulness as if it were a universal absolute.

In the absolute world we are all interconnected; those with the capacity to see within this realm have compassion for bin Laden and for our own internal wars. Yet we are also living in the relative world and need to both understand where people are at and, at the same time, respond with skill and wisdom, and choose the best way to stop adversaries from further harming others and us.

7

What Water? Moral Passion and Truth in David Foster Wallace

David Foster Wallace's 2005 commencement address at Kenyon College, known as "This is Water" (the source of all of Wallace's quotes below unless stated otherwise), leads off with the fable of two young fish who meet up with an older one. "Morning, boys, how's the water?" he asks them. The two swim on for a bit and then one of them looks over at the other and says, "What the hell is water?"

For those of us who crave the whole Truth with a capital T, as Wallace himself describes it, the fish tale is a promising start. Can the wise fish instruct the young ones to become conscious of the water, about our world that's right in front of and around us, yet remains unknown? Just what is the nature of that existence in which we dwell unawares? Will that awareness provide us some relief from the pain of everyday life? Can a fish even come to know what the hell is water?

Desperate to escape his own self-consciousness, and his lifelong depression, Wallace gives us some glimpse of a big Truth that would allow him, and us, to escape our own small minds, the underlying sadness of everyday life, and to realize the nature of water — and he almost pulls it off. In the address, he offers what sound like bits from a secular mindfulness talk. He shares a stunning vision of an advanced state of awareness.

Wallace was not contained by traditional Buddhism (or by anything traditional). He did study Buddhism and meditation but was too worried about whether his posture was right. He began a two-week retreat of Thich Nhat Hanh's but left early because he said the food was bad, as good a reason as any. In his talk, Wallace never mentions meditation, mindfulness, or Buddhism. Yet, as his biographer, D.T. Max (2009), writes, he was preoccupied with mindfulness and paying attention to the things that matter.

Wallace's quest to express what the hell is water offers a possible key to his — and our — later stage of development, one that Buddhism in its own terms describes as a way out of the fundamental suffering of our human existence. He comes close to providing a cosmic understanding of things and a way to get there as he struggled to put it all together. In Max's words, Wallace's last book, *The Pale King*, "expands on the virtues of mindfulness and sustained concentration," which comes close to the topic of the commencement address, the need to pay attention. In his notebook for the novel, Wallace writes,

> Maybe dullness is associated with psychic pain, because some-thing that's dull or opaque fails to provide enough stimulation to distract people from some other, deeper type of pain that is always there, if only in an ambient low-level way, and which most of us spend nearly all our time and energy trying to distract ourselves from. (Max 2009)

What is that other, deeper type of pain that is always there? Is most of life a desperate series of distractions to avoid feeling, confronting, and overcoming that deeper pain? How do we overcome it?

Wallace suffered from depression and was on medication for much of his adult life. He went off it after feeling that it was hampering his creativity and tried various treatments; he returned to his original medication but committed suicide shortly after. In an Integral sense, depression is a complex condition that includes emotional, social, political, spiritual, and developmental as well as biological factors, which may include one's relationship with various medications. This raises larger questions: Can being fully in the transcendent, absolute moment through mindfulness meditation, through attention, cure depression? On the other side, can medication solve someone's fundamental, ontological suffering and sadness? You can see that neither answer is satisfactory, which is why we need to think and see things in more encompassing ways.

One way we can try to make sense of Wallace's compassionate effort to reach the Truth and overcome his fundamental suffering is to look at his stage of self-development using Susanne Cook-Greuter's model (2005, 2013). In this framework, Wallace was a Construct-aware/Ego-aware person who wrestled with the contradictions inherent in that more evolved stage. Cook-Greuter describes some of the qualities at this level that seem to fit Wallace. People perceive the unitary nature of all things but do not yet fully embody it; they feel conflicted around paradoxes of existence and language; they express a commitment to serve others and make a difference in the face of our mortality; and they sense that language and symbols at best give us a partial truth, and that we are always separated from the non-duality of existence.

Without a developmental framework, it is easy to confuse Wallace's vision with the mindfulness evangelists of today who have little sense of how culture, social systems, and stages of development themselves are a kind of water. Secular mindfulness folks seek certain states of awareness. Yet they often are unaware that they themselves as well as others swim in the water of developmental stages, culture, and social structure. Without this understanding, Wallace, like the mindfulness believers, tends to conflate the absolute — the nature of being (ontology) — with the relative, the particular problematic social existence of our own capitalist society. Like them, his solution to the pain of everyday life ("the day-to-day trenches of adult existence") and what it means to learn how to think is "awareness." And to get there, he says, "the really important kind of freedom involves attention."

Attention is an intimate and meaningful action. Through attention, Wallace may be seeking a deeper awareness of the groundlessness of all existence, non-dwelling awareness itself, that which is beyond the duality of relative and absolute. In this sense we can say that attention *is* that. Loy (2010) thinks that this yearning for awareness is not actually my awareness, but that of the cosmos and its desire to become aware of itself through me. That is, Wallace may be at a later stage of development, and although his language is still one of personal choice, he does not just refer to individual choice as an ego-based endeavour but as a reflection of a freer, advanced consciousness. If we take attention for Wallace to mean pure awareness, the groundlessness of all being, then what he is trying to say, although his self-referential language gets in the way, makes more sense. Let's look at how Wallace wrestles with this.

You have a choice of what to think about, Wallace tells the graduates. Meaning and interpretation of things is a matter of "personal, intentional choice." Right away, though, Wallace is wise enough to recognize a paradox to this individualist stance that reflects his Construct-aware stage of development: blind certainty and close-mindedness on the part of the self is a problem too, he says. And one of the worst examples of the "total wrongness of something I tend to be automatically sure of" is my, and our, belief that we are the "absolute center of the universe; the realist, most vivid and important person in existence." So, yes, there is something else of which one needs to be aware.

Wallace warns the students, if you aren't conscious and aware enough to "choose what you pay attention to" and "choose how you construct meaning from experience" in adult life, you will "get totally hosed." He is encouraging students to evolve from an earlier, egocentric perspective to a later one that can take others' viewpoints into account.

Although this basic self-centredness is our default mode, Wallace says, we can choose to alter or even get free of this natural hard-wired default setting. However, he denies that he's lecturing about compassion, other-directedness, or all the other "so-called virtues" — he's beyond looking for answers from conventional society with its moralizing.

Wallace equates intellect with too much abstract thinking and rumination — to follow the mind as master is wrong, he argues. Wallace conflates and thereby dismisses all thinking with rumination; we can argue, however, that his point is that reason and thought alone are no longer going to provide us with answers to deeper truths, and in that sense he's right.

So if there is no conventional moral basis and thinking can't be trusted, how do you keep from being a slave to your head and to your mistaken default setting that I am the centre of all things? Wallace finds an answer in "simply paying attention to what is going on right in front of me, paying attention to what is going on inside me." On the surface, this is Secular Mindfulness 101. No moral platitudes, no thought, just choosing to pay attention. But to what? Like the secular mindfulness folks, he won't commit to categories of what or how to think. Wallace continues in this neutral, technical mode, and says that learning how to think means learning how to "exercise some control over how and what you think," and to be conscious and aware enough to "choose what you pay attention to and to choose how you construct meaning from experience." Notice there's a big emphasis on personal control and choice of constructing meaning. There is a seeming paradox here: you want to get out of your default mode that you are the centre of all things but only you can choose how to construct meaning from your own experience. This paradox can be resolved if we consider that for Wallace, the self is no longer operating from ego-invested interests but more from an evolved plane of free choice; Wallace, however, appears unable to articulate this difference, and without it he falls back to a position that relies on ego: it is I who can choose what I want.

From a conventional order of awareness, telling you to just pay attention to what is right in front of and inside you begs the question of what those things are and how they are described — how they are constructed, what they mean. From a later, Construct-aware stage, though, Wallace is relying on his developed intuition. Wallace has to choose to name what he thinks is problematic and what one should heed instead. He reveals that what he fears most for college grads is that they will each go through their respectable adult life "dead, unconscious," and a slave to a default setting of being "uniquely, completely, imperially alone day in and day out." But Wallace himself appears to take this profound aloneness, with its grinding work and consumerism, as a natural, default setting. Although he says that there are "whole, large parts of adult American life" that involve "boredom, routine, and petty frustration," he leaves it at that; he doesn't critically evaluate American society or consider a larger vision of how people can work together to create a more meaningful and fulfilling culture. Society can't provide any solution or even solace; any attempt to not feel lonely, dead, and unconscious must lie beyond any social endeavours and occur in some more evolved choice to opt for awareness — it seems to be an awareness that does not grasp, that takes no particular form in thought or society. Wallace appears to be discussing boredom and loneliness, and their solution, at an ontological or existential level.

Although he claims that this basic self-centredness is our default mode, Wallace does not blame Western culture and capitalist ideology. Yet he links his notion of attention to a social criticism of neoliberal America. The coordinates of Wallace's nightmarish, dead, unconscious, lonely, adult existence without conscious attention are aspects of a particular American way of life for a certain demographic. He warns the graduates of an "average adult day" of "your challenging, white-collar, college-graduate job," then elaborately outlines the kind of routine that he says his audience will face "day after week after month after year." It includes the cycle of boring work, driving in "slow, heavy, SUV-intensive, rush-hour-traffic," manoeuvring past other tired, hurried people in a "hideously lit" super-market, and dealing with a miserable checkout line and an overworked "frantic lady working the register."

If Wallace were at an early order of consciousness, we might lump him together with many mindfulness coaches who focus on just adjusting the individual to stressful conditions: you can't change much out there, so focus on yourself. The unjust, socially constructed conditions of consumerist society are not of interest to them and are taken as naturalized, given — they just are. Wallace also appears disinterested in and/or skeptical about working with others to change social conditions.

Yet his prescription is an antidote for self-centredness, at least on a personal level. He takes others into account, cares about them, and does criticize North American society. Wallace says: don't fall for the default mode of self-centred individualism and judgmental competitiveness of American consumer society. Get out of your head and at least have some understanding and compassion for others: try to imagine that they have difficult lives that are more tedious than yours, he says, and they may have reasons for acting in selfish ways themselves, reasons that might include caring for others that you can't know about. Wallace works to fight his way out of the self-centred default mode of personal choice. At best, though, he sees others as also stuck inside their own privatized, individualistic cars and heads, in need of a better way to choose how to make the most of their private experience.

Wallace then points to something that is neither egocentric nor social: I can at least choose to consider these possibilities, he suggests, and "if you really learn how to pay attention, then you will know that there are other options." By hinting at "other options," it sounds like Wallace is trying to choose something from an advanced state of awareness that transcends the ego/society dichotomy.

Even in his criticism of North American culture, Wallace refers to the "so-called real world of men and money and power" that hums merrily along in a pool of fear and anger and frustration and craving and worship of self. Our own present culture has harnessed these forces in ways that have yielded extraordinary wealth and comfort and person freedom. The freedom all to be lords of our tiny skull-sized kingdoms, alone at the center of all creation.

To call it a "so-called real world" suggests a deeper real-world that is more meaningful to him and to all of us than self-centredness, money, and power.

Some Sort of Spiritual-Type Thing

Yet Wallace is not content with just social criticism and social change; with your college degree you now have a "more socially conscious liberal arts" judgment and a correct analysis but that's just one more form of that self-centred default setting.

Wallace suggests choosing "some sort of god or spiritual-type thing to worship" — a spiritual and moral vision as a better way to consider things. He says if you don't include "some inviolable set of ethical principles" and instead worship money, possessions, beauty, power, or intellect — all things that enhance the default mode of self-centredness, and which this "present culture" reinforces — you will never feel like you have enough and these forms of worship "will eat you alive."

Yet Wallace still rejects the primacy of this moral perspective and says ethical principles are insufficient "default settings." He makes these secondary to the big Truth of awareness and choice on what you decide to pay attention to. Wallace then makes an astounding leap — he jumps from speaking about choosing to just pay attention to an even further "spiritual-type" visionary state that reconciles the ego caught up in the immanent daily grind with something transcendent:

It will actually be in your power to experience a crowded, hot, slow, consumer-hell type situation as not only meaningful, but sacred, on fire with the same force that made the stars: love, fellowship, the mystical oneness of all things deep down.

Later, he leaps again toward a similar reconciliatory state that combines the sacred with the ordinary at a highly spiritual plane: the freedom of "being able truly to care about other people and to sacrifice for them over and over in myriad petty, unsexy ways every day."

These evolved vision-states reconcile the temporal and finite, the everyday, ordinary things with the eternal experience of universal and sacred love. While some who meditate at any stage might experience this state at times, sustaining this vision arguably can only occur at a late stage of development. Wallace's leap toward this state as a way to reconcile these qualities makes sense if we speculate further about his own developmental stage. In Susanne Cook-Greuter's (2013: 87) model, Wallace's vision-state is in accord with someone reaching up to the next and latest stage, the Unitive: "Persons at the Unitive stage can see a world in a grain of sand, that is, they can perceive the concrete, limited, and temporal aspects of an entity simultaneously with its eternal and symbolic meaning."

Wallace, however, if he is at the earlier Construct-aware stage, cannot sustain this evolved state that sees both the sacred infinite and ordinary finite together. He dismisses it again! "Not that that mystical stuff is necessarily true," he says. "The only thing that's capital-T True is that you get to decide how you're gonna try to see it." There seems to be a disconnect between Wallace's full-throated moral and spiritual vision-state of the finite with the infinite and an attachment to "you get to decide what to worship," the capital-T True. You might think that this reconciling, mystical awareness should be his Truth — the water of which we are unaware — rather than you getting to decide how you want to think about something. But in the second leap he again reverts to the claim that what is most important is "attention and awareness and discipline," as well as "being educated, and understanding how to think," and that Truth is about the real value of an authentic education, which is "simple awareness; awareness of what is so real and essential."

The puzzlement of Wallace proceeding straight from observing one's thoughts to describing a state of non-dual insight about the universe is generally a quality of someone at the Construct-aware stage of development: "The more regular practice of turning inward and observing one's own mental processes also often leads to the spontaneous experience of a direct mode of being in which knower and known momentarily merge, and the personal self-sense disappears" (Cook-Greuter 2013: 81). So it may be that at the later Unitive stage of self-development, mindfulness, paying attention to one's interior processes, can lead to visions that merge subject and object as an evolved state of awareness. However, as Wallace may have found, most Construct-aware individuals cannot sustain these peak moments. For them, Cook-Greuter (2013: 82) says, "they experience moments of freedom from the ego's constant efforts at control and self-affirmation. Yet, such experiences are short-lived. As soon as one evaluates and judges peak experiences, the magic is broken." Self-consciousness wins out.

In Cook-Greuter's description, the Construct-aware person is pre-occupied with an inner conflict around existential paradoxes and the limits of rational thought and language to make meaning. Wallace's dismissal of thought is that of a person at this stage who realizes the limits of rational thought and language. He sees through the predicament that Cook-Greuter (2013: 81) describes of "living in language," which cannot express the reality of "knowing the impermanence of the embodied self." Wallace is nothing if not obsessed with existential choices toward a better life, with how to make meaning, and how language plays a part in that. Construct-aware individuals see a basic flaw in themselves as seeing oneself as the centre of the world, and he labours to let go of his ego attachment. At the Construct-aware stage, which Wallace appears to be, Cook-Greuter (2013: 79) describes the realization that "final knowledge about the self or anything else is seen as illusive and unattainable through effort and reason because all conscious thought, all cognition is recognized as constructed and, therefore, split off from the underlying, cohesive, non-dual territory."

Let's take Wallace at his word. Okay, the Truth is the *choice* to become aware, to become aware of your egocentric default mode and to then choose "other ways." Is this still a falling back toward a self-centred posi-tion, toward an egocentric self? Not if we value the free actions of each of us to make personal choices no matter the circumstances, to do so as embodied beings who are not following a prescribed moral or spiritual path with a known end or outcome, and who are willing to take risks in a messy, uncertain world. An awake, aware being at an advanced stage can be free to make personal choices coming from their own experience. At any given moment we are free to choose how to see things, what to think about; the more conscious, or mindful, we are of each moment in which we choose, the freer we are, albeit always within the context of our social existence.

John Steinbeck (2002: 131) strikes a similar chord in *East of Eden*:

> The free, exploring mind of the individual human is the most valuable thing in the world. And this I would fight for: the freedom of the mind to take any direction it wishes, undirected. And this I must fight against: any idea, religion, or government which limits or destroys the individual.

In developmental terms, this is not egocentrism but a later stage or order — the ability to move freely in different values systems; the emphasis on personal freedom without harming others; and the ability to direct thought and action from an inner core. It is akin to what Robert Bellah et al. (2007: 333–35) call "expressive individualism." This Whitmanesque individualism stands against the earlier "utilitarian" kind based purely on self-interest. Instead, it is the unfolding of each person's unique core of feeling and intuition in order to realize one's individuality — and for whom one may even "find it possible through intuitive feeling to 'merge' with other persons, with nature, or with the cosmos as a whole."

The water is the capital-T Truth of our non-dual and interdependent existence — the fire of consumer hell is of the same flame that made the stars, love and oneness, *as well as* the default thinking of privatized, lonely selves who believe they are the centre of the universe. Integral therapist Mark Forman, following Cook-Greuter, says that beneath the construction of meaning is a deeper reality, an "undifferentiated phenomenological continuum" (Cook-Greuter 2013: 88), a constantly changing "ground-of-being that cannot be adequately described in words" (Forman 2010: 147).

Wallace perhaps sensed the water beyond words and experienced states of knowing it, but tragically suffered from severe depression and ended his life. A close follower of Wallace's life and writings says:

> The book Wallace was too stuck in himself to complete [at the time of his suicide] is one in which he was observing how we all ought to become unstuck, sadly. The realization that you have

something of value to contribute to the greater world necessarily involves prying your mind off yourself for a minute. (Bustillos 2011; brackets added)

Depression, Mindfulness, and Development

For Cook-Greuter (2013: 85), when Construct-aware individuals "cannot integrate this awareness [of both the relative constructed world and a deeper absolute reality], their depression is about man's [sic] essential aloneness and inability to create lasting meaning through the rational enterprise." This is Wallace's anguish, his need to stretch language and individual meaning construction to its limit yet failing to reach lasting connection with the non-dual nature of reality. He sees through the limits of language and constructs yet can't get beyond them.

Mark Forman (2010: 204) proposes that a therapist who works with a Construct-aware individual can "remind the client of what he or she already knows by this point — that the identity that one finds when one 'forgets the ego' is freer, more real, and more fulfilled than the one that is left behind." At a healthy level of Construct-awareness, says Cook-Greuter (2013: 83), "most are capable of arriving at a dynamic and hopeful balance within these fundamental conflicts: They fulfill their perceived or chosen destiny independently and courageously in full realization of their basic despair and aloneness."

For those at this stage who seek to transcend it, a kind of deliberate meditative practice is beneficial. Forman (2010: 205) says:

By encouraging the practitioner to relax into both pleasurable and painful sensations and emotions, it is expected that he or she will begin to become aware of the basic energetic nature that underlies the sensation. Done repeatedly and consistently, and a matter of practice, deeper spiritual insights begin to emerge.

The Construct-aware practitioner, Forman says, can experience the underlying reality "as an expression of something spiritual of which one is a part."

Awareness of the non-conceptual, non-dual, sacred reality calls us to see, name, and practise this basic Truth, the water, in all areas of life; both inner and outer, a transcendence of egocentrism and of conventional moral prescriptions — Wallace rejected both of these — in which both choice and compassion are conscious and unconscious, in the sense of spontaneously arising. It is rare to reach this steady stage of awareness. In his emphasis on attention as awareness, perhaps Wallace was reaching for this transcendence, and seeking it in the immanence of ordinary life within the selfishness and drudgery of corporatized America.

We are left with another possible hint about Wallace's thinking from his unfinished novel, *The Pale King*. Wallace left a note that laid out the novel's idea that is akin to how meditation from a Buddhist tradition can lead to an awakening:

> Bliss — a-second-by-second joy and gratitude at the gift of being alive, conscious — lies on the other side of crushing, crushing boredom. Pay close attention to the most tedious thing you can find (Tax Returns, Televised Golf) and, in waves, a boredom like you've never known will wash over you and just about kill you. Ride these out, and it's like stepping from black and white into color. Like water after days in the desert. Instant bliss in every atom. (Max 2009)

Once we can stop distracting ourselves and sit with these feelings ("ride these out"), and reach behind identifying with them and our self and let these go, we become freer and joyful in all ways. This could be the deeper meaning of attention that Wallace strove to reach.

In North American society, to become awake in this way is all the more difficult to do; Wallace was critical of American culture — his sense that, as Max put it, "America was at once overentertained, and sad." It distracts itself to the extreme in order to avoid the underlying sadness of not facing itself. Max wrote that Wallace wanted to "show people a way to insulate themselves from the toxic freneticism of American life" and admired people who can "achieve and sustain a certain steady state of concentration, attention, despite what they're doing." You feel for Wallace, who wanted so much to break through his cosmo-onto-bio-logic-al depression and live in joy in "every atom" of his being. As Wallace told his audience at the end of his talk, we have to keep reminding ourselves, over and over, "This is water. This is water." May we all help each other do so.

Section III

Mindfulness in Schools

8

Interiority: The Persistence of Inner Life

Despite their claim to value emotional learning, schools tend to override the importance of the inner life. (See Chapter 5 on interiority, and what we refer to as the mind or self.) There is little interest in subjective qualities such as consciousness, meaning, values, feelings, critical thought, imagination, creativity. Schools see these as private experiences cut off from others and often refuse to acknowledge how they are a part of everyday, often unjust social relations. Schools seldom explore moral and spiritual values or engage in dialogue around these issues; they are left up to the private individual, regarded as off-limits in the curriculum.

Even mindfulness in schools lacks interiority in significant ways. Mindfulness has little to no moral foundation, no evaluative stance on what counts in terms of meaning and importance in the social and historical world. It is the practice of paying attention without judgment, a kind of inner behavioural technology, and avoids venturing into critically discussing values — what matters, what should count as objects of attention. Some mindfulness educators regard feelings as free-floating entities that just arise in mysterious ways; they speak of them as just "visitors," abstracted from social context (Greenland 2010: 162). Because they are immeasurable and regarded as private, they are not otherwise evaluated and seldom discussed. Mindfulness also shuns the interior framework of self-development, the knowledge and understanding of how stages of growth frame the states of awareness that occur during mindfulness practice.

A trend that contributes to the neglect of the inner life is the push to make school counsellors' work more about helping students attain measurable academic success than about promoting full self-development. Feelings were once the domain of school counsellors. Now they are more educated to regard feelings in instrumental terms, as things that get in the way of students doing better, succeeding in measurable terms at school and behaving in conventionally approved ways. School counsellors are now charged with attending to the functioning of the system of the school as a whole and to consider their identity as defined in meeting its mandate. This has weakened an important counselling task: addressing students' personal concerns other than academic achievement.

These counsellors now prioritize the needs of the school, implementing comprehensive counselling programs and delivering curricula to improve the school's academic success. The Wallace-Reader's Digest Fund and the Education Trust wrote the Transforming Schools Initiative over concerns with the muddled identity of the school counselling profession; it argued for the need to refocus school counsellors on helping students attain high achievement. It steered the profession toward this path by claiming that school counselling should chiefly be about academic success (Education Trust 2009), and their definition of a school counsellor is a clear reflection of this. According to them, school counselling is

> a profession that focuses on the relations and interactions between students and their school environment to reduce the effects of environmental and institutional barriers that impede student academic success. School counselors foster educational equity, access, and academic success in a rigorous curriculum to ensure that all students graduate from high school ready to succeed in college and careers.

To the extent schools at all endorse developing students' emotional and personal qualities, they tend to regard these as subordinate means to improve students' academic achievement rather than as intrinsic, valuable qualities in their own right. Student "academic achievement" and "college readiness" remain unexamined constructs; they are givens, the values of which are presumed to be self-evident and are seldom discussed, let alone evaluated. Even when school counsellors introduce mindfulness (Paterson 2016; Tadlock-Marlowe 2011), they frame references to interior processes — attention, emotional regulation, empathy — as individualistic, instrumental skills that uncritically serve to adjust students to the school's neoliberal expectations toward compliant behaviour and academic success.

A pervasive cultural trend that affects school counsellors and other educators and that aligns with the focus on academic success is the denial of subjectivity altogether. Contemplative educator Oren Ergas (2017) notes:

> Our public curricula may include diverse lessons in different subjects but self-knowledge is usually not one of them. Curricular time spent with pedagogies in which students are encouraged to explore their interior lives, is extremely scarce compared to the study of disciplinary knowledge and skills.

This shows up as the attempt to reduce the rich qualities of inner life to "nothing but" or as a function or epiphenomenon of something else that is more primary. The following approaches within the broader culture and in schools contain a piece of the whole, or a partial truth. However, in their quest to reduce or explain away inner life by other means, each tends to absolutize its perspective and operate as if it were the whole truth.

Inner Life as Nothing But Behaviour or Brain Matter

For some behaviourists, internal processes and experiences such as emotions, even consciousness itself, are nothing but observable behaviours or outcomes that they can modify and manipulate. Our school counselling students report that many administrators and teachers, most of whom are not sensitized to issues of student perceptions, experiences, and feelings, focus instead on the troublesome behaviour of students. When a student is distraught and expresses this in a disruptive way, many of these educators often are more concerned with the behavioural consequences. In such cases, they value classroom management as a behavioural issue in conventional ways; they regard keeping the students from misbehaving and following the rules as more important than what is going on with the student in terms of their feelings, their family and interpersonal relationships, or the social conditions of their everyday lives. The behavioural influence is even evident in the field of SEL, which says it is about teaching students how to deal with feelings. A behavioural bias occurs to the extent that students are taught cognitive-behavioural "skills" that are to be learned or enacted on an extrinsic, formulaic basis, but without ensuring that the students internalize — that is, value, understand, and make personal sense of — the meaning of the skills.

The insistence today on outcomes assessment, such as high-stakes test results, is a more pernicious example of focusing on student behaviour for academic performance. Education policymakers pressure educators, including school counsellors, to take objective data like test scores as the primary, if not the sole, representation of whom a student is. Their performance on the test that particular day — not the quality of what the student knows and values, what they find meaningful and motivating, or how they conceptualize knowledge — is now of overriding importance. This testing creates fear and anxiety and thereby stifles curiosity, critical thinking, and the questioning of authority.

For other materialists, emotions are just functions or epiphenomena of brain processes to be modified through various brain-altering techniques or treated with medication. Recent trends in neuropsychology research and the increased popularity in prescribing medication for children and in other psychotherapies reflect this belief: problems are all in the brain. It is important to distinguish arguments that poor social environmental factors negatively influence brain development from reductionist approaches that seek to find all causal explanations for human behaviour in the brain and that minimize the significance of subjectivity. For some theorists and neuroscientists, the self and consciousness do not exist; they are just things produced by the brain. Integral therapist Elliott Ingersoll refers to this ideology as the epiphenomenon or "side-effect" hypothesis, which regards the mind as nothing more than a side effect of the brain (Ingersoll and Zeitler 2010: 29–32). Arthur Zajonc, a contemplative educator, notes that experience gets "labeled 'epiphenomenal' and considered by some to be merely the froth on the wave of a neuro-physical reality. Yet it is here that we live our lives, that we suffer and rejoice, struggle to understand, to love, to act" (Palmer and Zajonc 2010: 62).

Inner Life as Nothing But Cultural Relationships

Some postmodernists reduce the self, feelings, and the notion of subjectivity to nothing but aspects of networks of intersubjective relations and cultural constructions, since they argue that there is no self in the first place that can "have" feelings, just infinite webs of culturally constructed relationships. This leaves no room for depth of interiority, only surface relations. Social constructionists claim that "it is no longer meaningful to talk about a core identity when identity shifts by virtue of the relational context in which a person is presently immersed" (McNamee 1996: 127).

While intersubjective relationships are crucial, subjective and individual differences get obliterated when everything, for example, is accounted for by ethnicity or race alone. It is rare for multicultural counselling to reflect on itself and it tends to remain at a relativistic level of development. Cultural relativism in the broader sense occurs when counsellors insist that all viewpoints and values are valid, that there must be no hierarchy of truth, and that no one can claim to know any objective knowledge — again, an absolute truth claim in itself.

Some counsellors become so enamoured of the notion that everything is just a relative social construction mediated by cultural relationships that they reduce all problems to that of cultural relations. One counsellor, R. Rocco Cottone (2013), suggests the rise of a "new paradigm" in counselling: radical social constructivism. In this notion, everything is understood through culturally defined relationships expressed through language. "There is no psychology of the individual," Cottone claims. "All thoughts, all words and all concepts such as free will and individual choice are communicated by others and reflect one's cultural context rather than one's individual psychology."

He goes so far as to conclude that, "there is no individual choice" since choice is socially constructed; "there is no free will" because that's just a "culturally loaded term consistent with Western cultural bias toward autonomous decision-making.... There is no individual moral conscience."

Cottone confuses two issues and then draws the wrong conclusion from this conflation. Yes, human experience occurs in constructed, cultural contexts that supply the meaning and language for understanding our thoughts and actions. However, he errs in concluding from this that therefore everything must be collapsed into cultural relationships and that there is no perspective of subjectivity or first-person experience. First-person experiences of free will, autonomous decision making, and individual moral conscience do exist — within cultural constructs of meaning, but they themselves are not reducible to cultural relationships. The experience of personal choice and conscience, and the individual awareness and reflection of these, even within cultural contexts, are their own phenomena. Cottone deletes subjectivity: he has no interest in exploring it since from his ideological position of radical social constructivism it doesn't exist. According to this position, there is no sense of self, just "biological organisms in a social medium" (Cottone 2013). His dismissal of the experiential qualities of autonomous decision making as just a "culturally loaded term" is another example of conflating a psychological phenomenon with culture — in this case, Western culture. His own negative bias about the "Western cultural bias toward autonomous decision-making" is further evidence of his conflation of a particular evaluation of a particular culture and the neutral fact that all terms, indeed all forms of human life, are culturally constructed.

Some social constructionist counsellors, then, prefer to see clients' experiences as a function of language narratives or stories that the client constructs and that then can be rewritten, reframed, or re-construed. While perceiving things requires cognitive construction, and reframing and developing new narratives can be therapeutic, it is inadequate and problematic to reduce all other aspects of life to language or to narratives that can be arbitrarily assigned meanings. Feelings are experienced directly and are also framed within developmental worldviews; they are not just reducible to or transformed or dissolved by arbitrary different language or narratives. As Mark Forman (2010: 265) notes,

> *the relativistic view becomes problematic when cultural, racial, or power issues are assumed to be the major causal or etiological factors, when neither the client nor the evidence in a given case suggests that they are.* It is also problematic when they lead the therapist to ignore individual subjective experience and stage growth. (original italics)

Inner Life as Nothing But Social Systems and Institutions

Ken Wilber (2007) points to the problem with systems theories that attempt to encompass and explain everything; systems leave out essential interior qualities, are reductionistic in their own right, and are thereby not Integral:

> Systems theory and most forms of ecology and eco-philosophy — generally fall short in their holistic quest, and instead of truly integrating the manifest world, they merely reduce all I's and all We's [individual and intersubjective interiority] to a web of dynamically interwoven Its — the Web of Life …; [absolutizing a universal Web of Life] eviscerates the interior domains in their own terms.

In education, some social justice activists and counsellors absolutize educational or social systems. They regard interior feelings such as self-doubt, self-hatred, and sadness as functions of oppressive social, economic, and political systems or structures, beliefs imposed by those in power that then become internalized and keep people feeling submissive ("internalized oppression" or "colonized mentality").

To their credit some social justice advocates rescue the significance of interior experience from those who disregard its validity altogether in favour of altering political and economic structures as the primary solution to everything. Most counsellors concerned with social justice rightly claim that such feelings need to be addressed and worked through at an experiential or subjective level, often with other members of the group that experiences the oppressed conditions, and even with those whom, with or without intention, contribute to the oppressive conditions. Nevertheless, some of those concerned with internalized oppression appear to subscribe to the notion that such feelings are secondary — that is, mere reflections or epiphenomena of primary structural injustices and oppressive social conditions, and that interior life is not a significant terrain of its own.

Some schools attempt to introduce structural or environmental means to resolve emotional and interpersonal problems. For example, schools may try to reduce students' feelings of envy, competition, and low self-worth regarding the pressure to wear fashionable clothes, and the ensuing disruptive behaviours, by requiring all students to wear uniforms. Other schools aim to provide computers to every student as the way to solve motivational issues in learning, or believe that smaller classes or smaller schools is the one answer. However, while it's undeniable that adverse social conditions, educational policies, and structural inequities influence student development, values, beliefs, and emotional well-being, and that certain changes can and should make a difference, the concern here is the overuse of environmental factors to account for all problems. This can lead to the mistaken belief that once these conditions or structures are eliminated, corresponding personal experiences — for example, self-hatred, sadness, and anger, or social patterns of homophobic bullying, racism, or sexism — also will just disappear.

Inner Life as Nothing But Relativistic Individualism

Recognizing the validity of experience and states of consciousness, however, does not mean there exists a private realm, cut off from and inaccessible to others, that is not a part of overall human life, social relations, and activity. This leads to the myth that opinions are not subject to objective verification and that believing whatever I think and feel must be true. This fallacy places subjectivity over everything and leads to solipsism, narcissism, and the denial of facts and truth ("truthiness") that are found in the social world. Kurt Andersen, writing about the history of the American taste for fantasy spun by creative entrepreneurs and con artists, says: *"If I think it's true, no matter why or how I think it's true, then it's true, and nobody can tell me otherwise.* That's the real-life reduction ad absurdum of American individualism" (Durbin 2017, original italics).

Many believe that anyone's outrage, including some who challenge oppression, need not be examined within its context; they take feeling outraged as the foundation of moral authority and as an unquestionable truth. Philosophy professor Kelly Oliver (2017) writes:

> Privileging *raw* feelings over the *cooked* analysis of them not only fuels anti-intellectualism, but also conceals the socio-historical context that produces those feelings … to authorize outrage

(whether on the left or the right) as foundational and beyond
analysis is to deny the ways in which race, class, gender, politics,
upbringing, culture and history shape our emotions. (original
italics)

Inner Life as Integral to Everything

From an Integral perspective, the subjective, first-person viewpoints,
experiences, and states of consciousness of counsellors, teachers, and
students are each irreducible and legitimized as important domains of
knowledge in their own right. Through meditation and intentional self-
development through the stages, we can train ourselves to reach more
subtle and formless states of consciousness; these qualities of advanced
states can become permanent.

Overall, we need to illuminate the complexities and ambiguities of
inner life on their own complex terms. In the face of the education bureau-
cracy, with its demand for behavioural accountability, a few educators
hold out for the importance of subjectivity and inner experience in the
field — for example, curriculum theorists William Pinar and Madeline
Grumet (2014). Contemplative pedagogy is another realm that values the
interior. An education proponent for a critical contemplative pedagogy,
Peter Kaufman (2017) asserts that it provides space in the classroom
for "first-personness," and it "revolves around introspection, reflection,
and attention." Cognitive psychologist Eleanor Rosch (2008) argues for
the importance of contemplative education as a path of inner wisdom:
"Blindness to all but the outer level of the mind has produced a constricted
view of psychology, an obstructed educational system, a dearth of wise
decision making, and a world in disarray."

Inner work, self-reflection, is crucial to wisdom and full human
development. Inquiry into one's personal thoughts, beliefs, feelings, the
meaning of one's family history, and states of consciousness; into one's
imagination; into those aspects of oneself of which one is unaware; into
troublesome and unhealthy thoughts; into how one's worldview and emotional makeup have been conditioned by ideologies, assumptions, and
experiences from one's past and from the dominant society; inquiry into
the very nature and development of the self: these are essential practices

that mindfulness programs in schools seldom engage or encourage — although they can and should.

However, an Integral perspective sees experience as embodied in the overall qualities of human activity. It is, to borrow a phrase from Marx and employ it in another way, the ensemble of human relations that grounds and defines, but does not reduce, subjective meanings and qualities of feelings and aesthetic experiences to those relations. Personal awareness and consciousness must refer to social life for it to have meaning; yet experience itself is not reducible to the realm of interpersonal and cultural relationships.

In Integral terms, core identity can be recognized and validated. This can occur despite the postmodern critique that claimed the death of the ego and deconstructed it away into many contexts; that is, this perspective is post-postmodern (McIntosh 2012). Integral theory, Ingersoll notes,

> proclaimed the birth of a far more complex individual. This more complex, expanded map of the self included the impact of relationships, shared beliefs, and meaning-making. In addition, we include the revival of the wisdom traditions and decades of studying the relationship between spirituality and psychology. (Ingersoll and Zeitler 2010: 11)

Mindfulness programs in schools overall fail to embrace the complexity of inner life. Instead of critically exploring consciousness, they settle for a mindfulness of raw emotions that leaves unexamined the nature of one's self and its embodied, social place in the world. Rather than seeking critically skilful inner wisdom to enhance human development, they employ mindfulness instrumentally to promote neutral behavioural and neurological functions such as focusing, calming, and self-regulation. In both cases, mindfulness ends up simply adjusting students to the conventional, troublesome norms of academic success that neoliberal schooling demands.

Another significant aspect of subjectivity missing from mindfulness programs is a critical awareness of the stages of self-development, to which we now turn.

9

Interiority: Self- and Moral Development

Mindfulness meditation in education needs to account for both states of consciousness and stages of self-development. Stages are part of a hierarchical order of growth — however, this use of hierarchy is not to be confused with a biased, Western model of arbitrary power that judges early stages of culture or consciousness as inferior to others.

According to the school counselling profession, a developmental approach, which considers the level of each student and promotes the full development of all students, is a significant aspect of the emerging consensus for what defines a professional counsellor; in the words of one counselling professional, the approach "sets us apart from other mental health professionals" (Thomas Clawson in Rollins 2010: 38).

Without an Integral awareness, though, the focus on development in counselling leads to over-attachment on one hand and lack of understanding on the other. Amid the anxiety to define the profession, one counsellor argues that his peers should continue to emphasize development instead of social systems in their advocacy work. This, he says, is so that the professional counselling identity will not be confused with the field of social work: "Professional counseling's uniqueness is contained in its historical focus on promoting growth and development in clients — not changes in social systems" (King 2010). This is a good example of a non-Integral position that over-identifies with one factor, development. It excludes other perspectives — in this case, social structures — and fails to see development and social structure as essential to each other and that they co-occur.

Yet school counselling programs, despite their stated commitment to provide developmentally appropriate interventions in K–12 settings that foster student growth, seldom promote post-conventional moral reasoning and self-development among themselves. Nor does the counselling profession, with few exceptions (see *Counseling and Values* 2007; McAuliffe and Eriksen 2011), appear to be interested in promoting later stages of adult development among counsellors or other educators. There is little commitment as well to help students examine aspects of themselves as objects of awareness from more encompassing perspectives. Even were this to occur, a critical cultural context of meaning is necessary.

Many mindfulness educators lack an understanding about the difference between states and developmental stages. Mindfulness practices can create a heightened state of awareness; a student or teacher, through practice, might notice or witness their feelings, thoughts, and sensations and come to distance themselves from and de-identify with them in a calm manner. Within a meditative state you can focus on something or experience a non-focused, spacious awareness of whatever arises. However, as Wilber notes, a person may attain an advanced meditative state through mindfulness but their developmental structure constrains their worldview; the developmental stage of self and moral development of the student or teacher frames how that state is interpreted and contributes to how the person thinks in response. He also points out that you can meditate for years and reach states of subtle awareness yet not discover the outer, structural stages of development; just as you can study the developmental stages of individuals and cultures yet not attain a more evolved state of consciousness.

Mindfulness educators seldom if ever apply or even acknowledge developmental models as a way to inform and help students, teachers, and the schools themselves. As we develop, explains Robert Kegan (1994), we turn our subjective, inner patterns of thinking into objects of our own awareness and reflection for later stages. We are then able to take a more encompassing perspective, to look back and see what we used to believe and think, and see those thoughts and perspectives to which we were once attached. We can think back to David Foster Wallace's metaphor about the two young fish who are asked about the water by an older, wiser fish. With a more encompassing viewpoint, the fish could learn to move beyond their limited worldview and see it from a more objective perspective.

Development is dialectical; it is not linear, mechanistic, or inevitable. This means we understand and accept where people are along the full hierarchy of growth stages, within their moral, social, cognitive, and spiritual realms. Integral meta-theory also accounts for insights and truths from historical epochs — in developmental terms, traditional, modern, and postmodern — each with its contributions and limitations.

Kegan's model of self-development is a variation on the basic hierarchy of egocentric, conventional, post-conventional, and unitive. Instead of stages he refers to orders: early impulsivity (first order); egocentric (second order), conventional (third order); post-conventional (fourth order), and unitive or universal (fifth order).

Educators and students may gain a contemplative experience or conscious state by practising mindfulness, but many still have at best a conformist and conventional developmental stage (third order) mentality that filters and limits their mindful state. In some mindfulness programs, participants, despite their practice, still adhere to loyalty to authority, strict rule-following behaviours, and uncritical, conformist thinking. Mindfulness practice by itself does not lead to critical questioning, moral reasoning, or skilful and moral actions. Nor by itself does it lead to later stages of autonomous thinking, the ability to hold ambiguity, and to think on one's feet from a post-conventional cognitive or moral developmental order. While mindfulness education programs encourage awareness and reflection of emotions and intentions, they steer a middle course through the developmental waters of interiority.

Educators generally teach and practise mindfulness in the context and service of producing conventionally successful students and teachers who can adjust to the demands of neoliberal society. Unlike depth psychology, they avoid the uncharted realms of unconscious emotional life; unlike Buddhism, they bypass later, ego-transcendent states and stages, or the wisdom to look more deeply at causes of unhappiness or at what is meaningful. For full and optimal human development, educators and students would need to be free to explore the shadow and contemplative aspects of human experience.

We can apply the practice of mindfulness meditation toward self- and moral development. Mindfulness can enhance and promote movement toward more encompassing stages of awareness that consider perspectives beyond one's own. This is one useful mode of mindfulness. If we can guide awareness toward noticing beliefs and values within our stage or order, we then can identify and discuss them, choose to let them go and consider the next, more inclusive perspective. In doing mindfulness meditation with an urban high school football team, I framed mindfulness practice in part as a tool for self- and moral development. I employed it in part as a means for the young men to let go of their attachment to an egocentric or conventional worldview about masculinity and other aspects of the self; they learned to witness their own assumptions and beliefs, and to envision later, more expansive moral perspectives (Forbes 2004; Orr 2014).

Educators need to consider people's moral developmental worldviews. Facts alone seldom change people's opinion, given that people interpret information through a worldview that organizes their thinking (Lakoff 2010). An important developmental task in schools is to help students move from a sociocentric or conventional worldview to a more post-conventional, liberal, or autonomous one. Conventional students tend to believe they must follow the rules and obey those in power. At this stage people identify with their family, religion, or ethnic group and view those on the outside as Others. Educators and counsellors who want to help students develop more encompassing, post-conventional perspectives frame their teaching through caring relationships, respectful listening, and dialogues that point out the contradictions and consequences of the students' ways of thinking. Alongside this, they work to change the social structure and relationships with Others; mindfulness can supplement all these actions.

Counsellor educators who take a "constructivist-developmental" approach to teaching counselling help students arrive at higher-order perspectives in which they can reflect on their own belief systems as well as those of others; they employ Kegan's model of self-development (McAuliffe and Eriksen 2011). Developmentalists and counsellor educators help move counselling students from conventional moral development — in Kegan's terms, a third order (tell me what to do; duty-oriented morality means maintaining the social order) — to post-conventional, self-authorized consciousness, or fourth order (there is no clear answer here, I can think on my feet; I can tolerate ambiguity). Given the complex demands on a school counsellor, Eriksen and McAuliffe (2006: 188) point out, "counselor educators aim to assist students toward a postconventional schema because it parallels the work of counseling. Postconventional people move beyond considering the current social order to be ultimate." Counsellors can practise Integral thinking to allow them to honour, understand, and work with all earlier stages of students.

A developmental understanding serves as a check on pure subjectivity; it accounts for the framework or worldview of consciousness. But we still need to place self-development within broader cultural and social contexts to avoid excessive individualist self-absorption. In the counselling and mindfulness work I did with the high school football team and in my classes, I placed developmental awareness within an inclusive framework of knowledge and practice. With the young men, we critically examined the particular political and social structure of schooling, football, and consumerism, and looked at ways they could use mindfulness to resist and challenge exploitative situations in skilful ways. In my school counselling courses, students have examined and reflected on their own stage of self-development from various models as part of their own personal and professional growth. We've discussed how later development, along with skilful mindful actions, can help them resist and challenge injustices and exploitation in schools and social settings, and promote healthier relationships.

It is necessary but not sufficient to help students evolve to Kegan's fourth order of self-development, which he rightly argues is needed to meet the complexities of postmodern society. But remaining at this level without a broader, balanced awareness can yield stagnant, self-contained individualists who do not experience or share deeper connectedness with others. A culture of self-satisfied fourth-order selves risks ending up as an unhealthy collection of individualistic, atomized egos, socialized to compete and succeed in a market-based society, who think in relativistic terms, and who are blind to cultural and social injustices. If mindfulness can contribute to helping people evolve to a healthy fourth- or even fifth-order consciousness as described earlier, so much the better, but it is not enough by itself.

Contemplating the Contemplative: A Higher-Order Practice

Within developmental terms, a later perspective enables us to reflect on belief systems themselves. This is Kegan's fifth order of self-development. Tom Murray (2009: 105) makes the distinction in terms of orders of self-development with respect to progressive and Integral education: "If every perspective is like a lens or filter which distorts perception and inference, then we can correct for these distortions to the extent that we understand something about the lens or filter itself (turning subject into object, as Kegan frames it)." That is, we want to reach a level of consciousness in which we can include awareness of our own systemic worldviews, reflecting back on our own belief systems and loosening our own attachments to them; from a meta-perspective we can see how we ourselves fit into educational systems as well.

Most identified progressive and holistic educators, Murray (2009: 112–13) argues, are not at this point:

> The progressive, alternative, reform, and holistic pedagogies … are associated with [Kegan's] fourth order (and reach into his fifth order). Integral approaches are more centrally fifth order. Applied to the domain of education, learners at Kegan's fourth order are self-directed (or self-authoring, co-creative) learners who can examine themselves and their culture, develop critical thinking and individual initiative, and take responsibility for their learning and productivity. At full fourth-order consciousness, individuals have mastered skills such as these, and in the process of doing so, likely became advocates of such skills and identified with them believing this level of skill superior to others. Typically, they have practiced and identified with one or a small number of progressive schools of thought....
>
> At Kegan's fifth order individuals begin to reflect upon whole belief systems, even their own fourth-order beliefs, as limited and indeterminate systems. They begin to dis-identify with any particular belief system, and experience themselves as embodying a variety of evolving belief systems, surfacing in different contexts. Questions of "who am I," "what do I believe," "what

is true," and "what is right" cease to have one best optimal answer ("it depends!") Rather than responding to situations by looking for optimal or win–win solutions (a fourth-order approach), fifth-order individuals see themselves as co-evolving constituents of each situation, and expect a problem situation or dilemma to transform them; they may continue to search for an adequate solution or approach to a problem — each developmental level transcends and includes prior ones, as [Ken] Wilber notes.

In my experience, many mindfulness and contemplative educators, as proponents of progressive or holistic education, are ensconced at this fourth-order level: they are unable to step back and de-identify with their own belief systems. I find this to be a crucial distinction that is lost on those advocates who bypass any critical perspective on mindfulness in schools. In article responses, I have observed some mindfulness program advocates in education and therapy to be defensive and even hostile — they appear unable to mindfully sit with their own discomfort, are quite attached to their own beliefs about mindfulness programs, and project their own intolerance onto critics. They conflate criticism of how mindfulness is employed with an attack on mindfulness itself. A number declare that critique is just being negative and unhelpful and that being critical serves no purpose. They see social criticism as a waste of time. Some argue that if you have not taken an MBSR course, you have no right to question anything about it, including the social context in which it occurs. This is akin to a fallacy of immediate experience: you can't know or evaluate anything unless you've experienced it yourself; if you haven't had cancer or experienced trauma then you can't know what they are and speak of them with others, or in education you can't evaluate an ethnic studies program unless you are of that ethnicity.

Yes, one's own subjective experiences are inviolable; but it is a relativistic and dangerous notion to conclude that those alone are sufficient to define all truth within the actual world. In line with the ideology of positive psychology, true believers in mindfulness prefer to just cite programs they think have a positive effect and some argue that everyone should do the same (Nowogrodzki 2016). They regard mindfulness in individualist and personal terms and are dismissive of broader critical analysis: It helped these people, it helped me — end of story.

An example of mindful awareness from a possible later, more encompassing stage of development that enables us to reflect on belief systems is a multicultural course created by some counsellors called Multicultural Social Justice Criticism (MSJC) (Marbley, Steele, and McAuliffe 2011). The counsellors reflect on the writings and actions of other multicultural teachers as well as social constructionism, and question their relativist perspective. They declare that "by placing the multiculturalism and social justice movements and scholarship themselves at the center of analysis, MSJC is a tool that may be used to guard against a nonreflective multiculturalism" (2011: 166). For example, they suggest that a relativistic quality of standard multiculturalism, the belief that there are no final truth claims about knowing, can be "considered a luxury afforded to affluent, dominant group members who are in the middle-class academy."

We can argue that the authors, while they do not locate this relativistic premise within a postmodern stage, come at it from a more developed perspective. They place a relativist assertion of truth within a social context (in Integral terms, the Its or Interobjective quadrant) that accounts for class differences of beliefs; doing so can help dismantle an attachment to one's truth claims as being absolute. (It is not likely the authors think that every idea in turn is reducible to the particular class position of the person asserting the statement — if so, they would be trading one postmodern belief for another.)

Theology professor Kathleen M. Fisher (2017) questions some of the beliefs of leading contemplative educators from a more elevated, dispassionate standpoint. She exposes the either/or thinking (a quality of conventional developmental thinking) of those who see contemplative knowledge and personal experience as superior to critical and analytic thinking: they believe academic knowledge splits off the knower from knowledge and that therefore this is inferior to personal experience gained through contemplative practice. These educators further split off the interior from the social world; one claims that personal insight has "far greater valence than a prompt from without."

Fisher notes that some contemplative educators who wish to teach empathy and compassion believe we must do so based on what Arthur

Zajonc and others call "an epistemology of love." Fisher quotes them as saying this approach to knowledge favours "subjectification and intimacy" over "objectification and distancing." Spiritual experience, loving what you know, is an essential way of knowing, they claim; elsewhere, Zajonc says that our approach to an object of inquiry via this epistemology should include qualities of love, such as gentleness, intimacy, and vulnerability (Palmer and Zajonc 2010: 94–96).

More than another either/or analysis, Fisher finds this argument troubling in that it not only sees subjective experience as superior to objective learning but tries to subsume all other knowledge in education under spiritual experience. She counters that reading, writing, and critical, analytic thinking also cultivate inner awareness, and unlike sole reliance on subjective experience, they include knowledge about others and the social world.

Fisher argues that for contemplative educators to require a teacher to make a personal commitment to contemplative habits "raises the specter of evangelization," and questions why a teacher who has benefited from a personal spiritual practice would feel the need to introduce it to students, any more than they would their religious or political preferences. "The fervor of the converted is very powerful," she says, and describes some pitfalls in contemplative education around adequately handling some students' vulnerabilities regarding religious, emotional, substance abuse, and developmental concerns. She notes the irony that the evangelical zeal undercuts the notion of contemplative practice, in which one engages in self-reflection and de-identifies with attachment to one's ego. This is not surprising, though, given the lack of awareness within much of contemplative education of developmental and other forms of critical and analytical thinking.

From a later developmental perspective, on a personal level, you can witness the ego itself. You are able to see how your ego filters experience through constructs; you can consider the significance of various viewpoints not just from socially constructed categories (Construct-aware consciousness) but from the most expansive possible perspectives, which include and arise from later developing levels of consciousness (Ego-aware consciousness). Construct-awareness, as Cook-Greuter (2013: 79–80) describes it, is alert to the pitfalls of language, as well as to concepts and rational thought itself, with its "profound splits and paradoxes" in which "good and evil, life and death, beauty and ugliness may now appear as two sides of the same coin." Ego-awareness occurs when the nature of the ego becomes visible to itself: "Final knowledge about the self or anything else is seen as illusive and unattainable through effort and reason because all conscious thought, all cognition is recognized as constructed and, therefore, split off from the underlying, cohesive, non-dual truth." This is the awareness of the "always present background or non-dual ground of being … the deeper undivided formless source of consciousness that our experience of interbeing arises in and out of" (Gunnlaugsen 2009: 36–37). It is a transrational, beyond-the-ego stage.

David Loy (2005) describes this awareness not in terms of a stage model but as arising from Buddhist practice; concepts can be liberated, he says, not eliminated, and thinking is deeper, since it is free of the delusion that the "self" is split from the "Other." At this point, critical thinking is enhanced, not eliminated. The elegant truth of this awareness holds in all cases:

> The idea isn't to get rid of all language, it's to be free within language, so that one is non-attached to any particular kind of conceptual system, realizing that there are many possible ways of thinking and expressing oneself. The freedom from conceptualizing that we seek does not happen when we wipe away all thoughts; instead, it happens when we're not clinging to, or stuck in, any particular thought system. The kind of transformation we seek in our spiritual practices is a mind that's flexible, supple. Not a mind that clings to the empty blue sky. It's a mind that's able to dance with thoughts, to adapt itself according to the situation, the needs of the situation. It's not an empty mind which can't think. It's an ability to talk with the kind of vocabulary or engage in the way that's going to be most helpful in that situation.

Education as Higher-Order Development

Educators can include, challenge, and transcend dominant school practices in order to benefit everyone. Rather than seeing self-development and education as means to help students and the nation compete for and achieve economic and material prosperity, or to help individual students succeed in conventional academic terms, we can see them as valuable endeavours in their own right. We include and transcend progressive education by calling for a worldview that moves beyond either/or thinking and by developing a more inclusive, self-reflective perspective.

The purpose of education is to recognize, experience, and contribute to optimal human development. A crucial aspect is to help us move toward an awareness of our non-duality or unity with all others and with the universe. A key quality of an evolving developmental approach is to include and transcend; to be inclusive of and respect different perspectives while adopting more transcendent, wiser, or truer ones.

Can we practise letting go of our attachments to our opinions, judgments, and worldviews with wisdom and skill? Can we take conscious responsibility for our own personal growth and for the well-being and goodness of everyone? Our sense of separateness has been a kind of mirage — and our awakened state of "I-amness" is one of unity with the entire cosmos:

> A human being is a part of the whole, called by us "Universe," a part limited in time and space. He (sic) experiences himself, his thoughts and feelings as something separate from the rest — a kind of optical delusion of his consciousness. The striving to free oneself from this delusion is the one issue of true religion. Not to nourish it but to try to overcome it is the way to reach the attainable measure of peace of mind. (Albert Einstein, in Calaprice 2005: 206)

Although the locus of our action is our embodied being, it is not about ego gratification or stress reduction. It is more about stress induction — creating challenges and destroying complacency (Bazzano 2013; Lopez 2012). It is overcoming the dichotomies found in language and concepts that polarize and alienate self from Other. This practice is not just to serve the needs of our ego, or of our own group or nation, or of a particular ideology, but for the sake of all sentient beings; at the deepest level we are they and they are us. "Transformative spirituality," Ken Wilber (1999: 30) declares, "is revolutionary. It does not legitimate the world, it breaks the world; it does not console the world, it shatters it. And it does not render the self content, it renders it undone."

Schools should include discussions about what it means to live a good life; in this respect, educators and school counsellors can make a significant difference.

10

Culture as Context: Malignant Normalcy

Culture from the Inside

We are all social beings, born into cultures and living within relationships, interconnected with others. Contemplative studies tend to focus on first-person (subjective, experiential) and third-person (objective, scientific) perspectives, often ignoring second-person (intersubjective) perspectives that have to do with cultural meanings and relationships. But consciousness is inherently intersubjective; it is formed through relationships and shows up as the ability to care about and understand others (Thompson 2001).

We can look at relationships on both micro (interpersonal) and macro (broader social norms and rituals) levels. Within our network of relationships, we create, share, and engage in beliefs, norms, and rules together through dialogue and interpretation. In implicit ways, these interactions often frame everyday meanings, values, and relationships, which we form anew with others.

Through our partners, family, friends, neighbours, communities, religion, ethnicity, and nationality, we experience relationships that are profound and essential parts of ourselves, and are significant to contemplative education. These are not the space within us or outside of us but between us, and are qualitatively different — what Olen Gunnlaugson calls a world- or we-space (2009; Gunnlaugson and Brabant 2016). Rather than individualistic or scientific approaches, seeing things from the perspective of our interconnectedness entails collaboration, mutuality, and dialogue. Schools can create contemplative, mindful we-spaces that enhance learning through shared inquiry and the "collective wisdom" within classes and groups (Gunnlaugson, Scott, Bai, and Sarath 2017: viii). They are our own conscious creations of connected, caring, healthy relationships that employ careful listening, openness, and honest, respectful dialogue. Creating such an equitable, meaningful school community is a moral issue to which mindfulness can contribute in conscious ways.

To practise mindfulness and contemplative education from an interpersonal standpoint is a radical transformation of the privatized, individualistic belief that contemplative experience occurs just in one's head. It is to see the contemplative as inseparable from our relationships and to embed it within the practical, moral activity that we enact with others — for example, in social justice work. Practising mindfulness in interpersonal ways opens us up to questions absent from first- and third-person viewpoints. In the actual context of our messy lives in and about which we contemplate (or not) — our relationships, our families, our engagement with others in our academic, political, spiritual, activist, and local communities — where are the interactions and dialogues between us about what is moral and good? How do we treat each other? How do we both talk and theorize about how we experience, interpret, and make new meanings and values together, including about contemplative practice itself? How do we bring mindfulness into our personal and interpersonal commitment to issues around race/whiteness, and gender and class equality — for example, in schools? (See Berila 2016.)

It is important to address the interpersonal (second-person) side — relationships — of spiritual development in contemplative education. Many people experience a personal relationship with God, Jesus, Allah, or another expression of the divine absolute, or Spirit, or supreme love, through prayer as defined and made meaningful within a particular culture. The divine Other's love may be morally demanding yet unconditional, forgiving, infinite, mysterious, and sacred; at a later, universal level, some experience the relationship as a mystical union (Fowler 1995). For atheists or secular humanists, a later stage of relationship may involve personal love for individuals and selfless, universal love of humanity. This kind of relationship is both symbolic of the need for loving devotion and also a deeply personal felt desire shared by many people; it thus needs to be included in accounts of the contemplative.

Those who engage in this spiritual or religious relationship do so along with others in a community that is itself a significant intersubjective culture or we-space. At later stages, a planetary We could emerge — if people were to perceive and experience the world as one dynamic organism. Attachment to the belief that one's worldview is the only right one dissolves. Differences are acknowledged and celebrated while at the same time realization of an underlying depth of unity and commonality occurs; the self is both unique and an inseparable part of a larger, caring whole. In public schools and higher education, contemplative lessons on diversity and social justice can embed and reclaim discussions about second-person contemplative practices and students' traditional religious and spiritual experiences, relationships, and values from ethnic and family traditions (Berila 2016).

Culture from the Outside

Without recognizing cultural context as a second-person perspective, mindfulness falls prey to the myth of the given — the belief that meditative (and all) meaningful experiences are not culturally constructed and understood in impermanent, relational terms but appear as objective facts, directly perceived rather than as interpretable, contested meanings that can be uncovered, discussed, and transformed within relationships. As a result, harmful norms unfold, hidden and unaddressed — for example, heterosexism, consumerism, and competitive individualism — that need to be brought to light. Our relationships, our participation in various meaning-making cultures, should be investigated from the outside.

Contemplative practice needs to be aware that within shared everyday space, people inhabit different worldviews, which we can observe in terms of cultural development. In basic terms, cultures are traditional, modern, and postmodern. From an Integral perspective, we can evaluate and appreciate all three, although each cultural worldview has a troublesome or unhealthy side. In the following, Integralist Jason Digges (n.d.) supplies a useful analogy of development applied to cultural frameworks.

Imagine you have an uncle, Digges says, who is a pastor who believes that the Bible is the eternal truth or dogma and that we can interpret it in just one way, That's a traditional perspective that values faith, duty, family, and order, and provides wisdom with respect to moral values of universal love. On the troublesome end, traditionalists can be intolerant of others, rigid, dogmatic, and deny scientific evidence.

Your dad, suggests Digges, is a businessman: for him, the scientific method, rationality, materialist proof, and measuring something are the only ways to determine something exists. He represents a modernist point of view that believes in progress and endorses success based on entrepreneurial values and merit. On the other hand, a modernist can be materialistic, selfish, and exploitative. Taking empirical science and technology as all there is makes for a world devoid of moral values, subjectivity, beauty, and mystery in a way that disenchants the world.

Your teacher encourages you to seek your own truth; for her, Digges offers, truth is relative and depends on many people's perspectives (for example, pluralism or multiculturalism); there are many truths and no one truth. She represents the postmodern position that at its best endorses environmentalism and racial and gender equality. The later postmodernists dismantle master narratives that rationalize political power and ideologies and seek their own relative truths and interpretations A postmodernist take can also overvalue relativism, deny any hierarchies of growth or truth, and reject previous traditional and modern contributions (McIntosh 2012). It claims there are no truths (itself an assertion of truth and thereby a contradiction), and that science and subjectivity (the self) exist solely as cultural constructions.

You might then say: they all seem right in part; I can see the perspectives of the others that each cannot and with which each person overidentifies. I want to combine them from a more evolved or Integral perspective. In this way, we can uncover the developmental order of subcultures, such as schools or organizations, in which one works and decide which qualities are healthy and which ones we would like to change.

As a secular program that has severed itself from a morally based tradition (Buddhism), mindfulness in schools swims in shallow cultural waters. It flounders with regard to moral principles and practices of social justice, and it lacks critical knowledge of and engagement with everyday cultures, their development and meanings. There is an emergent need to embed mindfulness within programs that uncover and resist the dominant ideologies and troublesome cultural practices in which we live, and to help us create new, inclusive relationships that work toward optimal personal development and universal social justice. Part of this can be called a critical, civic mindfulness: "Mindfulness in education offers an opportunity to reorient education away from narrowly conceived instrumental ends towards broader ethical and socially-engaged ones" (Ng 2015; see also Healey 2013).

Mindful educators seldom, if at all, question the problematic, socially constructed nature of schooling and school values within the neoliberal society in which they offer mindfulness programs. They do not ask whether one should adjust to or resist the dominant cultural norms. Our task, then, is to uncover, discuss, evaluate, resist, and change the problematic, implicit, unacknowledged norms of moral values and meanings hidden in the background of society, and to create a more caring, inclusive, accepting, mindful culture.

This is not to say pessimistically, like Freud, that all of human life is pathological. Nor, on the other hand, should we attribute emotional trauma to the fundamental nature of being human. That conflates Buddha's ontological statement, "there is suffering," with psychological trauma that stems from specific societal relations that can and should be changed. An interpreter of Buddhism, psychiatrist Mark Epstein (2014), for example, naturalizes and abstracts psychological trauma away from its social nexus and says that trauma is "simply a fact of life." Both approaches gloss over any actual historical analysis of society and leave things as they are. Well, everyone is sick, everyone is suffering; it's inevitable, we can't change anything, so just change your personal relationship to things, through therapy, through Buddhist wisdom, and adjust as best you can. As David Loy says, certain qualities of capitalist society at this historical time reinforce some basic existential problems, such as the sense of lack and the need to cling to a notion of a permanent, unchanging self; these call for urgent efforts to bring a more evolved consciousness to the world. As part of this effort we must uncover and seek to challenge together some specific problems of everyday capitalist culture.

Let's name a few unexamined troublesome cultural beliefs and ideologies, or thorny issues, a number of them interrelated, lurking unaddressed in everyday education today. They represent intersubjective and relational qualities, not just intra-psychic ones. These can be exposed from a social and critical perspective and practice, as part of a mindful critical pedagogy and as part of our own relationships. Because we both adapt to and create the norms and beliefs by which we live, these are contestable patterns of meaning that together people can discuss, challenge, and change.

Malignant Normalcy

Capitalist society's predominant paradigm remains focused on the isolated individual pursuing their competitive, narrow self-interest in rational, economic terms. As therapist Terrence Real (2017) points out, "Pathology is rarely an aberration of the norm so much as an exaggeration of it." Like unhealthy stages of development, taking a norm to an extreme — such as individualist, privatized self-interest or conformity to rules or gender roles — is unhealthy. Robert Jay Lifton refers to "malignant normalcy," normalizing troublesome and dangerous aspects of everyday life in our society. He warns, "What we put forward as self-evident and normal may be deeply dangerous and destructive" (Moyers 2017). Erich Fromm's (2010) term, "the pathology of normalcy" refers to people's attempt to conform to conventional society to avoid isolation and alienation, and he considers whether we can say a whole society such as ours can be lacking in mental health. In a broader sense, the term, like Lifton's, can also mean going along with troublesome or unhealthy aspects of everyday culture. As Krishnamurti said, "It is no measure of health to be well adjusted to a profoundly sick society."

The Myth of Meritocracy

In neoliberal society, the individual is both the source of any unhappiness and the solution — that is, each of us alone is responsible for overcoming our presumed deficits rather than together looking to analyze and change difficult social conditions. The powerful cultural myth of meritocracy reinforces this approach to the everyday, saying that the system is fair and that if someone works hard they will succeed at whatever they do. This is patently untrue: you and many others can work hard and yet not succeed. There are too many unjust, systemic inequities that benefit the wealthy and those with socially desirable traits — white skin, male, heterosexual, and able-bodied, among others. A further downside to this myth is that any failure falls back on the person, which leads to self-blame; it can't be the system, it must be me. People internalize the neoliberal belief that one can and should obtain success and happiness by purchasing, owning, and consuming things, and by marketing one's self as a personal brand (Giroux 2014a; Ravitch 2014).

This myth of meritocracy creates considerable anxiety and a sense of despair and powerlessness for many people, who blame themselves for their misfortunes (Kelly 2012). The lonely, isolated person is endemic to neoliberal capitalism; in this sense, the system itself is unhealthy and breeds mental problems and unhappiness. George Monbiot (2016c) asks, "What greater indictment of a system could there be than an epidemic of mental illness?" While neoliberalism, as a stage of capitalism, is on the wane, the myth of meritocracy is so ingrained in our culture and world-view that many tend to regard it as natural and inevitable. Like Wallace's water in which we swim, its pervasiveness makes it difficult to see and question. Neither does the mindfulness emphasis on the here and now help us envision possibilities for the future.

Scientism

Scientism serves as an ideological handmaiden of neoliberalism through the predominant assumption that in schools only measurable, observable phenomena are real, truthful, and the sole measures of personal success. If you can't see it or measure it, it isn't real or valid: education never happened. Examples are high-stakes testing, outcomes assessments, objective behavioural changes, self-regulation practices, observable changes in neurological correlates (brain imaging), and data-driven or evidence-based programs.

The Audit and Austerity Cultures

Auditing and austerity norms apply neoliberal and scientistic (i.e., market-driven) accountability practices to education on behalf of policymakers, managers, and those in power rather than students and teachers themselves. Teachers and students become self-managing persons who make themselves auditable. Education professor Peter Taubman (2009) describes how education policymakers borrow auditing and accountability practices from the corporate sector to reduce the complex qualities of educational experiences into quantifiable data and structure in classrooms across the nation.

Audit culture ties in with neoliberal austerity. The goal of austerity is to starve and deplete the public sector and public schools, and privatize public services. Neoliberals throw the burden of care, resources, and measurable accountability back on private individuals, whom they expect to do more with less. The austerity myth says it is just natural that there is never enough to go around. This mystifies how conservatives in power maintain their wealth and intend to destroy the public good through giving themselves tax cuts, cutting public spending, and telling the rest of us to tighten our belts.

Self-surveillance makes austerity easier for those in power: we learn to self-regulate and limit ourselves without the need for external coercion. Foucault introduced the notion of self-surveillance as part of the idea of governmentality:

> As Foucault noted, the effect of constant surveillance in prison is to instil anxiety such that inmates come to scrutinise their own behaviour and eventually adopt the norms of conduct desired by the disciplinary institution — whether or not the guards are in the watchtower. (Shore and Wright 2000)

This approach is applied to schools. Educators who buy into the audit culture have adopted external surveillance and can now discipline themselves; they have internalized the rules of those in power. Teachers or supervisors are no longer needed to monitor or discipline anyone; people now regulate or govern themselves on behalf of those in power through self-observation. Shore and Wright (2000) state that terms such as *self-management* or *best practices* in higher education disguise the fact that "audit culture relies upon hierarchical relationships and coercive practices. The self-directed, self-managed individual is encouraged to identify with the university and the goals of higher education policy: challenging the terms of reference is not an option." Neoliberal policymakers encourage teachers and students to adjust to the audit culture and a "culture of evidence," a term that a national body that accredits educator preparation programs urged our school of education to adopt.

Peter Taubman (2009: 128) asks educators, how did we lose our way?

> How did we allow the language of education, study, teaching, and intellectual and creative endeavor to transform itself into the language and practices of standards and accountability? What led us to think that if we applied practices imported from the world of business we could solve our educational problems, and how did we surrender our right to define those problems?

Self-auditing relates to mindfulness in schools as well. Solutions are gained through scientific and technocratic approaches; for example, the individual should employ the technology of mindfulness to improve their own wellness, social and emotional skills, academic performance, and self-regulation, and have these confirmed through brain imaging and other "objective" outcome measures such as educational audits and test scores. Professor James Reveley (2015) points out that mindfulness has become a powerful technology of neoliberal self-discipline; in schools, teachers and students regulate themselves toward appropriate behaviour and focused attention by being aware of their thoughts and feelings moment to moment.

Whiteness

Many white people hold the malignant cultural assumption — experienced daily by African-Americans, Latinx, Indigenous people, and other people of colour — that whiteness *is* the cultural norm, and are unaware that this is a troublesome assumption for others and even for themselves. Moreover, many are unaware their everyday life benefits to varying degrees by whiteness, in contrast to many persons of colour. In North America we live not having to think about the ways whiteness is a systemic advantage over others (in particular, African-Americans), who endure systemic barriers to mobility and, in the U.S., have been historically restricted from opportunities to accumulate wealth and pass it on to their family as can some white people. This is evident in housing and employment markets, schools and higher education, access to affordable and quality health care, and in everyday interactions with merchants and police.

While it does not excuse this problem, one explanation for what makes the advantage difficult to experience and acknowledge for many white working-class people is that at the same time they themselves struggle with everyday issues. Some live painful lives diminished by loss of gainful and stable employment, shrinking wages, attacks on unions, fewer affordable educational opportunities, declining well-being and health, lack of health care, alcoholism and substance abuse, the loss of government support for families and children, and the disappearance of stable and enriching communities. The things for which they have worked and feel they deserve, also known in the U.S. as the American Dream, have not materialized as they expected, and without an understanding of the systemic political and economic causes of this breakdown are left feeling puzzled, angry, and in despair. Some of those feelings, encouraged by right-wing groups, translate into racism, nativism, and xenophobia, and with some individuals, given the availability of guns and automatic weapons, rage and violence. Yet while their life can be hard, they need to see that their white skin is not one of the things that makes it harder.

Meanwhile, many of those white people who are better off, often due to neoliberal tax cuts and advantages provided to Wall Street and financial sector services — by both U.S. political parties — literally can afford to ignore the structural advantages that surround them every day and take them as a natural given. They see them as something they were rightfully born into and/or that they earned altogether. Yet many well-off white people themselves are anxious about losing their privilege in a competitive capitalist system that allows just a few to succeed, and in turn use their advantages to protect their assets and status through influencing laws and regulations that benefit them and their heirs.

Racism

A stronger argument for why white people of all classes can ignore their advantage is the racism that is deeply and historically rooted in the institutions and practices of colonialist, imperialist Western societies and that contributes to the belief that being white is the natural order of things. The U.S. has not only never addressed its racist history but has normalized racism on institutional and personal levels — for example, during and after the Reconstruction era, with Jim Crow laws, through the Civil Rights movement, and up to today.

There are a number of common errors made when tackling racism. One mistake is to blur structural and systemic factors with personal ones. When personal and systemic sources of bias get conflated, the systemic and institutional causes of inequality tend to be ignored. There is considerable lack of analysis, misinformation, and blockage of facts within and from the corporate and social media, the government, and elsewhere about broader social structural forces that contribute to people's pain and how they make sense of it. This ignorance contributes to racist beliefs among some white people about whom and what systemic corporate forces are screwing them over, rather than African-Americans, Muslim-Americans, women, and immigrants from Latin America, to whom well-funded right-wing proponents point as the problem. For example, the financial bailout of 2008 left millions of people at the mercy of policies that favoured the banks and ignored the plight of the homeowners who lost their homes and with whom the banks had made unscrupulous deals. A Greek econo-mist's description of what happened to many Europeans applies as well to many Americans: "It was not rising inequality that provoked undying anger among these discarded people. It the loss of dignity, of the dream of social mobility" (Veroufakis 2017).

A related problem is that some white people mistakenly experience society as a zero-sum game: "If other people are accepted as equals, I lose. What about me?" Although this runs counter to many people's experi-ences in more integrated urban areas, this response is not surprising given that capitalist society generates competition and uses class, race, gender, sexual orientation, and ethnicity to control and divide people as well as to co-opt a relatively small number who succeed. This experience, the result of systemic forces, in turn leaves a number of white people susceptible to unhealthy, distorted, and destructive states, beliefs, and practices. We must name, discuss, and strongly oppose these forces in personal, cultural, and institutional terms. For example, there are instances where some white people have felt entitled to arbitrarily call the police on African-Americans, in effect policing black bodies (Hattery and Smith 2017).

Some anti-racist white activists refer to all whites as being fragile, privileged, or racist. Many white people are uncomfortable talking about race; they feel accused and/or unwilling to see the changes they can make. In my experience of teaching well-intentioned counselling students, however, labelling most white people as racist, privileged, or fragile is not effective or wise. Such terms conflate systemic causes and personal qualities, and do not help people distinguish them. Applying the term *privilege* to individuals due to the attributes with which they were born works to negate their own lived experience, their background, family and personal abilities and efforts, since these are debased and dismissed as the results of undeserved and unearned benefit due to one's white skin colour. They thereby experience this label as a personal attack that often leads to feelings of defensiveness, shame, guilt, and self-blame. It contributes further to a defensive backlash when they protest this label and are then told they are "fragile" and unable to hear this. This is what a counsellor colleague refers to as a double bind: "Taking issue with the dismissal of one's personhood is not even considered to be possibly legitimate, instead it is due to that individual's fragility and inability to stay engaged with the conversation (as framed)" (Lile 2018). Another double bind that conflates systemic and personal issues is to claim that all white people are racist on an unconscious level, which leaves no room for protesting, since that again only "proves" they are "fragile" or are wrongly denying their racism. Instead of insisting on these terms, we need honest, respectful, mindful dialogue where people's feelings are heard — then discussed, challenged, and problem-solved in both personal and systemic ways.

Anti-racist work includes the need for white people to look hard at our own position within a culture and economic system that adopts whiteness as the favoured norm. Guilt, denial, and defensiveness are not helpful; nor, on the other hand, are intolerant, self-righteous, and harsh judgmental attacks against others. Instead, we need to take responsible actions to see and overcome racism while working for an inclusive, expansive society that encourages and allows for everyone to fully develop themselves. For those of us opposing racism, being mindful of our own conditioned thoughts, feelings, and behaviours, of our unwitting participation in racist systems, and of our own unexamined attributions toward others are both immediate and long-term projects. We need to examine the culture of the schools and institutions in which we participate in terms of the quality of the relationships and perspectives on racism, fairness, and equity. We need to work together with others and at times challenge them and ourselves in respectful personal, interpersonal, and structural and systemic terms.

The topics of whiteness and racism are virulent and difficult to address. Where possible, they require considered, skilful, nuanced, and mindful dialogue and self-reflection in educational and other settings. A genuine recognition of and respect for all people's experiences, and of the structural causes, complex differences, and power imbalances, as well as the deeper, underlying sense of universality, of common humanity, must be made explicit and tapped in order for dialogue, understanding, healing, and growth to occur. As a white professor and counsellor, I note that, along with white students' feelings, the often contrasting experiences and the deep pain and anguish that many African-American and other students of colour experience in these settings must be acknowledged and addressed with great care and respect.

In working with white people on whiteness and racism in schools and elsewhere, a contemplative approach seeks to do at least two things simultaneously that are in dialectical tension and are often not easy. One is to listen with openness to their experiences, feelings, and viewpoints, since all people want to feel heard, be treated with dignity, feel safe, and not be accused and dismissed (see Lopez 2017; Hochschild 2016). The other is to find a level of dialogue in which people are made unsettled or uncomfortable enough to feel the need to rethink (or think about for the first time) some of their own troublesome assumptions. Too little discomfort and people don't change; too much and people shut down.

Besides working on ourselves and listening to others in conversations, we need to oppose the harmful acts of racists and white supremacists and racial disparities in social institutions, and to fight for major political and economic changes that would legislate and enforce equality for all. In all cases, we strive to take action with the most evolved intention possible, conscious of our underlying commonality. Wherever possible, we need to keep finding and creating common ground.

Trauma

Traumatic experiences disrupt people's normal sense of time, space, and connectedness with others. The meaning of and belief in a normative, hopeful future or purpose, such as religious redemption or realizing the American Dream, may become broken, lost, and in disarray. Traumatic experiences can be both individual and collective, but both occur within a common culture. Traumas — such as the sudden loss of a parent or home, sexual or emotional abuse, or witnessing or experiencing violence and its aftermath, including addictions — are often experienced as individualized, isolated phenomena. A poignant and damaging source of trauma is lack or loss of healthy emotional attachment to a loving adult during the first years of life.

In broader terms, many people grow up in stressful, and stressed out, privatized nuclear families that are isolated from extended family and any real sense of community; they further lack diminished governmental and societal support and feel they must bear their own burdens by themselves. As a result, they experience and endure trauma in private due to harm from their family and parents, who suffer from their own unaddressed emotional issues of stress, depression, and anxiety. James Rowe (2016) points out that much trauma is inseparable from domestic and sexual violence, repressive state policies, and exploitative workplace practices — that is, unjust structural conditions that are nevertheless internalized as personal problems.

We can consider some trauma, then, in culturally critical terms as malignant normalcy; it is an unacknowledged aspect of many people's everyday lives in North American society. Psychiatrist Sandra L. Bloom (2013) sees the U.S. as having much unaddressed and unresolved trauma — as a nation whose ancestors were immigrants and formerly enslaved and colonized people, it remains marked by a history of economic insecurity, poverty, racism, disruption, and violence. Many have generational issues of loss and receive cultural messaging that tries to solve pain and conflict in compulsive ways — through violence, militarism, and domination over others as well as abuse and alcoholism, all of which are then papered over with denial. While mindfulness has been employed to help returning armed service members with post-traumatic stress disorder (PTSD), in a militaristic society geared for war it is no accident that even mindfulness has been perversely used to train soldiers preparing for combat deployment (Stanley 2014).

Racism as Trauma

Community trauma and that among poor children of colour in particular impacts neurological, cognitive, and emotional development (Maté 2010). Racism, both personal and systemic, is a form of trauma on its own terms. At an individual level there is evidence that being a victim of a racist incident can lead to PTSD; a psychologist argues that the Diagnostic and Statistical Manual (DSM), which defines mental disorders — a dubious, non-scientific, and politicized document itself — at least should be broadened to reflect race-based trauma (Williams 2013).

In systemic ways, racism itself is traumatic: police violence, poverty, the lack of safety for both adults and children, and experiences of daily discrimination contribute to greater incidence of poor health and emotional stress among many African-Americans and other persons of colour. One obvious example is that for years politicians ignored the drug epidemic among African-Americans in inner city areas and filled the jails with criminalized addicts who seldom received treatment. Now that there is an opioid epidemic affecting many white suburban and rural communities, there is a national outcry for more prevention and treatment services. African-Americans are always aware of the stresses caused by racial differences and divisions in a racist society. Sociology professor Michael Eric Dyson (2017) writes, "To be black in America is to live in terror." For many, the fear and actuality of unpredictable violence is a kind of trauma; author Ta-Nehisi Coates (2015) describes how this can disrupt ideal narratives of hope, redemption, or the American Dream that govern everyday life. One critic suggests that Coates's attempt at redemption from a racially traumatized world through what Coates calls "struggle" is through "relation, connection, and undirected evolution in the struggle to 'make … peace with' an end-less 'chaos'" (Eisner 2017: 112). (Others are critical of Coates's arguable belief that the chaos never can be overcome; see Steinmetz-Jenkins 2017.) The everyday pain of systemic racism is matched by the difficulty of addressing it in adequate, mindful ways; we are acutely in need of a redemptive, restorative culture.

Toxic Masculinity as Trauma

A culture that raises many boys to cut off their feelings and forces them to prove to themselves and others a harsh notion of masculinity — sometimes in the form of harassment, other times in dominant and violent ways — is a form of trauma, what researchers term *toxic masculinity*.

First, an important point: addressing the problem of toxic masculinity is not a critique of masculinity as a whole, of all boys and men themselves, and of qualities of healthy masculinity. An attack against all boys and men in personal terms — blaming men and discriminating against them just because they are male, and ignoring their own experience — is not only unhelpful but is unjust and can contribute to further emotional and social harm toward men. Some conservatives as well are wrong to conflate the critique of toxic masculinity with an attack on all men (Douglass 2017).

Within a culture of toxic masculinity, some boys and men carry an emotional burden, as do the many women who are familiar with and subjected to it. Kali Holloway writes:

> When masculinity is defined by absence, when it sits on the absurd and fallacious idea that the only way to be a man is not to acknowledge a key part of oneself, the consequences are both vicious and soul-crushing. The resulting displacement and dissociation leaves men yet more vulnerable and in need of crutches to help allay the pain created by our demands of manliness. (2017; see also Forbes 2004; Real 2017)

The cultural system of toxic masculinity deprives many boys and men, as well as girls and women, from freely developing their many-sided healthy selves and engaging in mutually respectful relationships (Fortin 2019). The system's effects prove traumatic in particular to many gay males from an early age and into adulthood via the homophobia that continues to exist in much of society. Some boys and men who feel shame and inadequacy at their perceived inability to live up to an exaggerated masculine ideal take out their frustrations on girls and women through objectification, unwanted attention, sexual harassment, and violence (Rozsa 2018). For others, the message that vulnerability is undesirable prevents them from feeling and working through their pain and hurt.

Jordan Stephens (2017), a British musician, says that the false power of patriarchy covers up the pain of many troubled boys "who wanted more hugs from their mum or have missed the company of their dad, or were victims of abuse or loneliness or just generally felt as though they had no time, space, company or even the words to describe how they felt." Much of this in turn contributes to women's emotional trauma, which many now are calling out within a wide variety of workplace and educational settings via the #MeToo movement.

As with whiteness, some of those boys and men who have been social-ized to think they need and are entitled to exert control over girls and women in toxic ways can confront their own false power as well as their own feelings and fears. With mindfulness, support, and therapy they can learn to let go of their conditioned patterns of thinking and develop healthier, undistorted thoughts, behaviours, and relationships with others and with themselves. At the same time, we all have a part in changing the broader toxic cultural norms and dynamics.

An Addictive Culture in Response to Trauma

Much of the dominant culture and economy thrives and is itself depend-ent on people feeling the need to purchase commodities as external fixes in order to feel happy, fulfilled, and physically at ease. Substance abuse and alcoholism are often attempts to medicate and soothe oneself against unresolved traumas — often a lack of loving attachment — from one's childhood. Gabor Maté points out the link between addiction and a background of trauma, and how the former starts as an attempt to solve or medicate an emotional issue. Addiction has social origins within many families that struggle with inadequate economic and social support, resources, and healthy relationships. However, the question, Maté says, isn't what's wrong with you, but what happened to you:

> If you start with the idea that addiction isn't a primary disease, but an attempt to solve a problem, then you soon come to the question: how did the problem arise? If you say your addiction soothes your emotional pain, then the question arises of where the pain comes from. If the addiction gives you a sense of comfort, how did your discomfort arise? If your addiction gives you a sense

of control or power, why do you lack control, agency, and power in your life? If it's because you lack a meaningful sense of self, well, how did that happen? What happened to you? From there, we have to go to your childhood because that's where the origins of emotional pain or loss of self or lack of agency most often lie. It's just a logical, step-by-step inquiry. What's the problem you're trying to resolve? And then, how did you develop that problem? And then, what happened to you in childhood that you have this problem? (Dockett and Simon 2017)

The U.S. and Canada are currently facing an epidemic: many people have become addicted to prescription opioids. There is money to be made by alcohol, tobacco, and pharmaceutical corporations; opioid drugs are over-prescribed. All the while, there is a shortage of treatment programs and services for emotional problems and substance abuse, which often go together. A sizeable illegal drug trade as well keeps the prison and law enforcement sectors in business, and punishment remains a greater priority than treatment and prevention (Preza 2017). Here, too, meaningful relationships, or lack thereof, play a significant part in addiction and its treatment. More mental health professionals now acknowledge that a major cause of addiction, lack of healthy social attachment, also points to its "cure": creating genuine connections with others (Hari 2017).

Mindfulness and Trauma

Some students in schools benefit from mindfulness to help them deal with stress; they can learn to recognize their pain and with support can consider healthier ways to respond (Fraga 2016). Meditation along with psychotherapy can help some people recover from trauma. Maté emphasizes the importance of helping people with trauma to experience their feelings:

If, as I argue, addiction is rooted in trauma, then the treatment of addiction has to aim beyond just stopping the behavior. That's where the addiction treatment falls down so miserably. Too often it's all aimed at behavioral regulation or behavior reform, with the thought that if people stop the behavior, then they're going to be okay. No, they're not — and they won't be fully okay until they deal with the fundamental issues. So the treatment has to aim at nothing less than the restoration of the individual to themselves and to their capacity to be with the present moment, whether the present moment is pleasant or not. That's what's too often missing from addiction treatment. (Dockett and Simon 2017)

However, mindfulness meditation by itself is not a panacea for trauma. Some mindfulness researchers have pointed out that meditation itself under certain conditions can trigger traumatic memories (Booth 2014). In other cases, it can lead to emotional disturbances such as alienation, fear, anxiety, panic, or a loss of emotions altogether, even among experienced meditators with no history of trauma (Farias and Wikholm 2015; Love 2018; News from Brown 2017). For those who suffer serious trauma and dissociate from feelings, mindfulness by itself can be harmful (O'Faolan 2017). Any practising of mindfulness in public school settings, which should only be introduced by an experienced meditation practitioner, needs to first address potential trauma that may get triggered among some students and link with a backup system of professional therapy and support.

A traumatic experience of some who meditate is the disorienting sense of losing one's self. What sometimes confounds and compounds this experience is their mistaken belief that through meditation you are supposed to dissolve your self. Skilled meditation educators must refute this myth and clarify the intention of meditation. The aim is to come to de-identify with and establish a compassionate relationship with one's self, not to deny or negate it altogether, since for most of the time we still need a healthy relative "self" to function well in the relative world. This is why it is also important to assess a meditator's degree of well-being and stage of self-development, and alongside mindfulness to promote general emotional health, personal growth, and a caring, inclusive culture and society.

Social Media:
Fuelling Anxiety, Addictive Dependency, and Outrage

As part of the attention economy, social media are programmed to attract and capture people's attention in order to increase profits from advertising. This technology induces a constant state of heightened alertness and anxiety in addictive ways; we see this dependency in some children and the younger generation of teens, whom one researcher, Jean M. Twenge (2017), calls iGen. Twenge argues that since 2011 we can trace to some extent an increase in mental health issues such as depression and suicide among teens to the increased use of smartphones and social media. "There is compelling evidence that the devices we've placed in young people's hands are having profound effects on their lives — and making them seriously unhappy," she says. Fewer of them hang out together and instead spend more time on their phones, and those who spend more time than average on screen activities are more likely to be unhappy. Why? "For all their power to link kids day and night," says Twenge, "social media also exacerbate the age-old teen concern about being left out." Many who use social media more often, particularly girls, are on their phones in their rooms, alone and often distressed, which increases times they feel excluded when they see friends getting together without them. "Social media levy a psychic tax on the teen doing the posting as well, as she anxiously awaits the affirmation of comments and likes." This culture isolates teens from adults, encourages competitive and invidious comparisons with others, and does little to help them deal with unhealthy relationship patterns. Social media's addictive quality in some cases adds to these problems (Denizet-Lewis 2017).

Social media also heightens polarization in a culture war that relies more and more on unreflective outrage. Philosophy professor Kelly Oliver (2017) argues that while social media can help form communities, it is also "often fueled by emotional reaction rather than thoughtful response. Life is flattened to fit the screen.... Social media works by leveling and ripping bits of life from their contexts as a form of entertainment or news — the more outrageous, the better." She laments that in educational settings as well as politics it also works to shut down discussion, research, and debate through shaming and cyberbullying. While mindfulness can help individual students to remember to turn off their phones, it needs to be enlisted further to help them address the unhealthy uses of social media on a cultural and systemic scale.

Positive Psychology, the Self-Help
Movement, the Wellness Industry, Grit

Like mindfulness and social-emotional learning (SEL), these trends offer popular therapeutic solutions to societal problems that they claim lie within the individual. They play well into reinforcing conformity to the individualist, competitive, and marketing aspects of neoliberal culture.

Some mindfulness programs in schools align with the ideology of positive psychology: be happy, be positive, and be optimistic. This undercuts the mindfulness adage that you should just observe, accept, and be with whatever comes up, including negative feelings, and exposes the agenda of mindfulness as a means to generate pleasant, cooperative students. There is a "shift in focus toward positivity and well-being," says education professor Katherine Weare in the preface to her co-authored book with Thich Nhat Hanh, *Happy Teachers Change the World: A Guide for Cultivating Mindfulness in Education,* and that includes positive psychology, pro-sociability, and happiness to alleviate suffering (2017: xxxv). Note that the title reinforces the individualist belief that it is solely the happy teacher, regardless of the conditions of the school and community or the values of educational policies, who can change the world — by being happy. "Grit" is the individualistic belief that children just have to buckle down and become resilient in the face of failure, and that each student can succeed through determination.

Yet an emerging critical literature uncovers the ideological undercurrents of positive psychology, the marketing of spirituality, the therapy industry, and self-help culture. Critics show how these trends reinforce individualistic adjustment to neoliberal values and institutions (Binkley 2014; Carrette and King 2005; Cederström and Spicer 2015; Ehrenreich 2010; Moloney 2013; Rakow 2013).

Mindfulness works hand in hand with positive psychology, which is an individualistic and conventional ideology (Baer and Lykins 2011; Ecclestone 2011). By promoting positive emotions and avoiding negative ones, it serves corporate workplace interests and props up and blames individuals by overselling the potential of individuals to transcend their difficult circumstances (Coyne 2013; Ehrenreich 2010). Under the guise of health promotion, it seeks to further corporate control in the name of workplace harmony (Hedges 2009; for a critical appraisal of positive psychology, see Brown, Lomas, and Eiroa-Orosa 2018).

The lucrative wellness industry also focuses on individualistic solutions that ignore the very social conditions that give rise to stress and anxiety. One reviewer of such programs, writer Amy Larocca (2017), notes that even the well-off are unwell:

> There's something grotesque about this industry's emerging at the moment when the most basic health care is still being denied to so many in America and is at risk of being snatched away from millions more. But what's perhaps most striking about wellness's ascendancy is that it's happening because, in our increasingly bifurcated world, even those who do have access to pretty good (and sometimes quite excellent, if quite expensive) traditional health care are left feeling, nonetheless, incredibly unwell.

A reason some privileged women with access to traditional health care still turn to wellness fads is that the U.S. medical business, beyond its expensive, rushed, and impersonal service, further ignores and mistreats many women, who overall receive less quality health care than men. Wellness purveyors provide undivided attention to women's unique personal needs and greater compassion than do many doctors and hospitals. However, one writer, Annaliese Griffin (2017), points out that much of the wellness industry exploits this and has convinced many women that science and medicine can't be trusted altogether; this enables them to sell products and services based on misinformation. While the medical industry requires radical change, she points out, "it's important to remember that the dollars we drop on salt lamps and Moon Dust aren't the same thing as agitating for change — and that retreating into wellness is an option just for the privileged set." More women now are questioning the trend of doctors to assign meditation for pain relief as a way for the medical profession to offload the responsibility of care to women themselves instead of investigating social and physiological sources of stress (Yahm 2018).

As for "grit" — which includes endurance, resilience, and optimism: we know that class, race, and the educational level of parents have a greater influence on a student's success than student effort (Nathan 2017). Journalist David Denby's (2016b) trenchant critique of grit, worth quoting at length, exposes its morally shallow, individualistic, and corporatist values. It also serves as an apt description of what is wrong about the way mindfulness is often used in schools. In a list of attributes endorsed by proponents of grit (as often with mindfulness), he finds

> nothing in it about honesty or courage; nothing about integrity, kindliness, responsibility for others. The list is innocent of ethics, any notion of moral development, any mention of the behaviors by which character has traditionally been marked. [Advocates] would seem to be preparing children for personal success only — doing well at school, getting into college, getting a job, especially a corporate job where such docility as is suggested by these approved traits (gratitude?) would be much appreciated by managers. Putting it politically, the "character" inculcated in students … is perfectly suited to producing corporate drones in a capitalist economy. Putting it morally and existentially, the list is timid and empty. The creativity and wildness that were once our grace to imagine as part of human existence would be extinguished by strict adherence to these instrumentalist guidelines.

Denby further points out the inadequacy of "grit" as an explanation, and its avoidance of how inequitable social conditions contribute to success or failure:

> Family background, opportunity, culture, landing at the right place at the right time, the over-all state of the economy — all these elements, operating at once, allow some talented people to do much better than other talented people. [A grit proponent] — indifferent to class, race, history, society, culture — strips success of its human reality, and her single-minded theory may explain very little.

Denial of Suffering and Death

Positive psychology and the wellness industry's emphasis on optimism and happiness reflect this culture's inadequate way it deals with suffering and death — through denial. There are few meaningful mourning rituals at a community level; mourning is seen as a private affair that one is expected to get over after a certain time and/or to engage in positive emotions as a coping mechanism. Positive psychology encourages an almost exclusive focus on positive emotions, which provide "beneficial effects" used to cope with loss (Wortman 2011).

Western culture regards death as something to overcome and for the grieving person to get on with life; the culture wants no quarter with contemplating death, let alone accepting it. When it comes to such sentiments, the poets Walt Whitman, who praised death, and Wallace Stevens, who wrote that "death is the mother of beauty," are without much honour in their own country. The poet Rilke (2011) wrote:

> Death is our friend, our closest friend, perhaps the only friend who can never be misled by our ploys and vacillations. And I do not mean that in the sentimental, romantic sense of distrusting or renouncing life. Death is our friend precisely because it brings us into absolute and passionate presence with all that is here, that is natural, that is love.

Some contemporary writers like Megan O'Rourke (2012: 217–18) have provided wisdom as a counterbalance to the conventional denial of sadness, melancholy, and grieving:

> It's not a question of getting over it or healing. No; it's a question of learning to live with this transformation. For the loss is transformative, in good ways and bad, a tangle of change that cannot be threaded into the usual narrative spools. It is too central for that. It's not an emergence from the cocoon, but a tree growing around an obstruction.

About death, novelist and essayist Marilynne Robinson writes:

> We experience pain and difficulty as failure instead of saying, I

will pass through this, everyone I have ever admired has passed through this, music has come out of it, literature has come out of it. We should think of our humanity as a privilege. (Stein 2012)

Zombie Culture

Death is transfigured in one way through zombies, which have become a popular cultural trope in films, novels, video games, and TV series. Among other meanings, zombies have become a metaphor for how the corporate-capitalist state and culture reduces life-affirming social activities for the public good into deadened commodities for private pleasure, generating harmful and punitive policies. Zombies are devoid of soul, imagination, and critical thinking, and are reduced to survival; we live in a destructive zombie culture that lacks vision and compassion for others and reduces people to manipulative data, says education scholar and cultural critic Henry Giroux (2014b; see also Egginton 2015; and Browning, Castillo, Schmid, and Reilly 2015).

Zombies represent the staying power of neoliberalism itself — not a living, useful system, if it ever was, but not yet dead and still here. Despite the financial collapse of 2008 and in worldwide elections in 2016 and 2017, in which neoliberalism lost ground to right-wing nationalists and populists who want protection from global market forces, no clear progressive alternatives are arising yet to take its place. George Monbiot (2016b) calls neoliberalism the "zombie doctrine" because after its collapse in 2008 there was nothing to replace it: the zombie walks. Historian Eric Foner said, "Neoliberalism … lingers on like a zombie walking the earth, it has no intellectual legitimacy anymore" (Kreitner 2017).

Many feel powerless and anxious about the future in the face of climate change, terrorist bombings, and global corporate domination. "Zombie stories give people the opportunity to witness the end of the world they've been secretly wondering about while, at the same time, allowing themselves to sleep at night because the catalyst of that end is fictional," says Max Brooks, who wrote a book on which a zombie film was based (Barber 2014). At the 2017 G-20 summit meeting of world leaders in Hamburg, Germany, a collective of protesters against capitalism paraded slowly in the streets dressed as zombies; they later cast off their costumes to reveal colourful clothes and hugged each other. According to the collective's website, the zombified figures were "supposed to embody a society that has lost the feeling that another world is possible" (Way 2017).

Similar interpretations about the popularity of zombies fall under our fear of loss of control over our past, our selves, and our mortality. One writer sees them as representing our past and our inability to come to terms with it, reminding us of novelist William Faulkner's comment that the past is never dead, it's not even past. He suggests that "all zombie stories are in some way about how a past that cannot be changed threatens to consume the world that is living" (Marche 2013).

A zombie researcher, Sara Juliet Lauro (2013), sees the link with our realization that we're less in control of our brains than we think we are — we're the zombies. Another of her insights is that today we share a heightened sense of tragedy that we are embodied and have to die — zombies at least never do. And, of course, "cellphone zombies" are everywhere and in at least one large city have been banned from looking at their phones while crossing the street (Mohn 2017).

Researcher Chris Goto-Jones and artist Ricardo Bessa see a link between mindfulness meditation and portrayals of the zombie apocalypse, two models of post-selfhood that seek to free themselves from the anxieties of a capitalist society and, according to Goto-Jones, "the demands of an ego driven to exhaustion by instrumental rationality" (Adraque 2015). Goto-Jones (2013) considers the zombie as representing the fear of what it would be like once the ego dies after the end of capitalism; it serves as a means to scare us away from imagining a liberating post-capitalist consciousness. He is doubtful whether mindfulness can serve to free us from capitalist control and instrumentalist consciousness and generate an alternative future, since mindfulness is "a new form of ideological domination that enables people to endure the alienating conditions of capitalism without calling for material revolution, redistribution, or institutional change." Neither zombies nor mindfulness provide a hopeful post-capitalist vision.

Can mindfulness itself be zombified? Ron Purser and I observed that the author of a *New York Times* column, "Meditation for Real Life," turned everyday events ("How to be Mindful at the Gym," "How to be Mindful at the Doctor's Office") into a self-conscious, controlling practice that knocks out any spontaneity or pleasure, all in the name of mindfulness (Gelles 2017). What we called the zombification of mindfulness "is the deadening of something that is alive. Gelles' mindful zombie is relieved of having to make difficult choices. The moral imperative is that you must attend to everything you do" (Purser and Forbes 2017). A Buddhist scholar, Richard Payne (2017), thought the *Times* column trivial; he saw it as an indicator that mindfulness as a fad has peaked, yet predicted that like other fads, "this one will probably continue a zombie existence in a parallel universe where disco balls are still popular, leaking into our own from time to time."

Another analogy with zombieism parallels the way mindfulness reinforces deadening neoliberal values and practices. Professor Eric Cazdyn, in his book *The Already Dead* (2012), describes a new medicine paradigm that allows patients to maintain themselves with chronic diseases; there is no future of either dying or being cured, only an endless present. He calls this condition "the new chronic," wherein hopeful notions of cure and revolution disappear in favour of present stability and maintenance. Like zombies, patients dwell in the timeless present and are the "already dead." A reviewer of Cazdyn's book, Erene Stergiopoulos (2017), sees this dynamic extending beyond medicine into the way capitalism operates overall and serves to stifle resistance to unjust conditions:

> The conditions of contemporary capitalism that favour management over cure extend beyond illness and into social struggle: Instead of fighting for revolution, the new chronic leaves us instead to fight to maintain the status quo. It's the same logic that encourages the most marginalized to make do in a system positioned against them, rather than question the historical and social conditions that left them disadvantaged in the first place.

To take it further, much of mindfulness, with its relentless loyalty to an indeterminate, never-ending present, favours the maintenance of and adjustment to current existing conditions of neoliberal society. Mindfulness teachers are often fond of telling people to see and be with "the way things are"; after all, there is no actual past or future, they preach, these are just usually troublesome thoughts in your head, there is only the now. Instead of gaining insight into the past and envisioning and fighting for a better future, mindfulness employed in this way also encourages a new chronic of the ever-present. It deters people from seeing how existing inequitable social conditions are fluid and how we can change them through historical time.

Lack of Culture …

Left behind by mindfulness education programs in the wake of the neoliberal wave is the cultural capital of many schools and communities of colour in urban areas. It is rare that mindfulness school programs acknowledge these and work with and within them to discuss and employ shared skills, strengths, and interests. Overall, the lack of a meaningful culture beyond the accumulation of commodities and individualistic and competitive success, the loss of community, caring, and connectedness, the sense of fragmentation and isolation, is one of the great tragedies of American culture that mindfulness programs in schools do not address.

Mindfulness promoter Jon Kabat-Zinn (2006: 143) has his own analysis of and solution to what's wrong with us — our "entire society is suffering from attention deficit disorder — big time." But instead of a cultural critique and suggested ways out through and with others, Kabat-Zinn frames the problem in personal terms, as a psychic illness. Individuals are ill with a disorder and poorly equipped to be mindful and adaptive enough to cope with everyday life. Never mind the attention economy, the way corporations compete for, demand, and grab our attention through the social and corporate media with relentless and ubiquitous advertisements, or how stress is created by greedy banks and corporations, privatized health care, and unemployment and underemployment.

Kabat-Zinn's individualistic analysis and solution, that mindfulness is the way to overcome virtually every societal deficit, reflects the broader cultural value of personal self-regulation or self-management as the answer to any problem. Instead of examining and participating in our shared culture, individuals provide their own expertise to solve their personal problem of inattention. This is designed not to change the capitalist system that contributes to stress and attention deficit, but as a way to adjust and accommodate to it. It further burdens the individual with constant self-surveillance and mystifies the nature of those cultural and societal ills that are in need of critical analysis and collective change.

… and a Culture of Lack

In everyday ways, we experience a "culture of lack" — Buddhist activist David Loy's (2002) term to describe a capitalist culture that induces feelings of emptiness, craving, and that one is never enough. Underlying this is a more fundamental sense of lack, which fuels capitalism's dependency on consumerism and addiction that requires our endless search for external goods or relationships to better or complete ourselves and to avoid having to face and feel our own feelings. At a deeper, ontological level, Loy points to the anxiety and insecurity of people in the West who attempt to shore up a self that is not a solid, permanent entity. We work to prop up and promote a self that feels increasingly anxious, fragile, and put upon from all sides, because it is not something we can make secure in the first place. It is no wonder that distractions serve as means to avoid our basic insecurity and anxiety about the self; they are a way to divert us from having to face this awareness about the impermanence of the self for which conventional society has no satisfactory answer. Loy (2015: 120) says:

> There is an almost perfect fit between this fundamental sense of *lack* that unenlightened beings have, according to Buddhism, and our present economic system, which uses advertising and other devices to persuade us that the next thing we buy will make us happy — which it never does, at least not for long … a consumerist economy exploits our sense of lack, instead of helping us understand and address the root problem. (original italics)

Kabat-Zinn's brand of mindfulness shows little interest in either the cultural or foundational causes as to why many people feel the need to distract themselves. Too often as well, with regard to many of these matters, mindfulness programs in schools have little to say.

11

Society as Context:
Neoliberal Education

Wisdom is sold in the desolate market where none come to buy.
(William Blake)

Like David Foster Wallace's young fish, who are unaware they are swimming in water, many of those who practise mindfulness in educational settings are oblivious to the powerful undercurrents of neoliberal structural inequities that constrain mindfulness and contribute to everyday stress. In this way, mindfulness serves a function in schools. Along with SEL programs, mindfulness is expected to mitigate the stress that stems from neoliberal society itself (Forbes 2016a, 2012; Hsu 2013; Zakrzewski 2015). Schools, such as some in Massachusetts, encourage students to employ mindfulness to regulate their emotions, in line with the individualized, therapeutic trend in neoliberal education, "so they can concentrate on learning" (Vaznis 2016). Not only is this a shallow, instrumental use of mindfulness, we need to first ask: what counts as learning, who determines it? Why are so many students at odds with school learning?

Mindfulness educators are fond of saying that we tell kids to pay attention a hundred times a day, but we never teach them *how*. The "how" is supposed to be mindfulness, the sustained practice of noticing your thoughts, feelings, and sensations, and bringing your focus back to a particular point or object over and over again. The hidden question, however, is: why do we need to tell children to pay attention in school in the first place? Why are so many of them distracted, bored, and restless? After all, we have all seen that when children are interested in something they can engage in absorbed and sustained attention. Do educators look at what is wrong with school itself, and themselves, the water in which they swim, as a source for why they have to tell students constantly to pay attention? As with mindfulness proponents, some school psychologists have seized on mindfulness as an instrument to further standardized objectives such as academic success and self-regulation; they don't bother to question whether these are worthwhile for students in terms of educational and developmental values. In one review (Renshaw and Cook 2017: 6), they describe mindfulness "as a skill set that can be learned like any other skill," as a coping or "well-being-promoting skill," and as a subset of SEL competencies, self-awareness and self-management. This is an instrumental use of mindfulness — it furthers individualistic, neoliberal competition in schools and avoids critical questioning of educational meaning, quality, values, or social context.

The aforementioned school psychologists are happy to cite a meta-analysis of mindfulness programs with youth that yielded "small positive effects" and think that is strong enough to ward off previous claims that the research base for mindfulness interventions is too weak to concretely justify further intervention. Buried in a special issue of *Mindful Magazine* glowing with uncritical descriptions of school mindfulness programs is the admission from a researcher, Lisa Flook of the University of Wisconsin-Madison, that "we don't have conclusive evidence at this point about the benefits or impacts of mindfulness on youth." She at best sees "the promise of interventions and trainings on outcomes related to grades, wellbeing, and emotional regulation" (Gerszberg 2017).

Not only does the research evidence on mindfulness remain scant, the overvalued concern with the need to obtain some kind of objective proof pre-empts the need to evaluate the purposes, values, and social meaning of mindfulness programs in the first place. This is due in part to the unquestioned allegiance to the dominant paradigm that just discrete, measurable behaviours or data count as actual truth or knowledge. There is a blind, driven faith that mindfulness, or any other experience, can be proven true through narrowly defined, objective measures that forego examining and questioning any broader purpose and meaning.

Within this objective, behavioural research paradigm itself, the evidence is not just weak at best, the methodological challenges to provide credible evidence are complex and daunting, in particular the need for comparison conditions and random assignments (Felver, Celis-de Hoyos, Tezanos, and Singh 2015; May 2017; Hanley et al. 2016; Resnick 2017). A meta-study of the research on the effects of meditation on "pro-social" behaviours (compassion, empathy, connectedness, reduced prejudice and aggression) concludes that it "suffers from methodological weaknesses and is partly immersed in theoretical mist" (Kreplin, Farias, and Brazil 2018).

Mindfulness educators need to first ask: what are the purpose and value of mindfulness interventions, and how and why are such programs employed in schools? Mindfulness becomes instrumental in gaining "small positive effects" with weak methods toward unexamined ends. This occurs within a neoliberal political and social climate whose merits themselves are not questioned, are contestable, and are often detrimental.

Within this context, a core market-based value that accrediting agencies push and that many teacher and school counselling education programs internalize is the demand for "continuous improvement." The insistence on constant accountability of teachers and counsellors, and for school effectiveness as measured by test scores and surveillance of performance, becomes an endless, never-satisfying quest. The quality of interactions and experiences between students and educators in the process of inquiry is of no interest, just more and better results that measure so-called success, achievement that always recedes into a future that never arrives. As a number of my colleagues and I can attest, the endless pressure from having to strive without end for "improvement" defined by others feels like a futile exercise and takes an emotional, exhausting toll on educators and students alike. Moreover, we have not found this kind of demand for evidence to be useful in how we conceptualize and practise our work, nor has it resulted in wiser students or better-quality programs.

In education, neoliberal reforms are driven by a false premise. While there is an impoverished sector of society that does not do as well as others, the claim that the U.S. public education system overall is a failure compared to other nations is a myth (Lind 2012; Ravitch 2014). This justifies neoliberal reformers' argument for less public education and more privatized, market-based solutions (so-called choice in the way of vouchers and privately funded charter schools as means to make schools more productive or competitive; for a report on the problem with charter

schools, see Network for Public Education 2017). In this way, the neoliberal reformers fail to follow the very thing that the successful nations
they praise do: invest more federal money in public education and teacher
education, and reduce structural poverty.

Many educational reformers see students as economic investments in
the future. They regard and treat education as a means for students to gain
employment so that the U.S. can better compete in the global economy. Of
course, education should contribute to economic well-being and national
prosperity for all. But education cannot and should not be reduced to
an engine of success or an economic commodity itself; education is too
vital, valuable, and complex an endeavour to serve as a handmaiden of
corporate interests.

Mindfulness by the Book

Schools operate within a society in which the market and its values
dominate and which is governed by policies that serve these interests.
Education policies conflate education and economic success, and regard
students as human capital. For example, the No Child Left Behind (NCLB)
and Race to the Top policies were intended to build up schools in order
for the U.S. to compete in the global economy. According to the Obama
White House website:

> In today's global economy, a high-quality education is no longer
> just a pathway to opportunity — it is a prerequisite for success.
> Because economic progress and educational achievement are
> inextricably linked, educating every American student to gradu-
> ate from high school prepared for college and for a career is a
> national imperative. (K–12 Education n.d.)

In schools, then, we need to look at how education policy frames how
mindfulness is employed, and ask why this is happening now on such
a large scale and who stands to gain. Business professor James Reveley
(2016: 497) writes:

> The capacity for personal prevention and self-surveillance that
> school-based mindfulness training inculcates in the young …

is central to the self-managing figure that neoliberalism prizes. When institutionalized as a form of therapeutic education, therefore, mindfulness meditation is not ideologically neutral but rather morphs into a neoliberal self-technology.

We need to acknowledge and resist the dominant social conditions under which mindfulness in schools operates and instead together ask what the most genuine purpose of education should be; we should insist on a meaning in which mindfulness enhances both self and social development for the highest good.

Within a corporatized structure of work, mindfulness in part becomes a means to increase both productivity and compliance (Krupka 2015). In similar terms, mindfulness can become a way to ramp up an education system that will create compliant students who can manage their own behaviour, focus on their assignments, and calm themselves when angry or frustrated with school. Rather than questioning, discussing, analyzing, resisting, and changing troublesome, stressful education policies and cultures such as high-stakes testing, poor quality schools, the closing of many schools in urban communities, and unjust disciplinary policies, students are taught to look to their own feelings and skills as the source of their stress, despair, or anger. As they calm themselves with mindfulness they may then be better prepared to be passive, unquestioning consumers and cooperative workers who will help their corporate employers better compete in the global economy. An article in *Forbes*, the business magazine, approvingly reported "mindfulness helped kids during high-stakes testing, by reducing their anxiety and boosting working memory" (Walton 2016). Within schools' neoliberal, competitive culture, stress becomes decontextualized and interpreted as the personal failure of an individual to become successful; one must compete against others on an otherwise meaningless high-stakes, test, adapt to the demands of productivity, and be a team player.

The problem in the U.S. and Canada of increased stress and distress such as depression and anxiety, particularly among youth, needs to be reframed within the context of capitalist societies instead of as privatized experiences that can be alleviated with individual mindfulness. Mark Fisher, author of *Capitalist Realism: Is There No Alternative?* (2009), asked:

Instead of treating it as incumbent on individuals to resolve their own psychological distress, instead, that is, of accepting the vast *privatization of stress* that has taken place over the last thirty years, we need to ask: how has it become acceptable that so many people, and especially so many young people, are ill? (*Blind Field* 2017, original italics)

In a careful observation of a popular mindfulness program in British schools, researcher Daniel Simpson (2017) found that "students learn self-pacifying skills, but not to question the sources of stress in societies ruled by corporate values." Neoliberalism has no interest in any critical socio-logical or cultural analysis of why so many people suffer in the same way; the more individuals take personal responsibility for their own emotional distress, the less likely any focus will be on the inequitable and deceptive institutional and structural aspects of everyday life that give rise to such distress. Annaliese Griffin (2017) points out that "medical outcomes in the U.S. are largely predicted by race and socioeconomic status, and it is minorities and poor people who face the worst consequences when toxins get dumped and regulatory systems break down." Without critical aware-ness of the broader social and cultural context, mindfulness can become a disguised pedagogy of social control. Funie Hsu (2016) discusses the example of mindfulness used in schools to extend students' capacity to focus and pay attention, and to increase executive functioning:

While focus and self-regulatory skills are important in academic success, they are being developed in an educational context where measures for achievement have become decidedly incentivized and consequential (e.g., the former policy of NCLB). Training students to enhance their attention, therefore, translates easily into neoliberal applications.

Consequently, students can calmly take high-stakes tests and raise their (and their schools') scores. Alienated inner-city children can accept their inadequate learning conditions and not act out their anger. Demoralized, burnt-out teachers can adjust to and comply with being audited and micromanaged, follow scripted Common Core classroom lessons, and teach to the test to raise the scores on which their jobs now depend. These are the kinds of outcome metrics borrowed from the corporate sector and imported into schools as part of the aim to privatize and gain profit from public schooling. We'll examine some ways in which mindfulness practices unwittingly reinforce the neoliberal status quo.

The constant pressure in schools on children to achieve, compete, and produce — and at ever-younger ages — leads to stressful feelings and negative consequences for children and teachers. Some educators serve up mindfulness as the lubricant that makes the gears run more smoothly. In the video "Healthy Habits of Mind," by Mindful Schools (n.d.) in Oakland, California, a teacher says she accepts that reading and writing are now taught in kindergarten: "the reality is, that's what's expected right now." The teacher sees that her children cannot do the tasks because they "cannot focus long enough"; that is, the tasks are beyond their level of development. Nevertheless, she says that since we are going to ask them to do these things, we need to give them the tools to do it. She offers them mindfulness to help them focus and de-stress in order to adapt to the academic pressure. The teacher does not question the neoliberal premise promoted that young children must forego play, free exploration, and other life-enhancing activities in order to read, achieve, and prepare for standardized tests at an earlier age. A researcher and former teacher of many years found that today, "5-year-olds are spending more time engaged in teacher-led academic learning activities than play-based learning opportunities that facilitate child-initiated investigations and foster social development among peers" (Brown 2017). Educator Natalie Flores (2016) identifies mindfulness programs in early childhood education as contributing to the "schoolification," or school readiness, of young children: the focus is for children to acquire formal, pre-academic skills instead of cultivating their holistic, developmental, and play-based qualities.

Nor do many mindfulness educators challenge other injustices and pressures that start early, such as the higher rate of suspension of African-American students, which begins in preschool and kindergarten and leads many down the school-to-prison pipeline (Lee 2014). Few mindfulness educators bring awareness of this systemic pattern of social injustice into their work (Hsu 2013). Even with some more benign alternative programs, such as restorative justice, that may use mindfulness, the primary aim is to promote a more orderly school environment by which students regulate themselves through self-discipline and accountability (Mindful Teachers 2014). Mindful restorative justice programs still favour students' self-regulation to conventional school environments. They leave things as they are rather than call out and challenge the structural and institutional inequities and injustices that lead to certain students being frequent offenders.

It is not accidental that proponents employ mindfulness in impoverished inner-city schools, which hold numbers of disaffected, indignant, and at times disruptive students of colour (Schwartz 2014). Mindfulness programs such as those offered by Mindful Schools in Oakland, the Mindful Life Project in Richmond, California, and the Holistic Life Foundation in Baltimore are motivated to support these youths' social and emotional well-being and improve their academic success. Yet without critically understanding and challenging the neoliberal education agenda, mindfulness practices geared toward stress reduction, conflict resolution, emotion regulation, anger management, and focus and concentration slip into functions of social control and reinforce individualistic responsibility. In one participating high school, teachers can send distressed or disruptive students — ones in the halls or those getting into physical or even just verbal altercations — to the Mindful Moment Room for individual assistance with "emotional self-regulation" (Mindful Moment Program n.d.). Suspensions went down and attendance and promotions went up. However, the root causes of the considerable stress, suspensions, and angry behaviour, as well as what needs to better occur in the school and community, are not addressed — just the emphasis on conforming to school expectations. There is legitimate anger and frustration over many social injustices that many students of colour experience, as evidenced in the Black Lives Matter movement. Students who witness or who are prey to violence, among others, also suffer from trauma; it is not evident that educators, mindful or not, challenge students' sources of pain and support them in questioning the goals and culture of the school.

We can see how preparing youth to be diligent corporate consumers is conflated with mindfulness via Gap's "Back to School" series of short YouTube videos (Gapkids Back to School — Meditation 2017). These feature Andres Gonzalez, one of the leaders of the Holistic Life Foundation, which provides mindfulness meditation to inner-city elementary school students in Baltimore. The series is part of a larger Gap campaign called "Forward with." A public relations piece states: "The GapKids 'Forward with' campaign is a celebration of progress. It's about extending the idea of 'dressing' beyond clothing to the traits and behaviors that will lead to kids' success" (Gap 2017). One of the people it highlights as helping youth in unconventional ways is Gonzalez.

In one video, young African-American students provide a "tutorial" on how to meditate, while in the other they sit and meditate on their desks. The narrator, presumably Gonzalez, says they are trying to get the youth "to direct their attention upon themselves"; he says that if we can get these kids to "slow down, pause, breathe and be present, then they are ready to do anything." What stands out in the video is the seamless transition in the blurb below the video from the narrator's quote to a sentence that directs the viewer to "shop the new collection" at the "Gap to School" website and hashtag. Mindfulness is fluidly linked to a corporate brand aimed at children.

The point is not to negate or downplay the work of the Holistic Life Foundation, but there are troubling questions not discussed on their website. With GapKids choosing Gonzalez as someone who helps "advance children through positive reinforcements outside the traditional educational curriculum," does Holistic Life receive corporate funds in return for being in an advertisement? Do students get clothing or a discount from GapKids? Do students know and approve of their being included in an advertisement for a major clothing corporation? Do they get to reflect on what the relationship might be between being mindful and endorsing a corporate brand commercial, or whether there should even be one? Do they get to learn about the Gap's India child labour scandal of 2007? Or whether, according to a Human Rights Watch report in 2015, the Gap still relies on stitching done in abusive sweatshops in Cambodia (Winn 2015)?

Holistic Life teaches students to focus on and take personal responsibility for themselves through mindfulness; they then tell them they can do anything. GapKids promotes personal traits and behaviours that lead to "success" in a neoliberal society as well as viewing commodification and branding as a natural part of childhood and schooling; its parent company has a history of questionable ethical manufacturing practices in low-income countries that exploit children and women. All these practices come together in that they share an individualistic and consumerist focus that ignores social context, and they are ripe for a more inclusive, critical kind of social mindfulness.

In examining one inner-city Mindful Schools program videotaped as a success story, activist educator Jennifer Cannon (2016) explains its use of racialized discourse and a deficit framework: a white mindfulness teacher intervenes and rescues out-of-control, troubled youth of colour. The teacher functions as a disciplinary/authority figure and teaches them that hard work, effort, and self-discipline through mindfulness leads to success — but how that is defined and by whom is nowhere to be found. Cannon points out that the mindfulness instructor reforms the individual student, not the education system, offers no structural critique or critical exploration of the students' lives and social conditions, and does nothing to build on the students' and community's own cultural capital or agency.

Some policy proponents, including those who are well-off, mandate that public school students take high-stakes tests; their own children, however — many of whom are sent to private schools — need not. The irony is that privileged students feel intense pressure to succeed and compete to get into prestigious colleges; they accept the myth that they alone are responsible for their success. Some find that mindfulness meditation relieves some of the performance pressures and helps them sleep better, diminish stress, and refocus on schoolwork so they can stay competitive within such a pressurized system (Davis 2015).

With the considerable bureaucratic demands placed on teachers, more are feeling stressed and seeking mindfulness, too. Patricia Jennings, an accomplished mindfulness educator and researcher, offers mindfulness training to stressed-out teachers so they can remain calm, work better with students, improve their "productivity," and adjust to the demands of their job. The subtitle of her 2015 book, "Simple Skills for Peace and Productivity in the Classroom," could serve as a neoliberal classroom mantra. Teachers learn how to calm themselves, pay better attention to their own thoughts and feelings and to their students, and create a better-managed (peaceful) classroom. Two educators endorse the "utility of contemplative practice" in teacher training to help teachers manage and reduce the stress of the profession caused by "social and cultural changes, such as educational reforms" (Impedovo and Malik 2015). This approach is typical in that it doesn't bother to challenge the external stressors endemic to neoliberal schooling (those "educational reforms") that lead to teacher stress, demoralization, burnout, and attrition, which the mindfulness advocates seem to regard as facts of nature. In 2018, a year of militant teacher strikes, U.S. teachers, mostly women, quit at a record rate due to low pay, stagnant salaries, and neglect of funding for public education (Hackman and Morath 2018).

Through mindfulness training, the message to teachers is that they should take it upon themselves to be present and adjust to demands for "productivity" and outcomes, rather than practise mindfulness as part of a critical pedagogy that questions and challenges the policies and conditions that create their stress and unhappiness. Jennings herself says she is not out to change the factors that contribute to teacher stress, burnout, and dropping out — such as children's poverty and trauma, and administrators' pressures to meet standards — but to help the teachers become the change they wish to see in the world using an individualistic approach (Kamenetz 2016). While no one should be expected to change structural inequities by themselves, a critical social mindfulness includes partnering with teachers to identify, discuss, strategize, and work to bring about needed cultural and policy changes with others.

Absent from schools are valuable ways that mindfulness can enhance the full development of students and educators together: reflecting on moral purpose, gaining and discussing insights into the nature of one's socially privatized self, and questioning and acting on the social and political contexts in which mindfulness is practised. We need to challenge an unreflective practice as well as the problematic social context it reinforces. We must employ mindfulness as part of an explicit, progressive approach that questions, resists, and transforms the troublesome aspects of education practices in neoliberal society.

12

Social-Emotional Learning and Mindfulness

Contrary to what some mindfulness proponents believe, just practising mindfulness does not lead to skilful, healthy, and compassionate behaviour. For example, while some contemplative educators note the importance of social and emotional learning, they suggest that "once knowing activates our feelings, we are moved to action.… Our intimate understanding of others and their needs prompts compassionate action" (Palmer and Zajonc 2010: 98). A leading researcher in mindfulness with children, Mark Greenberg, according to an interviewer's interpretation, also feels that "inherent mindfulness helps us to realize that we live in an interconnected world and puts us in touch with the golden rule" (Boyce 2012: 76). The assumption in each case is that contemplative practice leads straight to right thinking and even right action; that once you are in a contemplative state you will naturally gain insight and engage in compassionate, skilful behaviours that display your sense of interdependence with others.

The problem is, feelings of compassion or empathy by themselves do not motivate and enable you to engage in or carry out skilful, wise action. Without learning and applying proper interpersonal means, mindfulness alone does not guarantee that the student will know what and how to say and do from a more developed framework. While you can contemplate your feelings and attain a heightened state of mind, you still need to know how to practise actual effective relational actions with others and, moreover, consider and discuss what those are.

In an attempt to address this issue of proper behaviour, some mindfulness educators pair mindfulness with teaching students social-emotional learning (Lantieri and Zakrzewski 2015). Educators consider SEL skills to be the most optimal and healthy psychological and interpersonal skills students need in order to do well in school and in life. Some regard them as the highest available moral standards they can offer in schools, since they can't introduce Buddhist and other religious ethical precepts into secular educational sites. Teaching these skills is supposed to help students better deal with strong feelings, get along with others, resolve conflicts, and learn "compassion."

An impetus for educators to teach SEL is to regulate students. This allows for less disruption and more control by the school. Some SEL proponents provide this rationale:

> If students become more skilled at monitoring and regulating their emotional impulses, then they should become less likely to cause disruptions in class, get into fights on the playground, bully other children in the hallway, experiment with drugs, and commit crimes. (National Association of State Boards of Education 2013: 2)

All of this is underwritten by the bottom line of neoliberal education reform: schools are realizing that if students can better manage their emotions and stay focused, they will do better in school (that is, their test scores will improve). Learning about feelings, then, is instrumental — but not an end in itself, as part of students' personal growth to become decent people; rather, it is useful in order to improve their schoolwork.

While SEL claims to be a universal secular ethics, it is used here as a set of behavioural practices that reflect the individualist ideology of neoliberal society. SEL does not examine the emotional and relational sources of students' behaviour. It does not analyze how emotional life and action are inextricably related to the complex, rich, and often problematic social nature of the lives of students, teachers, and community members. It ignores the cultural and structural contexts of race and class. Recall from the section on anger in Chapter 6 that when SEL is used to manage student anger, it neglects issues of racial discrimination and the experience of students of colour. In neoliberal fashion, it places the onus and blame back on the individual student.

The competencies or behavioural skills favoured by SEL fit with neoliberal achievement-oriented values designed for conventional levels of success in a competitive, corporatized, market-based society. Like mindfulness, SEL programs are either unaware of or endorse this worldview. No less than the co-founder of CASEL, the leading organization that promotes SEL, sees developing SEL skills as a "really good return" on economic investment (Shriver and Bridgeland 2015). He says that employers "seek the very skills programs of social and emotional learning foster: teamwork, problem-solving, character, and grit" — which also lead to "improved test scores." Employing corporatized language, two SEL educators note with approval that leading economists, including a Nobel Prize laureate, call for schools to teach these emotional, "soft" skills since they yield the greatest returns on educational investment and lead to greater success in life (Brackett and Rivers 2014). According to the authors, the laureate thinks this is a cost-effective way to increase "the quality and productivity of the workforce through fostering workers' motivation, perseverance, and self-control" (2014: 3). They endorse the increasing efforts to "move toward better preparing youth to enter and contribute to a competitive and global workforce." These neoliberal goals go hand in hand with SEL.

The language of SEL is a far cry from representing values of optimal human development for all. Instead of even discussing the intrinsic qualities of education, SEL skills and their descriptions reflect free-market values that help students in standardized academic achievement and signal a technocratic, entrepreneurial, corporatized worldview that values individualistic self-control, pseudo-objectivity, and conventional success (CASEL 2018a). Skills are described as the ability to "accurately" recognize one's emotions and thoughts; "accurately" assess one's strengths and limitations; achieve self- and stress "management"; attain relationship skills such as cooperating and resisting "inappropriate" social pressure; and "responsible decision making." With a nod to positive psychology, they value a student having "a well-grounded sense of confidence and optimism" (CASEL 2018a).

Teachers and students can be mindful of thoughts and feelings and learn the latest skills that pass as secular ethics yet remain within conventional and conformist social structures that govern and restrict their awareness. It is not surprising that some states have standardized SEL skills for all their schools (Kansas became the first; Elias 2012); standardizing facilitates regulation through "objective" assessment and makes it harder for teachers to apply principles in creative ways to respond to children's diverse needs. This normative framework represents a particular individualist stage of cultural development. It does little to contribute to helping students evolve to later perspectives; it reinforces many of the self-centred values and practices that dominate capitalist society in the first place.

Overall, SEL skills are not about helping students develop emotions as part of their interior life. They are behavioural skills taught to students, rather than embodied principles and practices that students can and should co-create and develop through meaningful engagement and dialogue. With educators disinterested in interior life, focusing on these rehearsed skills does not ensure that students will take them to heart. Child psychologist James Garbarino (2000) argues that such skills need to be spiritually anchored, connected to their deepest meaning for youth. To what extent do students embody and make the skills their own? Can they apply the principles in a new stressful scenario that would show they do not just memorize the skill in a mechanical way?

There is little teacher education and preparation in SEL, and many teachers are "on their own" to learn about and teach SEL skills (Schoenert-Reichl and Zakrzewski 2014). Even were there to be mandated training through all states and provinces, though, the larger point is that SEL is no ethical, universal gold standard — educators and students need to discuss, practise, interpret, and evaluate social and emotional skills with respect to the social context of values and whose interests they serve. We still need to ask: who determines what counts as "managing," "effectiveness," and "success"? What kind of values and society do we prize? Without this inquiry, SEL and mindfulness can turn into a rote technology taught to achieve predetermined, normative behavioural outcomes. Their focus on outcomes does not elevate students' consciousness; it does not encourage critical questioning of and insights into the place of feelings within their own relationships.

One encouraging program at an alternative school framed SEL skills within a critical pedagogy that was relevant to the lives of urban African-American students. Instead of the usual "non-differentiated" SEL approach, the program merged critical pedagogy and culturally relevant material, using resources from the students' community (Slaten et al. 2015). The authors say that this "critically conscious approach to SEL" allowed the school to "inform students of the social and political context that may have contributed to their marginalization in the education system. Applying critically conscious principles would result in different types of SEL interventions and changes to school practices." They did so through small groups that discussed how race, class, and gender impacts their school experience, infusing the school curriculum with learning about the history of marginalized people, and by engaging in critical dialogue that emphasized students' strengths as well as resources, all of which led to actions to create healthier systemic change and individual emotional health, and social well-being.

Compassion

A set of social skills that many education policymakers endorse falls under the rubric of compassion. Educators want students to learn compassion, care, acceptance, and openness with and toward others; to this end, they promote SEL and mindfulness. Schools have an interest in teaching compassion, as proponents aim to help students get along with and be of assistance to others; these are prized abilities in the corporate and service-oriented workplace, as well as skills that are seen as instrumental to academic and interpersonal success. Some educators see compassion, or altruism, as a positive emotion and a "key outcome of SEL" (Zakrzewski 2014). A vague, general term, *compassion* is the ethical residue of Buddhist-based mindfulness teachings; it has found its way into the schools (and in other settings) in an acceptable, secular form. Proponents believe that mindfulness itself facilitates the skill of compassionate empathy with others; here again, many claim that just by practising mindfulness students will come to act with compassion toward others in ways that are ethical, skilful, and teacher-approved. Roeser et al. (2014: 224) believe that mindfulness training has implications for ethical development and can shape individuals who, in the words of neuroscientist Francisco Varela (1999: 4), "know what is good and spontaneously do it." Making considerable speculative leaps, they argue that a person trained in attention through mindfulness can better see and feel what is virtuous and non-virtuous in everyday life. Furthermore, with stabilized attention and calm emotional reactivity, they believe, for those who receive mindfulness training, "the clarity of their awareness and representations of social interactions *may* be enhanced in ways that foster their ethical development" (Roeser et al. 2014: 230, italics added). This weak hypothesis leaves much in explaining how attention training can lead to ethical awareness and action; yet this is the faith-based cornerstone of many secular mindfulness programs: just paying attention, without critical regard to social and moral context, leads to ethical behaviour.

As with other actions, while practising mindfulness for some may lead to more compassion, this is not guaranteed. We need to look at each individual's skilful behaviour, intention, level of self-development, emotional health, and, importantly, their moral worldview. We also need to look at the program or school that aims to teach compassion. Do the compassion educators identify cultural, moral, and political contexts? Do they account for implicit beliefs, values, and political structures?

Because mainstream teaching of compassion occurs within a culture of individualism, competitiveness, and differing privileges, spurred on by neoliberal policymakers who want to improve students' abilities to cooperate with each other and with authority, it thus becomes an abstract, privatized, instrumental skill one possesses or fails to possess that fortifies only the personal qualities of each individual. Proponents likewise provide no developmental or intersubjective frameworks for analyzing how and why compassion is taught. Is it practised to please the teacher and because everyone else does it? Do students reach a later stage of understanding and engage in compassion for the best of intentions and for its own sake?

It is the height of irony to bring children into a supremely uncompassionate society and then claim that we can "teach" them compassion — and hold them responsible when they don't get it. Teaching compassion as an individual skill to students without critically acknowledging their actual conditions — think of neighbourhoods decimated by retrenchment and unjust social, environmental, and economic policies — is akin to spiritual bypassing: embracing something "positive" in absolute, abstract, and individualistic terms that gloss over and avoid the way people must cope within their relative world.

Neuroscientist Dan Siegel says that the self is connected to everyone and everything, that we are a whole ecosystem. Yet he then falls back on a decontextualized, ahistorical, abstracted framework that takes the privatized individual, with a focus on the brain, as the starting point. This leads him to pose a dilemma from which he then must work his way out, from the individual brain to all of humanity. He asks: how do we help humanity "broaden our sense of self to include other people, other organisms, and the entire living ecosphere … how can we take human consciousness and enable it to go past the brain's obvious vulnerability of thinking the self is just a body" (1440 Multiversity 2017). Siegel boxes himself in from the start with a given assumption: We all think we are disconnected, privatized bodies, not because of anything to do with our current privatized, atomized, self-centred society, but due to something inherent in the brain's "thinking." Note that according to Siegel it is not the person who thinks, but the brain — another mistaken conflation.

However, it is not the brain that is the problem; it is the concrete relations of a particular individualistic capitalist society that are operating to create a deluded consciousness in which many people think their selves are just their bodies. This kind of confusing problem-posing abstracts the individual away from one's social relations and then further locates the source of thinking within the brain. It creates confounding dilemmas that lead us away from the need to address, resist, and transform the very society and social relations in which we live.

Empathy

The term *emotional intelligence*, as conceived by psychologist Daniel Goleman in his 1995 eponymous bestseller, became popular as society shifted from an industrial to a service economy and emotional work became a desired skill of corporate management (see Goleman 2005). Empathy, managing one's emotions, and getting along with others were seen as skills that could lead to a successful career and more profitable businesses. It is not surprising, though, that there is less science and more ideology in the loose network of concepts that comprise emotional intelligence (Matthews, Zeidner, and Roberts 2004; Purser and Ng 2017).

Psychologist Adam Grant (2014) musters evidence that emotional intelligence is not correlated with good moral qualities and that we need to account for such a stance:

There is growing recognition that emotional intelligence — like any skill — can be used for good or evil. So if we're going to teach emotional intelligence in schools and develop it at work, we need to consider the values that go along with it and where it's actually useful.

Empathy is a key quality of emotional intelligence and is an example of a useful skill within the service economy and the school system that supports it. Empathy, then, is not a benign universal quality; we must ask how it is used, by whom, and for what ethical purposes. An example of an instrumental use of empathy is "empathic discipline," when teachers learn empathy for the purpose of reducing school suspensions among "wilfully defiant" and "disruptive" African-American students (see Kirp 2017). The reasons these particular students are defiant and disruptive in the first place — the oppressive aspects of schooling and the mismatch with students' life experiences — are never addressed; the goal is to keep students controlled and compliant in school. Sure, all teachers should learn and practise listening with care and understanding as a matter of course, just as all school counsellors are taught to do, and it could improve the quality of relationships between some of them and some students. Nevertheless, the fact that teachers adopt "empathic discipline" to reduce school suspension rates makes the school's needs more important than the students' lives. It skips over addressing systemic problems in the school that contribute to students' defiance and the quality of the schooling they receive. To take these issues on could lead to a more honest and direct practice of empathy between the school and the students.

Daniel Goleman, following Paul Ekman, says there are three kinds of empathy: cognitive, emotional, and compassionate, and claims the latter is superior to the others (Goleman 2007a). But Goleman's argument is a pseudo-debate leading to the false conclusion that the proper kind of empathy, which cannot be determined in the first place, can lead to the proper kind of action in any given situation: it begs the question of what is proper and who determines that.

Cognitive empathy, he says, is the capacity to understand another's perspective and feelings. However, since it is neutral in moral terms, cognitive empathy may be used for nefarious purposes, as when a dictator employs an empathic understanding of his enemies' feelings in order to maintain his own power. Next, emotional empathy is when you share sensations along with the other person and are attuned to the other person's emotions. Here, he says, the problem arises when you can't manage your own upsetting feelings and burn out, or when you detach (to avoid burnout) to such an extent that you become numb, indifferent, and uncaring. Last, compassionate empathy, or what Goleman calls empathic concern, occurs when "we not only understand a person's predicament and feel with them, but are spontaneously moved to help, if needed."

But "empathic concern" cannot help us evaluate the best action or way to help in an actual situation — "spontaneously" or not, as Goleman says — and even whether help is needed. Goleman tries to avoid addressing controversial, political, value-laden content or exposing his own assumptions about any "predicament." However, once he, or anyone, provides examples, we discover what those nice generalities, such as empathic concern, in fact mean to the mindfulness proponent — where the person stands, in real-world terms. Thus in his book, *Social Intelligence*, Goleman (2007b) gives himself away about the kind of values, actions, and systems of which he approves. He cites billionaires Bill and Melinda Gates as exemplifying the highest level of empathic concern and favours "modifying the economic system" with empathy to create a "compassionate capitalism." Goleman thus endorses the individualistic market — as do the Gateses, with their undemocratic foundation — to provide health care as a commodity rather than as a right, and applies market logic to education by operating public schools that need to compete and demonstrate their commodity value (Aschoff 2015). Compassionate or conscious capitalism relies on empathy to prop up the capitalist system, which turns basic human needs into commodities for private profit — should that be the neutral "science of human relationships" that Goleman favours?

Some on the left also fall into conflating a type of empathy with an actual political position. Author Robert Wright (2016) argued that arming the Syrian rebels, a policy of which he disapproved, stemmed from "emotional empathy" — we felt badly for the oppressed Syrian people. He instead favoured "cognitive empathy," the ability to take others' perspectives — in this case, that of the Syrian dictator Assad, which he claims can lead us to adopt a moral "progressive realism," in particular the ability to "*tolerate* oppressive or belligerent foreign leaders" but not back them (original italics). The larger point is that appeals to abstract individual qualities such as empathy, and their supposed neural correlates, mystify the actual ongoing actions that proponents of empathy endorse and value, ones that we are required to evaluate and act on in concrete social, political, and historical terms. We cannot draw wisdom and knowledge on the proper skilful response from arbitrary attempts to determine the amount and kind of empathy someone claims exists or is necessary.

In a neoliberal culture, individualism weakens empathy as a potential practice of social solidarity. It reinforces rather than challenges the systemic injustices of the status quo. Political science professor Gary Olson (2013) argues that this practice leaves systemic injustices intact:

> Our hegemonic culture's social engineering allows for and even encourages individual expressions of empathy, including the volunteerism of philanthro-capitalists. Because such acts only treat symptoms and not sources, they are culturally sanctioned, pose no structural threats, and function to attenuate the acceptance, legitimization, and institutionalization of social empathy on a grand scale.

Worse, says author Tristam Vivian Adams (2016), capitalism organizes empathy for its own ends. Capitalist society requires two psychopathic extremes in the workplace: some jobs require considerable feigned empathy, charm, sensitivity, and friendliness, as in customer service. In others, there can be no empathy at all; people need to be cold and pragmatic and never crack in the face of danger and pressure.

Mindfulness programs teach awareness of emotions. But they do not address or analyze how emotional life is related to the social nature of the lives of students, teachers, and community members. Experiences of trauma, addiction, anxiety, and depression of course require healing, dialogue, and support. But mindfulness programs do not see these, along with anger and sadness, as responses embedded within social relations and systems that often require both critical reflection and social transformation toward greater caring and justice. Mindfulness instead becomes one more individualist endeavour that extracts personal experience from its social context and adjusts individuals to swim better in the polluted waters.

13

Neuroscience: The Search for the Golden Egg

Goldie's Goose Lays an Egg

> The same way you brush your teeth every morning, you should brush your brain with meditation and remove the build up of fear and worry which prevents you from experiencing the happiness you are seeking. (Hawn 2011)

I'm observing a middle school MindUP class in Bensonhurst, Brooklyn, spring 2017. The principal has brought the program, created by actor Goldie Hawn, into the school and certain classes are following its curriculum, lesson by lesson (MindUP n.d.). In this classroom ten bored, restless children — eight boys and two girls — sit in a circle. A counsellor and four teacher paraprofessionals sit on top of the desks surrounding them; the teacher stands up front.

The teacher labours to get through the prescribed curriculum lesson. "What were we talking about last time?" he asks. No one answers; he prompts them. "It begins with 'A.'" Nobody knows. "Amygdala," he says. The teacher describes what it does. They go on to the hippocampus — which holds memories, he says. There are frequent interruptions. "Be focused," he tells them. The paras speak to some of the children and tell them to pay attention. The students are told to practise breathing. After a disruption, the teacher gives one boy a "strike"; one more and he gets a restriction; to another, one more and there will be no "prize." Another boy is in a bad mood and does not want to meditate; he wouldn't follow the instructions to breathe in and out. The students practise blowing through a tissue — "not too hard or easy — *that's* mindful breathing." Notice the breath, sounds, thoughts, images, and feelings, the teacher says. "What do you feel when you breathe?" the teacher asks afterwards, but misses the moment to ask what are they feel sitting here now — boredom, restlessness, wanting to have fun.

How can mindfulness help us with our thoughts? "What do we say to our thoughts?" the teacher asks. He gives the answer: "Not now," and then says to bring attention back to our breath. The teacher needed to switch the seat of a boy who was goofing around. The boy resisted, and instead the counsellor came down off the desk and sat between him and another boy inside the circle. The teacher talked about what to do when we get angry. "SOLER: Stop. Observe. Let it go. End. Return to our breath." He again missed the chance to discuss the anger and unhappiness in the room. For the lesson on mindful listening, the teacher hit a Tibetan bowl and asks the students to focus and raise their hands when the after-tone stops. At the end of the period the students were to meditate. They closed their eyes and sat still. Afterward the teacher gave out points to each student. Twenty-five points was "excellent," and a few students received them for sitting still.

The session at last was over. The teacher had managed to cover — in effect, impose — the lesson amid the unarticulated resistance and apathy of the students, and ignore the disconnect between talking and listening about feelings and the actual feeling experiences of the students in the room.

Goldie Hawn, the creator of the MindUP program, believes that students need to know what occurs in their brain, which she calls the "context" of mindfulness, and that processing information is what is important (Schnall 2011). She uses the literal language of brain processes and describes her MindUP curriculum in schools as "brain-based learning." The curriculum even builds in lessons on neural correlates for elementary school children:

> So we do a kind of brain break, which is sitting quietly, and they
> focus on their breathing and they listen to a sound…. And that's
> just for a couple of minutes, but what they understand is the

neurological correlate to that, so it's contextual.... And so they learn about the amygdala and how that is fight-or-flight — they learn that it can save us, and they learn that it can get in our way … they know that when they do that, it opens up what they now call the PFC, or the prefrontal cortex, which is really the seed of learning. It's really when your brain is prepared and focused to receive information, to analyze information and to remember information. And that's part of the lesson. (Schnall 2011)

MindUP and other programs that seek solutions in the brain think that the brain is the mind. Hawn conflates the two. Neurological activity correlates with human activity and real-life problems — but they are not the same. Contrary to her point above, the brain is not "contextual"; human purposive, moral activity is. In Hawn's example the actual context is being a particular student in a particular school classroom with others and within a rich constellation of social, cultural, and political factors. To make sense of activity requires dialogical interpretation and everyday cultural context. How the neurological changes are regarded, what they mean, are not presented as a priori truth but require intersubjective, socially constructed interpretation and understanding from a particular framework. What is information? What is important information to know, who decides, for whom, when, and why? What does it mean to "receive," "analyze," and "remember" information" — does that sound to you like a meaningful way to account for education? It is not the brain that needs a break, the child does.

Yet people are being taught to think they now have brain problems to be solved by brain management. The danger is that instead of legitimating and supporting work in mindfulness and counselling practices, the focus on neuroscientific findings obfuscates the implicit values and worldviews that educators and counsellors should adopt and endorse. "Brain-based" curricula have implicit, unspoken values that have developmental, social, and cultural meanings; they are not automatically conveyed from findings of brain activity. Neither are answers to how to behave in skilful or moral ways, how to think, or to find the meaning of happiness. We need to first recognize that someone — say, a corporatized educational bureaucrat from Pearson publishing company — chooses what information is important and valued to learn in the first place. Such perspectives and values themselves, chosen by certain people in power, are not foregone conclusions; rather, they reflect contestable meanings about education. We need to discuss, question, and openly evaluate what counts as education rather than letting that be seen as an incontrovertible truth hiding behind so-called objective "brain-based" facts.

Trying to find wisdom and meaning and context in brain activity is a myth, like the story of the goose that laid the golden egg. Recall that the greedy bastards, enthralled with the goose — which, as a living thing, kept laying golden eggs — decided that the gold must be inside the goose; so they cut it up and killed it. Where's the gold? Whoops, no goose, no gold. Ah, let's look inside the brain to find all that information; if we get to the PFC, the "seed of learning," we'll get the gold, Goldie Hawn might say. Result? A goose egg: no critical evaluative human activity, no gold. Any research findings into the brain, as well as "brain-based" curricula require cultural interpretation, dialogue, and contextual meaning — developmental, social, cultural, historical — in order to avoid falling into the myth of the given. Human meaning is not found in discrete data; it is a holistic quality found in the purposive, moral, and changeable social activity in which one is embedded.

Hawn makes her values clear in the quote at the top. She's a believer in positive psychology. She thinks kids should scrub their brains every day with meditation in order to rid themselves of "bad" things like fear and worry that get in the way of whatever happiness you are seeking. Never mind being with what is, including sadness or pain that may come from actual things going on in a difficult family or community — or a lousy school. Mindfulness is to make you happy, which of course is never defined — it can be hedonistic and self-indulgent. Positive psychology ties in well with neoliberal responsibility — don't look at the social conditions that contribute to your and others' unhappiness, focus on yourself and your brain, keep going, stay happy. Teacher Tina Olesen points out:

> While MindUP claims to be teaching non-judgmental aware-
> ness of thoughts and feelings, it actually teaches a child to judge
> any thought or feeling besides optimism and happiness as *bad*.
> It shows him [sic] how to escape the warnings of his conscience

with pleasurable feelings — to make himself feel good even when he has done or experienced something that he ought to feel bad about. (Wickelgren 2012)

In MindUP, Goldie Hawn attempts to convert Buddhism to neuroscience while trying to cover up its Buddhist roots. Religious studies professor Candace Gunther Brown (2015) calls this out. She writes that Hawn

> developed a written curriculum in order to introduce Buddhist "contemplative practice" into the classroom "under a different name." Hawn calls the MindUP curriculum a "script" written for audiences averse to Buddhism and wary of religion's intrusion into public schools, yet hungry for moral revitalization…. The MindUP "script" tells the story that Buddhist mindfulness meditation is really "secular" neuroscience. The script replaces the terms "Buddhism" and "meditation" with "neuroscience" and "Core Practice" to denote the thrice-daily practice of mindfulness meditation in the classroom.

The problem with this, Brown (2014a) says, is that the core practice of the program, mindfulness, which includes the focus on the breath and practising non-judgmental awareness, by itself does not help students "develop moral and ethical virtues of 'empathy, compassion, patience, and generosity.'" Those require an ethical framework of values; it is unclear, Brown says, how mindfulness makes one virtuous, except as a principle of the Buddhist eightfold path of awakening.

The turn to neuroscience to justify mindfulness education programs obscures their social, moral, cultural, and political context. In North American culture, much of the justification for almost any activity such as mindfulness relies on the need to prove its efficacy, indeed its existence, with measurable scientific data, and neuroscience appears to have supplied the gold standard. Author and columnist Steven Poole (2012) is critical of the misuse of neuroscience and points out that the "real achievements of brain research are routinely pressed into service for questions they were never designed to answer." He argues that there is a tendency when looking at brain activity to "misleadingly assume we always know how to interpret such 'hidden' information, and that it is always more reliably meaningful than what lies in plain view."

A considerable problem with neuroscientific data on mindfulness is that the evidence for finding the neural mechanisms at best is not definitive. In a meta-analysis of neuroscience studies of meditation effects, researchers conclude that "studies suffer from low methodological quality and present with speculative post-hoc interpretations. Knowledge of the mechanisms that underlie the effects is therefore still in its infancy" (Tang, Hölzel, and Posner 2015). Rather than just a science in its infancy, neuroscience is unlikely to ever yield clear findings that show a correlation between neural processes, meditation, and complex, interpretable changes in human activity (Satel and Lilienfeld 2015).

A preliminary problem is that there is no clear agreed-upon definition of mindfulness meditation itself; it does not constitute a unitary construct (Basu 2018). This has led to too many research studies that rely on a variety of inconsistent methods, a minimization of the adverse effects of mindfulness, and the exaggeration of its benefits, which remain inadequately supported. In a thorough review of the literature, researchers expressed concern about the "pervasive mindfulness hype" (Van Dam et al. 2017). They warn that various possible meanings of mindfulness must be clarified in research, studies must be replicated, and researchers must remain modest about generalizing their findings from clinical trials and neuroscience (for summaries, see Sheridan 2017; and Van Dam and Haslam 2017).

With respect to the "pervasive mindfulness hype," Willoughby Britton (2012), a neuroscientist at Brown University who researches meditation, says:

> I think there's a deeper cultural phenomenon going on which I'm going to try to illustrate with what I call the Blobology effect. The Blobology effect, very simply said, is that when you show people … when people see colorful blobs on a brain scan, they can be convinced of anything. They can be convinced of anything even if what you're saying makes no sense or if it's absolutely preposterous. And even further, people will believe brain scans over their own experience.

The problem for neuroscience is the holistic nature of the brain itself. Neurobiologist Moheb Costandi (2015) points out that "the brain is not composed of discrete specialized regions. Rather, it's a complex network of interconnected nodes, which cooperate to generate behavior." There is no way to determine a one-to-one correspondence with one region and one behaviour, which always requires interpretation. There is no way to predict which part of the brain will generate certain socially defined activities.

Professor of Buddhist philosophy Evan Thompson (2016) says this as well in his closing PowerPoint keynote address at the 2016 Mind & Life Conference:

> The proper level of description for any cognitive function (e.g., attention) is the whole embodied subject or person, not brain areas or networks. It is unlikely that there is a one-to-one mapping between particular cognitive functions and particular brain areas or neural networks. Therefore, it is empirically unwarranted to map the cognitive functions involved in meditation in general, and mindfulness meditation in particular, onto particular brain areas or the differential activation of particular neural networks.

Neuroscience attempts to replace understanding the socially formed self with brain research; there is a lack of intersubjectivity in neuroscience, the context of relationships, which would enable us to make meaning of results (Fong 2013; Wilber 2006: 290). There is no singular event occurring in the brain or in meditation; both the experience of meditation and the presentation of brain activity require examining the explicit cultural, moral, and political contexts in which they occur and which are necessary to understand how their meaning is interpreted. Philosopher Catherine Malabou (2008) argues that with the rise of neuroscientific discourse as a cultural influence, the language of brain "flexibility" is more often used to legitimate neoliberalism's demand to adapt ourselves within a corporatized world in all aspects of our lives. She argues instead for people to become more conscious of the brain's "plasticity" and thereby choose to employ this awareness as a counter-force to the dominant order (see also Slaby 2010). Philosophy professor Tamsin Shaw (2016) says that knowing the neural correlates of reasoning "can tell us nothing about whether the outcome of this reasoning is justified. It is not the neuroscience but rather our considered moral judgments that do all the evaluative work in telling us which mental processes we should trust and which we should not."

The point of mindfulness in schools is not to increase brain function. It is to generate decent people who can critically evaluate moral values and embody and enact them to create a better world. Such students are intellectually curious and can engage in deep, critical inquiry. They can experience their many-sided selves, develop and enact their highest expressive capacities and talents, and are socially just and competent world citizens.

Brain-Based Counselling and Learning

As a counsellor and educator committed to personal and social transformation, and as one who had first come to mindfulness meditation through Buddhist teachings in late adulthood, I looked to and connected with the growing field of contemplative education for ideas and inspiration. There at the conferences were my academic colleagues, the contemplatives, who encouraged students to meditate as a non-conceptual, experiential form of knowing, to note what thoughts, feelings, and sensations were arising in the mind with the aim of helping them learn and behave with more insight, equanimity, and care. Joining them, I was surprised to discover, were the neuroscientists, who sought to find the neural correlates of meditation and its potential benefits to the brain and students' well-being.

Besides seeking any helpful results, it also seemed that for many meditators the turn to neuroscience was a way to validate their contemplative practice in secular terms, to cloak the field in the more acceptable and respectable mantle of objective science rather than the yellow robes of Buddhist monks. The Association for Contemplative Mind in Higher Education, the Mind & Life Institute, and the Contemplative Studies Concentration at Brown University were held up as prototypes for this emerging model of contemplative education: combine first-person perspective, the experiences of the person meditating, with third-person perspective, which consists of objective scientific data that legitimates and strengthens the practice. But too many pieces were missing: the actual context of our messy lives in and about which we contemplate (or not) our relationships, our families, our engagement with others in our academic, political, spiritual, activist, and local communities. Where were the interactions and dialogues between us about what is moral and good?

The emphasis on neuroscience, rather than on critical discussions about meaning, values, and power, has been no less true within the field of counselling. "Neuroscience represents a paradigm shift for counselling and psychology," according to counselling professor Allen Ivey (Murphy 2012). Leaders in the field, such as Ivey, call counselling and neuroscience the "cutting edge of the coming decade" (Ivey, Ivey, Zalaquett, and Quirk 2009). Counsellors and other helping professionals, they say, are looking to brain activity to help guide them in their work with clients.

Neuroscience, however, has not shown itself capable of impacting well-being. Through rhetorical scientific language it legitimates science as an authority over moral issues and serves to cover over any discussion of what is to be valued. Ivey et al. make some unremarkable, unprovable, and contestable claims about the relationship between the brain, meditation, and counselling. They say that since the brain can change and grow new neurons, then meditation, SEL, and counselling can facilitate attention and executive function, leading to changes in neurochemical processes that contribute to well-being. They suggest that effective executive functioning in the brain contributes to positive thinking and that empathy leads to more positive stories that in turn create new neural connections.

To say that meditation and other activities can alter the brain or create new neural connections due to its plasticity is a truism. Any repeated activities that contribute to persistent mental consequences affect brain activity and the brain lights up during many activities (Satel and Lilienfeld 2015; Sawyer 2013). Not only is there no way to determine the correspondence between neural areas and socially constructed and interpretable constructs and actions, the concepts of well-being, positive thinking, and positive stories themselves are ideological and therefore contestable and subject to debate.

Ivey et al. (2009) further believe that there is a link between social justice, a fundamental value of the counselling profession, and the healthy development of the brain. Poverty, they point out, contributes to stress, which in turn impairs neural development: "Racism, sexism and other forms of oppression send damaging cortisol into the brain." This belief conflates mind and brain, skipping over interpretation and meaning.

Racism, sexism, and "other forms of oppression" do not damage the brain; neither does chronic poverty *per se*. Rather, it is the effects of chronic stress from experiencing and interpreting socially constructed, oppressive relations such as racism and chronic poverty that could damage the brains of some people through producing excess cortisol. Forms of oppression and chronic poverty are relational terms, the meanings of which people interpret and understand within historical, cultural, societal, and interpersonal contexts. These conditions cannot affect the brain *per se*, which is a physiological entity. Missing in Ivey et al.'s analysis is an explicit acknowledgement and critical understanding of contexts and their relationship to meaning and values within them. These cannot be read off of neurological processes or divined from studying particular images of the brain; while brain activity is correlated with certain activities, those activities are made meaningful and interpreted by certain people under certain social conditions.

Ivey et al. value particular attributes in the abstract: attention, resiliency, emotional control, positive thinking, empathy, and social justice. Knowing how people employ these skills, however, requires that we examine the particular social conditions and purposes they are intended to serve. They do not ask, toward what ends are resiliency, emotional regulation, and even empathy to be put to use? Given the value neutrality of such terms, one could argue that a dictator could also hold these attributes, and even employ empathy in the service of what he considers to be social justice.

Missing from Ivey et al.'s argument is a critical social framework that links brain activity with social action. For example, education professor Aislinn O'Donnell (2016: 32), citing philosopher Franco Berardi, argues that "capitalism through the constant solicitation of attention through a range of media, technological tools, and marketing strategies is connected to the brain and the nervous system"; our brains are made of "flesh, fragile and sensual organs" and are not "formatted according to the same standard as the system of digital transmitters." Because of how a stressful economic system operates, O'Donnell argues, there is an increase in "panic, depression, attention-disturbance, hyper-activity, solitude, existential misery, anxiety, and so on."

Ivey et al. claim that neuroscience provides "data-based evidence for what counsellors have believed for decades: that the counselling process can change the human brain … new ideas produce new neural connections" (Murphy 2012). But should new neural connections become valued ends in themselves? Is the most important goal to change the human brain itself? Even with changes in the brain, do those changes by themselves guarantee, let alone correlate with, the occurrence of more "positive" individual actions, relationships, and societies? From what and from whose perspective are those changes "positive"?

A related troubling concern is whether a counselling approach is legitimized only if there is neuroscientific data that is believed to correlate with the practice. While objective scientific knowledge is important and not just another relative perspective, as some mistakenly believe, to insist that a counselling practice is worthwhile only if it leads to some uncertain changes in the brain is scientistic (i.e., ideological foolishness). Ivey et al. contribute to this tendency when they note: "Neuroscience provides a new, broader and practical scientific base for counselling and validates what we have always done. We now have scientific evidence for empathy's concrete existence" (Murphy 2012). But there is no correlation between brain activity and qualitative differences in empathy — those must rely on social and cultural context. Besides, do we now need neuroscientific evidence for qualities of established social practices in order to consider them valid in everyday life?

Counselling psychologist Paul Moloney (2016: 282) says that, in the end,

> it is you who are frightened, not your amygdala. Sociological and historical studies of emotional experience and expression agree that our interior lives are not just matters of biology. They are also about the weight of our personal biography, of the relationships in which we are enmeshed, and of the differences in power and influence that set the terms of mutual engagement.

Executive Functioning: For What Purpose?

Executive functioning is an umbrella term that includes cognitive processes that enable us to pursue a goal and manage things in life. Executive functions include planning, decision making, regulating emotions, and judgment. Neuroscientists are interested in these as they are identified with certain parts of the brain. Mindfulness educator Susan Kaiser Greenland (2011) defines executive functioning as a "family of attention-related processes involved in planning and carrying out goal directed behavior." Other functions, according to Michael Baime (2011), another mindfulness educator, are the ability to hold two concepts in order to compare and evaluate plans, ideas and memories, and linking memory with sensory input in order to make sense of the present moment in light of what we have learned from the past. These functions are said to predict school readiness as well as reading and math aptitudes (Greenland 2011). As such, they are of increasing interest to educators and school counsellors.

Given its link to emotional regulation and behaviour, executive function also interests mindfulness proponents in schools. Mindfulness "training," in Greenland's terms, encourages children to focus on one thing — for example, breathing, bodily sensations, or a task — and this is thought to enhance attention skills. In mindfulness, a student practises stepping out of reactive thinking to witness their thoughts or experiences.

The problem is that executive functions are defined in amoral, neutral, and technical terms, so they can be applied to any situation. A *New Yorker* cartoon shows two men looking at a billboard that says, "Stop and Think." One says, "It sort of makes you stop and think, doesn't it?" About what? Toward what moral, valued ends and in what kind of social relationships should we apply executive functions? Let's say we discovered, plausibly, that Hitler or bin Laden had measurably high executive functions — exceptional capacities for focused attention, planning, decision making, and controlled emotion regulation — for example, calmness amid stress, even empathy insofar as knowing what their enemies feel, even compassion for their loved ones and fellow citizens. We then must ask, are these neutral qualities of executive function sufficient and desirable in themselves, with no need to look at the actual social world?

In the business world and elsewhere, we see a rising interest in "brain hacking." Brain hacking is not a neutral practice for the good of all. For example, managers employ mindfulness in business to reign in workers' wandering thoughts and to increase performance and productivity (Allen 2017). Are those who teach about the brain helping students question the rise in profitable brain hack apps that with little evidence claim to enhance efficiency and well-being (Tlalka 2016)? Are they exposing the corporate programmers and designers who develop brain hacks that induce youth and adults to addictively check their phone and send out constant Instagram messages to reduce their anxiety (Tabaka 2017)? Even the remorseful anti-digital backlash that seeks to make technology less addictive is led by profit-making tech developers. Their marketable solutions again put the onus back on the individual rather than addressing the structural nature of predatory capitalist corporations (Tveten 2018).

The appeal to neuroscience and neutral terms like executive function obscures larger questions. How do we talk and theorize about how we experience, interpret, and make new meanings and values together, including about contemplative practice itself? Where is a discussion of the ethics and values one endorses in terms of what one should be doing? Is there interest in what the student experiences and knows? Is the student practising mindfulness meditation to take a high-stakes test sponsored by a publishing corporation? We need interpretation, as well as investigation, of how we live and ought to live our full-bodied, complex human lives within the social world. Has the goose that lays the golden eggs been killed and cooked?

Neuroscience in Context

Neuroscientific data can be useful to the extent it can support — but not substitute — explicit moral positions that promote optimal human development, interdependence, and social justice. Such evidence may help show that troubled behaviours and social relations can and do contribute to experiences of stress, the effects of which are observable in the brain and body, and which in turn are harmful in physiological, emotional, and social ways. For example, along with Gabor Maté, we can argue that healthy human development and more developed brains need meaningful connections and healthy relationships. These in part depend on adults who themselves have grown up in a society where they are well attuned to themselves and others and are present and emotionally available to children. An emerging area of research suggests that children's brain development and neural circuits are impaired when they grow up in what they experience to be stressful and adverse environments that include mistreatment or abuse. In an interview, Maté says:

> What we have to understand here is that human beings are not discrete, individual entities, contrary to the free enterprise myth that people are competitive, individualistic, private entities. What people actually are are social creatures, very much dependent on one another and very much programmed to cooperate with one another when the circumstances are right…. The child's brain development depends on the presence of non-stressed, emotionally available parents. In this country, that's less and less available. (*Democracy Now* 2012)

Unlike Ivey et al., Maté takes a political stand for optimal human development that contextualizes within capitalist society the body, brain, and neural circuits, and qualities of processing emotions, interpersonal relationships, community, and society. Maté engages in cultural criticism from a more inclusive perspective. He is critical of this class-based society for its excessive emphasis on individualism and a competitive market mentality that fails to produce and support emotionally available parents for all children. This impoverished social world in turn can affect healthy development; he states his values about the quality of relationships in our culture. Good emotional attachments contribute to neurological growth, although neurological evidence is not required to consider the significance and moral validity of this perspective in its own right. The aim is not to just change the brain *per se*, it is to contribute to the healthy cognitive, social, emotional, and moral development of all children.

Educators such as Parker Palmer argue that optimal learning occurs by making connections and seeing whole patterns; they refer to neuroscientific evidence to strengthen their points. Palmer appeals to neuroscience to support his cultural criticism that many schools leave students feeling they have lost a competitive contest. Beyond the sorting of students into winner and losers, he feels,

> we know from research that the brain's weakest function is the retention of isolated bits of data…. The brain is a patterning organ, and it thrives on making connections, which is why I say that good teachers have a "capacity for connectedness." But for a

very long time the public school system has been dumping data bits into students' heads and calling it "education." It's a system that targets the brain's weakest function, and that's going to leave a lot of people feeling stupid. The kind of learning that goes deeper and lasts longer comes from engagement and interaction.… This contest to see who can memorize the most factoids has been ramped up by No Child Left Behind and Race to the Top, with their emphasis on high-stakes testing. Legislation of that sort flies in the face of a half century of research that says that the more full-bodied the learning experience is, the better it is retained. As neurobiologist Candace Pert has said, the brain may be located in the cranium, but the mind is located throughout the body. (Von Stamwitz 2012)

Palmer indicts a society whose education system values isolated students learning factoids over engaging in meaningful interactions and practices with others. Neuroscience can help us realize we each have a "social brain" that links us together. As neuroscientist David Eagleman says:

We are a single vast superorganism, a neural network embedded in a far larger web of neural networks. Our brains are so fundamentally wired to interact that it's not even clear where each of us begins and ends. Who you are has everything to do with who we are. There's no avoiding the truth that's etched into our neural circuitry: we need each other. (Tweedy 2017: xxxvi; see also Cozolino 2017)

But such evidence by itself cannot serve as an objective standard for evaluating healthy personal and moral development and social relationships, or provide a prescription for what we ought to do. That requires our own critical and conscious participation as social beings who together create a healthier society and a better world.

Section IV

An Evolving Contemplative Education

14

Visions for a Counter-Program

Emergent Mindfulness

We need to think critically about mindfulness as well as ways to enhance its scope and inclusivity and to deepen its meaning; mindfulness needs to be more mindful (of) itself. An evolving practice calls for us to realize and enact the non-duality and inseparability of all aspects of life. On new ground it enjoins the wisdom and values from Eastern contemplative traditions — a way to realize the fundamental awareness that underlies all experience — with Western prophetic ones — the moral demand for universal justice based on our inseparability as we participate in and create our human history, even our own evolution. To paraphrase David Loy, in absolute terms the world is fine and timeless as it is; in a relative sense, though, it still requires radical action through time (history) to make it a loving home for all.

This is an Integral project within education. It does not just focus on individual mindfulness as a way to adjust to and cope with stress and injustice; it is a practice in which school community members further analyze, resist, and change those sources of stress and injustice. We invoke the wisdom traditions along with modernist, scientific knowledge, research, and critical thinking; we bring a progressive, postmodern awareness of multiple culturally constructed and developmental perspectives on self-hood, gender, race, ethnicity, and sexual orientation. Through mindfulness practice we sort out the conditioned thoughts and feelings we experience, ones in which we believe, and those with which we identify from the dominant ideological messages of an inequitable society. Through mindful social action we resist and challenge existing conditions and relations of power, greed, and delusion. The project includes the best of what mindfulness programs in education offer — helping students, teachers, and administrators to be calm, focused, and more self-aware — embedded in a critical framework. It recognizes people's levels of self-development and starts accordingly, seeking understanding and inclusivity. In terms of those who separate personal spiritual growth (getting awakened) from political social action (getting "woke"), Integralist Terry Patten (2018a; see also 2018b) says:

> For those who have awakened, it is time to "get woke." For those who are woke, it's time to be awakened.... Our task is to transform ourselves and our world — simultaneously. It is time to recognize that the inner and outer work are interdependent and function best when they function together.

Development Transcends the Secular/Religious Divide

At a deceptive surface level, some secular mindfulness proponents think secular mindfulness and Buddhism are just two sides of the same coin. Followers of Kabat-Zinn, who believes that his mindfulness program is the "universal dharma," argue that, after all, they both alleviate suffering. This is a false equivalency (see Lindhal 2014). By splitting mindfulness from its moral and soteriological roots in Buddhism, secular mindfulness has become a practice that also helps people adjust to inequitable and stressful situations in society reproducing self-centred, individualist practices that serve to reinforce the stress, delusions, and ill will from which people seek to escape. It doesn't touch upon the ontological nature of suffering let alone offer a way toward alleviating it in that absolute sense.

An evolving critical framework recaptures the foundational moral basis of mindfulness on new ground. While modern psychological healing and deeper salvation found within earlier traditions can complement each other, this framework also distinguishes them. It further adds psychological, scientific, cultural, and social systemic perspectives that lead toward optimal growth and awareness. It transcends the secular/religious divide by viewing consciousness in terms of development. At later, evolved stages and states of consciousness, whether secular or religious, consciousness includes and transcends all worldviews.

Laughing Men

There's a photo of three well-known mindfulness proponents — Richard Davidson, Daniel Goleman, and Jon Kabat-Zinn — laughing, looking relaxed, and enjoying themselves (Krauze 2017). Davidson thinks "there is an increasing interest in strategies like yoga and meditation that can help people adjust to modern circumstances" (Barclay and Belluz 2018). Sure, let's meditate so we can "adjust" to some vague, inevitable "modern circumstances" — like gun violence, sexual harassment, climate change denial, and tax cuts for the rich. Goleman endorses "compassionate capitalism" (Fisher 2008), because, you know, you can work a system based solely on a bottom line that benefits a few and become awakened at the same time — cool. Kabat-Zinn sees what he does "as Dharma expressing itself in the world in its Universal-Dharma-way" (Fisher 2010). No other ethics or wisdom tradition is needed, just his own program.

Is that the best we can do?

Notes for a Counter-Program

The fundamental aspects of a critical, evolving program arise, interlink, and operate with each other. They include subjectivity, development, objective enactment, culture, and society. The project is guided by an overarching vision of caring, social justice, and optimal development. At the same time, it evolves in unpredictable, creative ways through active engagement with ourselves and community members. The project can start small and start anywhere. As a school mindfulness program, it should offer an opt-in model of informed consent (Brown 2019). In describing these modes of mindfulness, I borrow terms from Ken Wilber and add my own (Wilber 2016; Forbes 2016a, 2016b).

Subjectivity: Waking Up, Cleaning Up, and Growing Up

An evolving mindfulness values the development of universal wisdom and compassion for everyone, in all aspects of education and society — not just in privatized, individualistic terms. It demands that the purposes of those mindfulness practices, and the developmental, social, cultural, and political conditions under which they are employed, be addressed and discussed: We're giving attention to what? Regulating feelings to what end, under what conditions, and in whose interests? In short, it commits to not adjusting to unexamined or unhealthy relationships and educational institutions that perpetuate greed, ill will, and delusion, but to experiencing and bringing about the most evolved qualities of human development for all people, from all walks of life.

An evolving contemplative program takes an explicitly moral approach that is not relativistic and that is neither just left up to individual preference or to faith that the process of paying attention to our thoughts will just guide us toward wise compassion and more skilful moral action. Within this critical framework of committing to the well-being of all, we begin to identify ways the mind has been conditioned and colonized by unwholesome ideas and beliefs from dominant society (see Pyles 2018). This guided practice can help expand one's consciousness to include more perspectives. Over time, through dialogue with others, through working this way in relationships and within the culture of a school, by reflecting on stages of self- and moral development, and by identifying and practising skilful actions, a conscious approach toward both self-development and universal justice can arise. This means there is a loosening of attachment to the notion of a privatized, selfish self, to one's own beliefs. It means the sense of self is transcended by a greater, universal concern for the well-being and happiness of everyone in the highest and broadest possible sense. In subjective terms, we look at and link together: waking up — meditating to reach later states of consciousness; cleaning up — mindful psychological work on oneself; and growing up — mindfulness to grow through stages of self-development (Wilber 2016).

Wake Up/Stay Woke

Meditation and mindfulness practices in schools can encourage students and teachers to examine critically the nature of the self, to cultivate the inner life, and to understand feelings not as free-floating objects but as arising from the actual social contexts of people's lives. Beyond relaxation for self-regulation and test taking, school community members can explore the various *states* of awareness that arise through meditation and link these to their personal lives and relationships. At deeper levels, people begin to become conscious of awareness itself, and can reflect on language (Construct-awareness) and even the self (Ego-awareness).

As an individual practice, mindfulness meditation involves resting without effort in a space of awareness, with a focus on the breath. As you dwell in this space, you begin to observe and take note of your experiences — identifying and labelling thoughts, judgments, values, opinions, and sensations — while holding them with compassion and non-judgment, like a loving parent. Over time you learn to notice your attachment to these and recognize they are not you, and they are not solid entities — they come and go — and you begin to let them go, to de-identify with them. You begin to take your own mind, and other people's concerns, in less personal terms, and can reach meditative states that allow for this in deeper ways. Ken Wilber calls this practice "waking up" (Wilber 2016).

As part of becoming "woke," school community members meditate in part to see how the ego is conditioned by specific troublesome personal, social, and cultural beliefs and conditions; reflection on this can happen alone, or with teachers, counsellors, peers, and parents. They can link thoughts, beliefs, and feelings with broader interpersonal, cultural, and social concerns. For example, within class or group counselling discussions about values, students can witness and label thoughts, feelings, and sensations in terms of which ones are unhealthy and unjust. They can see which ones they have internalized, conditioned by the messages of their family, social media, and corporatized society — materialism, sexism, racism, homophobia, perfectionism, competitiveness, and others.

Focusing on the "here and now" requires seeing that any moment is always socially constructed and interpreted, and should include critical thought, moral evaluation, historical analysis, and a critique of broader socio-economic relations. Without this perspective, the sole focus on the present moment can reinforce the privatized, individuated self and troublesome emotional states that are isolated and severed from one's actual everyday social relations and context (Purser 2015). In the absence of linking one's experience with social conditions, anxiety, anger, frustration, and despair become personal failures.

Instead of serving as a technology for students and teachers to simply advance within or adjust to the dominant social order, mindfulness practice can connect inner awareness to moral relationships and the social world. Instead of the neoliberal preference to avoid thorough self-reflection, mindfulness proponents can stand for a critical mode of subjectivity. Mindfulness education can encourage students and teachers to value exploration, contemplation, and creativity as part of an alternative meaning of success in education rather than one based on competition and measured in narrow, standardized outcomes. As a means of self-examination for teachers, it provides them a space for exploring their own interior nature outside of conventionally defined meanings and roles in education (Ergas 2017). Students and teachers can cultivate self-compassion and with awareness extend it to others as they witness and hold their own experiences with loving kindness.

Clean Up/Cleaned Up

School counsellors can bring mindfulness to bear on personal issues for students, using it as an adjunct to help those who choose to engage in individual and/or group counselling to explore and heal themselves and each other, and to do emotional work. Examples of areas to work on are personal goals, habits, concerns, desires, and values, as well as feelings of fear, anxiety, anger, and sadness; likewise, traumatic experiences, relationships with family members and friends, family history, sexual identity, and substance use and addictive thinking and behaviour are also beneficial topics. Depending on how much counsellors can work with them, students may further explore qualities about themselves, such as biases, that are unconscious, shadow, or dissociated pieces of their realities. Psychotherapist Keith Witt (2017, 2014) describes the shadow as "the sum total of our learning, drives, habits, values, preferences, and needs flooding constantly up from our non selves to our conscious selves" — the aspects we don't realize about ourselves but which affect us in significant ways. We want to commit to recognizing and letting go of our toxic habits — for example, unhealthy anger, distorted beliefs, selfishness, rigidity, and harmful, prejudicial thoughts and actions toward ourselves and others — that block us from being aware and grown. Wilber (2016) calls this psychological work "cleaning up." Rather than a self-centred, self-help practice within an individualistic, competitive society, students can set their intention to work on themselves as part of a responsible commitment to a greater good, including in that the well-being of others with whom they are connected.

Grow Up/Grown Up

We can employ mindfulness to practise moral and self-development. This is a missing piece in many school mindfulness programs. People can reach a meditative state and still not be developed in important ways, so besides waking up (through developmental states), it is just as important to grow up (through stages) (Wilber 2016). Stages of self-development filter mindful states as interpretive frameworks; that is, one can meditate and reach an advanced state of awareness but remain at an earlier stage of self-development, and this affects how they interpret their state. For example, a student might be mindful and experience a state of calm, yet still be at an early stage of self- or moral development — egocentric (it's all about me), or even sociocentric (I want to go along with what my teachers, school, or my family or peers tell me to believe in). We want to start with whichever level students are at and see how they can grow.

We also want to discuss with students: what does it mean to be grown up? What does a grown-up do? What is grown-up anger? What does James Baldwin mean in the larger sense, as well as in the context of his writing, that African-Americans and whites are bound together in love, when he said, "Love does not begin and end the way we seem to think it does. Love is a battle, love is a war; love is a growing up" (Baldwin 1961: 136)?

The aim is for all students and educators to develop fully our unique intellectual, personal, social, and moral capacities. School community members can learn about models of different lines of development and their structures; these show that orders or stages of growth include and transcend earlier ones and become more encompassing perspectives. Here we want to ask: through what self-developmental stage do we interpret our mindfulness? School community members then can identify their own stage of self- and moral development. Through mindfulness they observe the habits and patterns of their mind, which frames things based on their own worldviews and to which they remain attached: in general terms, egocentric, conventional, or post-conventional. Education researchers Antti Saari and Jani Pulkki (2012) state:

> Meditation, as a method of dissolving the ego, can be considered as an educational tool for addressing the roots of many social and environmental threats. Dissolving the ego means to strip one's cultural, social and psychological conditionings that have created a false ego of delusions and endless cravings.… Through meditation, the barriers to moral development can be slowly reduced and new prospects for human development opened.

Used in a conscious way, mindfulness itself shares a pattern with self-development: we step outside our own subjectivity — feelings, thought patterns — and observe and hold each aspect with compassion from a later, more inclusive perspective (Kegan 1994). With mindful awareness we then can observe our own stage or order of development and, if we choose, can commit to responding from the next one. For those who wish to go further and consider the subcategories of the basic stages, we can apply developmental models from, among others, Robert Kegan, Susanne Cook-Greuter, Mark Forman, and Ken Wilber.

Growing Deeper

At later developmental levels, mindfulness educators can step outside and examine their own beliefs in their attachments to mindfulness itself and to view mindfulness critically, as one particular system within a broader program of education. We can promote healthy awareness within one's current personal or cultural stage; when individuals or groups are stuck at their stage or have outgrown it and are ready to move on, we can help them develop toward the next one. Some may evolve toward later stages and experience a fluid, universal, non-dual way of being.

At these later stages of development, mindfulness becomes an immanent practice, transcending the conventional meaning of the self, the self-other duality, and how we relate to Western notions of time and space. Mindfulness in this deeper sense overcomes the function of individualistic stress reduction and adjustment to neoliberal society. It even extends beyond the popular trend at some mindfulness conferences to graft itself in random ways to moral practices of social justice, since in these later stages they are now inseparable. At the later stages, we can dwell in the relative and the absolute at the same time, and freely flow between them. This dwelling is transcendent in that it reflects the desire — and in some cases, the ability — to raise one's level of consciousness to experience the sacred; it is immanent in that we experience a sense of the sacred now, in everyday life.

Enactment: Transforming Instrumental Mindfulness

Mindfulness programs in schools overall remain within the narrow framework of individualist skill building and adjustment to neoliberal education goals in behavioural therapeutic terms. To ensure lower stress and greater efficiency for teachers, mindfulness educators, along with social-emotional learning proponents, want students to demonstrate greater calm, increased focus, display more positive and optimistic affect, acting collaboratively and with kindness, and emotional self-regulation in order to be more successful learners and behave in conventionally approved ways and increase societal success (see Waters, Barsky, Ridd, and Allen March 2015).

At a conventional level some teachers and students report that these practices can and do help them relax and cope with stress, to calm enough to reflect on better ways to respond to certain situations, to better pay attention and concentrate in school, and to improve personal relationships. This instrumental mindfulness, though, strips down a contemplative practice to a morally neutral technique. Moreover, without critical awareness, it serves to reinforce the beliefs, practices, and policies of an individualistic, therapized society, adjusts students and educators to unhealthy norms, and does nothing to challenge the unhealthy and unjust systemic, cultural, and institutional conditions that contribute to the many school problems that mindfulness is then brought in to resolve. It emphasizes behaviour and skills to the detriment of exploring with any depth consciousness and meaning with respect to experience, moral values, and the nature of the self.

To the extent mindfulness programs teach healthy, compassionate, and empathic behavioural skills, they should be recontextualized to enable students to question and challenge unjust and alienating school practices that impact their lives. Skills should be relational and embodied — intrinsic activities that contribute to both self-development and the creation of healthy and caring relationships in the school, community, and society.

A number of my working-class African-American counselling students have said it is not helpful when the counselling profession tells them they simply need to practise self-care; it better needs to recognize how their lives tend to differ from those of many white upper-middle-class students who have more resources. Students need to reflect critically on their everyday embodied lives in cultural and societal terms in order to understand what it means to care for themselves in the face of emotional difficulties and objectively harsh conditions. As one journalist notes, "For many young people, particularly those raised in abusive families or who live in neighborhoods besieged by poverty or violence, anxiety is a rational reaction to unstable, dangerous circumstances" (Denizet-Lewis 2017).

At a later stage of awareness, mindful self-care skills can be transformative and radical acts — if they are framed by the conscious intention to help one be a healthy person who cares not just for oneself but also for others as part of a means to resist and transform injustices and help bring about a more inclusive, caring, and democratic society. Social work activist and educator Loretta Pyles (2018) says that in this way self-care is "an act of resistance to disconnection, marginalization, and internalized oppression." In this spirit, feminist and African-American activist Audre Lorde in 1988 said, "Caring for myself is not self-indulgence, it is self-preservation, and that is an act of political warfare" (Mirk 2016). Without a more evolved consciousness, though, this call for self-care can be co-opted as a slogan for marketable, self-indulgent, and puritanical practices (Kisner 2017; Pyles 2018).

We also can deepen the meaning of becoming a better student. School mindfulness programs can employ contemplative education by engaging students to reflect not just on themselves and the nature of the self, but in critical, reflective inquiry into the nature of their objects of study. Aislinn O'Donnell (2016: 43) says that by developing attention, mindfulness programs might help students turn outward, which helps them decentre the self and attend to the objective world rather than being stuck in "projections and fantasies of the self." Students take up science, the arts, literature, history, and the study of society from a contemplative state of awareness. They learn a particular way to focus their attention without judgment on an object of study and take the time to look, listen, and then think. For many students, when framed as part of an emergent practice, this experience can be transformative and is worlds apart from competition, memorization, learning solely to pass a test, studying to please parents or teachers, or just getting through school. When it is not a rarefied practice severed from its social context but embodied in a critical approach to optimal development, contemplative education becomes a meaningful practice for both students and educators. This is likewise one way to counter the distracting and deleterious effects of social media and technology on youth. In a larger sense, a critically conscious, contemplative education can challenge the dissatisfaction with the Cartesian approach that contributes to educators' and students' "chronic stress, fragmented attention," and lack of time; it can offer meaning, wholeness, and a way "to link inner and outer worlds," connecting "the psyche and soma" (Morgan 2014).

With respect to neuroscience and data, rather than a reductionist materialism or a glorification of science as the sole arbiter of validity, mindfulness educators can study if and how critical mindfulness enhances healthy neural development, and how broader cultural and structural practices might enhance or diminish brain development and overall health (via the interpretive experience of harsh, unjust conditions). They can use and generate data to discover new truths, and evaluate or support — but not to validate or "drive" — wise, skilful, mindful educational projects.

Those involved in schools should question and resist the dominant, "evidence-based" neoliberal paradigm in education, which insists on assessing everything, as well as the myth that mindfulness experiences are not valid unless educators can squeeze them into and define them by measurable outcomes and behaviours (Worthen 2018). With an evolving mindfulness, we experience a broader notion of education that embodies intangible qualities of sensibility, self-development, awareness, compassion, wise judgment, relatedness, and a meaningful education. These cannot be measured by outcomes such as academic success, stress reduction, and behaviour management. It is not accidental that research on mindfulness programs yields minimal results given that mindfulness is reduced to impoverished measures that fail to capture the richness of both subjective and interpersonal experience as well as what people hold as right and good. Citing Paul Grossman's and Nicholas T. Van Dam's (2011: 220) critical review of mindfulness methodology, O'Donnell (2016: 39) argues:

> At present, mindfulness is in danger of being co-opted in the "evidence-based," "what works" agenda that has proven so problematic for many of us working in educational settings, as, by prioritising performative indicators and valuing only that which can be measured, [it] risks instrumentalising what is a rich existential and ethical practice and using inappropriate forms of evaluation.

In contrast, researcher Marie Holm (2016) offers a qualitative approach to mindfulness research that focuses on the "processes by which mindfulness is applied and how it develops"; she argues for more ethnographic and anthropologic studies rather than ones that begin with top-down premises.

Culture (We)

Creating Conscious Culture

Evolving programs see mindfulness as an intrinsic aspect of interpersonal relationships and part of the call for social justice and a moral life. They do so in order to heal and cure various traumas many students experience every day, and to develop and enrich a culture of wise, skilful, compassionate, and loving people (Bloom 2013). Along with practising mindfulness with individuals or in classrooms, schools themselves need to create healthy, critically mindful cultures or we-spaces in order to develop relationships that foster trust, safety, respect, inclusiveness, caring, compassion, acceptance, healing, and connectedness. Students and all community members need to feel heard, valued, and respected and have a real say in their education. They can discuss the extent to which their unique, richly constructed and intersecting identities share commonalities with and impact others. A conscious, caring culture serves as a partial antidote to the alienating, privatized aspects of capitalist life that contribute to stress, loneliness, and increasing mental health problems and substance abuse. It's a way of practising being fully attentive, fully present with each other. Wilber (2016) calls working on relationships "showing up."

School counsellors and other committed educators require considerable interpersonal and group skills, including mindfulness and deep empathic listening, to deal with and work through conflict, difficult emotions, and the variety of worldviews within communities. Using their training to attend to the cultural quality of the school, counsellors can advocate, collaborate, and lead in this work by establishing rules and rituals for safety, mindful dialogue, and active listening. Within these cultures, people can then create caring, respectful, healing relationships that take on and transform many of the issues that affect the quality of the community — bullying, selfishness, racism, arbitrary power, competitiveness, homophobia, sexism, and other concerns that often remain hidden and unacknowledged.

For example, within a second-person process called cogenerative dialogue, or cogens, students have a significant voice and choice in what occurs in the classroom. They talk about and reflect on the learning process and structure with each other and the teacher. Teachers and students then collaborate to identify and implement positive changes in the classroom's teaching and learning practices. Some faculty and students in the Urban Education program at the CUNY graduate school link cogens with mindful practices. As they take on what they call "thorny" issues that stretch a bit beyond people's comfort zones, they listen to each other and become aware of their biases. Participants note that "these may be the only times these issues can even be taken on and discussed openly in an educational setting. To do so successfully we argue that aspects of mindfulness can be used in the classroom to help create these spaces" (Alexakos et al. 2016).

A mindful school commits to the full development of all members and to the school culture itself. Instead of ignoring or minimizing them, the school culture welcomes, includes, and draws on the resources, cultural capital, and contributions of all school and neighbourhood community members (Cannon 2016; Yosso 2005). Some urban schools use hip-hop culture — art, dance, and rap — to give students relevant expressive choices; students themselves may generate and link hip-hop culture to both discussion topics and their relationships within these schools (Emdin 2014).

Making Culture Conscious of Itself

An evolving mindful school investigates its own culture, helping its community members develop an informed awareness of their social relations and the environment they create. This approach studies, uncovers, and challenges hidden cultural biases, assumptions, attachments, rituals, and practices that operate within the school culture, becoming mindful of unaddressed, insidious patterns in interpersonal relations that may operate in ways that limit the well-being of everyone. Examining the discourse of the school culture in this way serves as "antivirus protection" against implicit, psychological patterns and worldviews that are problematic or unhealthy and that lurk in the background and infect mindful practices. This is a way to guard against the myth of the given, believing that unexamined, everyday norms are the natural order of things instead of seeing how meaning is culturally constructed — made and created together with others, impermanent, and changeable with them. I call this "wising up."

Troublesome patterns within both the school and larger North American culture — including racism, sexism, homophobia, and xenophobia, as well as issues of anxiety stemming from social media, stress and trauma, and other strong emotions for people of colour and for white students and faculty — can be addressed, sat with, questioned, discussed, and negotiated together within a healing, contemplative we-space. This awareness enables educators and students to investigate, discuss, and resist these implicit everyday cultural norms, relationships and cultural experiences. They can practise and create healthier alternative caring relationships that are both dialogical and mindful.

For example, around social media, school members can notice and label unhealthy and questionable thoughts, feelings, and sensations that are conditioned by dominant society's messaging; they can investigate social media and the attention economy as sources of anxiety. They can ask and research, in whose interest is it to have so many of us hooked on this technology? How is it that our attention is so easily captured by ubiquitous advertising and click-bait sites? Who benefits? This is a critically engaged mindfulness that resists the attention economy and opens the possibility for more sustainable forms of community (Doran 2018b).

Students can investigate through mindfulness how to create critical distance from and step outside existing social conditions and toxic institutions. Psychologist Steven Stanley and his students perform mindful "breaching" experiments. They mindfully notice and suspend conventional, conditioned assumptions and then reflect on everyday conduct and cultural norms such as consumerism within an urban downtown area (Stanley, Barker, Edwards, and McEwen 2014). Public health researchers Amanda Wray and Ameena Batada (2017) employ contemplative practices such as visualization, mindful reflection, and critical pedagogy to engage students in social justice activism that interrupts everyday social injustices and illustrates our interconnectedness.

Participants who are critically mindful can ask: what is the developmental level of the school culture? The school can see where its culture fits as a whole — whether people are attached to or over-identify with self-centred, conventional, or individualistic patterns — and use mindfulness practices to change and build healthier, more inclusive relationships.

To view cultural norms and values from a developmental perspective helps the school in a number of ways. First, it enables the school to break free of relativism. Proponents of relativism think that all beliefs are valued the same and must be non-hierarchical. Relativists thus regard their own position of non-hierarchy as hierarchically superior to any other form of hierarchy, which makes it difficult to even evaluate positions. Developmental thinking identifies and situates relativism itself as one particular perspective that school community members can discuss, apply where useful, and transcend.

Second, an evolving contemplative education that investigates various levels of culture in developmental terms also interrogates and challenges individualism, the myth of an unchanging, separate self. It can move people toward the awareness of our interdependence with all beings and with the Earth itself, a later stage of awareness. At that point we realize we are an inseparable part of these relationships, and we work to resist and change institutions like corporations, the media, and the military that reinforce Ego-attachment — what David Loy calls the "wego" — on a cultural and intersubjective scale as well as in personal and objective terms.

Third, a developmental perspective on the culture of a school allows for critical investigation and dialogue about mindfulness and social justice issues themselves. A school can examine the extent to which these practices are belief systems to which people have become attached and point to later stages of awareness that recognize attachments to mindfulness, critical pedagogy, and approaches to social justice. At later stages, school members come to see how they are already part of a larger, interrelated vision and practice.

Deeper Sharing

Myths arose within and across earlier traditional cultures to provide a moral grounding and for us to make sense of the world, our place in it, and ourselves. Some postmodernist films, novels, and music take early myths and bring them into the present. We can begin to explore and create myths that are even post-postmodern. From a broader, contemplative understanding, those who have been wounded or have a difficult or regrettable past can create a healing, loving culture in which people find common ground, one that's good for all of us. In mythic and emotional terms, this is a redemptive journey from trauma; in prophetic terms, it is redemption and forgiveness on new ground that is akin to curing ourselves.

The appeal, for instance, of the futuristic movie *Mad Max: Fury Road* is that it is a story of those who, in the words of the director's quote at the end of the film, "wander the wasteland, in search of our better selves" and who are able to leave their broken world behind and begin anew. A reviewer suggests that for the main characters, "in the end, their underlying goal is to reach a point where they can finally show the compassion and humanity that, until now, they have been forced to repress due to the ruthlessness of their environment" (Perrotta 2015). Two education scholars, Dan P. McAdams and Brady K. Jones (2017), point out that people who have experienced trauma can reconstruct new meanings and that doing so with others plays a crucial part in healing:

> In the most successful outcomes, posttraumatic growth entails constructing a redemptive story around personal trauma and integrating that story within a broader, self-defining life narrative. Making meaning out of trauma through life narration is as much a social phenomenon as a personal one, and it is decisively shaped by culture.

A contemplative project is to re/create post-postmodern myths with others. In schools, these can be constructed in imaginative ways with students, incorporating writing, video, music, and the arts. By tapping into deeper contemplative states along with self-reflective practices and knowledge of developmental stages and social conditions, we can find emergent, immanent ways to heal and grow. Media professor Kevin Healey (2016) envisions "civic mindfulness" as "lucidity writ large," which includes a way for us together through the media to write "empowering cultural narratives." We can dream together while maintaining consciousness through contemplative practices, he says; we can create a lucid dream environment toward our higher capabilities through transforming our media environment and the digital economy.

Another contemplative cultural practice is to bear witness together: to be with and hold pain, sadness, and suffering with love and forgiveness. This is both a way of being with others and a conscious resistance to the dominant cultural norms of selfishness, isolation, attachment, and denial.

Society: Mindful Resistance and Social Mindfulness as Transformative Practice

School community members can identify, investigate, and uncover systemic barriers in their own community and society that impede social justice — also a "wising up." Through classrooms, groups, and workshops, together they study and resist unjust practices, policies, and social structures that impact their lives, and strive to create equitable ones. These are aspects of civic mindfulness and mindful resistance. Author Robert Wright (2016), who began the Mindful Resistance Project, says:

> It's after your mind settles down that you can start observing your feelings with new care and clarity, and so begin to free yourself from the grip of the counterproductive ones. Settling down, in other words, is phase one in arming yourself for mindful resistance. A peaceful mind can be a fearsome mind.

James Reveley (2015: 90, 80) sees the potential for school-based mindfulness, when not just an individualized pursuit, to be a resource that supports collective resistance to neoliberal structures and policies.

Techniques of emotional self-management, he argues, could provide students with the "emotional skillset to resist the governance regime" and "release the resistant potential of the educational subject as a creative, socially transformative force." Mindfulness, he argues, has the potential to "support resistance to neoliberalism, rather than just functioning as neoliberalism's educational handmaiden." Political scientist Dean Mathiowetz (2016) says that because meditation is about "doing nothing" and is non-instrumental, it paradoxically can promote openness to others' perspectives; it can support projects that resist hierarchy and can serve as a resource against "the oligarchic forces of our time, in the name of citizens and democracy."

Social and educational activists see the necessary link between social activism and embodied spiritual practices such as mindfulness and yoga (Petty 2017). James Rowe (2016) cites Angela Davis, who, he says, sees that "mindfulness might become a revolutionary force if it is embedded in social movements that target oppressive systems." He notes that meditation sessions were significant practices during the 2011 Occupy Wall Street event in New York (2015). With respect and skill, activists need to challenge our and others' thinking when we are unaware of how our beliefs reflect dominant and/or oppressive social structures. bell hooks (quoted in Rowe 2016), wrote that skilful mindful awareness can help to "release the attachment to dominator thinking and practice."

This awareness can also help activists let go of some of their own attachments to rigidly held beliefs. Rowe points out that some in the Occupy Wall Street movement could have benefited from examining attachments to their own feelings in mindful ways — for example, their ambivalence toward working with and through established institutions of power such as unions. Other important mindful work for activists is to notice and discuss the extent to which emotionally charged social identities are clung to and held as essentialist, unchangeable, and expressed in just one way; or, on the other hand, denied altogether (see Lee 2017). Mindful social action depends on a practice of openness that allows people to realize both our unique differences in terms of experiences based on gender, race, ethnicity, class, and sexuality as well as our underlying unity and commonality. For those with more societal privileges, skilful listening and bearing witness to the pain, anger, and difficult feelings of those who feel unheard and disrespected is essential. For those who do feel unheard and disrespected, it is just as important that they speak out and challenge the rules of reason and respectability when they sense these are oppressive and rigged against them (Ng 2017).

Instead of educational practices that reinforce market-oriented individualism and that foster self-promotion and self-blame, a civic mindfulness furthers conscious agency in which people develop themselves as social beings and global citizens, part of an inclusive, democratic practice that creates a shared sense of common good. Buddhist scholar Edwin Ng (2015) defines civic mindfulness as "the use of mindfulness to help people cultivate the ethical and political sensibilities for more robust civic participation, alongside the cultivation of mental health and personal wellbeing." Kevin Healey (2013) argues that "systemic issues cannot be addressed through stress-reduction programs that assume the beneficence of unregulated markets.... While everyday mindfulness addresses personal stress, civic mindfulness addresses stress in the body politic, including abuses of power and breaches of the public trust."

An emerging civic or social mindfulness aligns with the movement to create schools that are more equitable, as well as to end poverty, wealth and income inequity, racism, sexism, homophobia, and xenophobia. Henry Giroux (2014a) sees the struggle for democracy and for public and higher education as linked with "the broader struggle for reclaiming a democracy that fulfils both its most radical ideals and its commitment to the common good, public values and a capacious notion of justice." Civic mindfulness endorses the principles of the Manifesto for a Revolution in Public Education, written by community activists and educators and which offers a clear critique of neoliberal education, a vision of equality of opportunity, and schools that, among other necessities, include "quiet places for contemplation" (Change.org n.d.).

Aislinn O'Donnell (2016: 40) argues that the conscious practising of mindfulness in a school can contribute to a "more radical critique of schooling" that in turn can lead to organizational changes:

> This could invite careful examination of the responsibility of educational policymakers and of schools themselves in cultivating cultures and curricula to create "outer conditions" that

are more supportive to students and teachers in their efforts to develop more subtle, nuanced, open practices of attention and compassionate awareness. I suggest that it is insufficient, and even unethical, to focus solely on "inner conditions" if such changes to "outer conditions" can be made.

School communities can engage in mindful social action, in which they work with others on local, national, and global levels to take on local school policies, state and federal neoliberal educational policies, systemic bullying, and deep-rooted structural barriers such as corporate influences on school, government, and society as they defend and demand universal quality public education, sustainability, and interdependence with all others. I call this "acting up."

Besides working mindfully with trauma in cultural, interpersonal terms, people can better engage in collective mindful social action by addressing trauma through mindfulness and embodied practices. James Rowe (2016: 217) says that the language of trauma is a "way for activists to name the intimate effects of interlocking systemic dominations. Attending to the intimate effects of structural violence through mind/body practice can strengthen movement-building by improving the health of participants, slowing cycles of trauma, and expanding collective agency."

Another important social practice is contemplative or mindful anti-oppressive critical pedagogy. From a feminist perspective, education professor Deborah Orr argues that mindfulness can help expose and undercut the binary mind/body assumption that grounds much of "the logic of domination" (Orr 2002; see also Cachon 2015). Women's studies professor Beth Berila (2016) extends this practice of combining mindfulness with an anti-oppressive critical pedagogy: using a feminist approach, she promotes the mindful and compassionate exploration of students' experiences and critically inquiring into their own beliefs and value systems. Students practise mindfulness to help them sit with discomfort around the complexity of identities and experiences of internalized oppression and privilege, and they can reframe resistance through this process, too (see Pyles 2018). This is an activist stance that embeds mindfulness as a means of raising consciousness and empowering action toward social justice. Berila's website (n.d.) says, "Anti-Oppression Pedagogy teaches how to analyze systems of oppression, while contemplative practices cultivate an embodied self-awareness. Mindful anti-oppression pedagogy merges the two to cultivate an embodied social justice."

In a similar vein, sociologist Peter Kaufman's (2017) critical contemplative pedagogy combines Freirean critical pedagogy with contemplative education. He shows that both share the dimensions of non-duality, interdependence, impermanence, intentionality, and the inseparability of the political and the personal. The emergent approach to mindfulness outlined in this book shares some of these qualities.

Rhonda Magee (2016, 2015), a leading mindful social justice educator, developed an approach she calls ColorInsight Practices. These "combine mindfulness-based practices with teaching and learning about race and color to increase awareness of how race and color impact us all, and give rise to insight and greater understanding." In my own work with high school football players, I employed mindfulness as part of an anti-oppression critical pedagogy that invited the young men to witness and then examine some of their troublesome thoughts, beliefs, and feelings about conventional masculinity as they arose and to consider the extent to which they were attached to these (Forbes 2004; Orr 2002). Funie Hsu (2013) points to the need to investigate with mindfulness the structural aspects of the school-to-prison pipeline that negatively affect many African-American students. There are countless educational policies impacting students and teachers that call for a mindful, questioning critical pedagogy.

At the same time, we need to work for societal restructuring and transformation, to envision and practise alternatives to capitalism, as is already happening within some organizations and communities (see Hickel and Kirk 2017). Henry Giroux (2017), quoting social science professor Nancy Fraser, says that this depends in part on the ability to "articulate the legitimate grievances of Trump supporters with a fulsome critique of financialization on the one hand, and with an anti-racist, anti-sexist and anti-hierarchical vision of emancipation on the other." More than just a political and economic critique and program, we need to envision and enact a caring, loving society that meets all people's needs for meaning and connection. Law professor Peter Doran (2018b) links critically engaged mindfulness with the idea and practice of the commons; he calls for a "mindful commons" that creates new, caring forms of attention that shatter dualities of "rationality over subjectivity, material wealth over human fulfilment," and capital accumulation over human needs.

Traditional and Emergent Mindfulness for Schools

In a Brooklyn high school where I consult, school counsellors have developed a four-session mindfulness curriculum for ninth-grade English classes. They start with the topic of how to reduce test anxiety, a common student concern. The four sessions are on introducing mindfulness, anxiety, anger, and self-care. This initial series of presentations is traditional. It offers practical uses of mindfulness in individualist terms to help students cope with anxiety and anger and enhance personal self-care — they practise identifying and being with feelings, breathe and return to the breath, and learn personal skills and ways to self-regulate. That's a good start.

However, if the counsellors were to leave it at that, this approach would be:

- individualistic, therapeutic; problems are psychologized, seen as residing within the person
- technical, using skill-based practices not based on moral foundations
- unaware of developmental, cultural, and social/political contexts in education
- used in the service of adjusting students and teachers to school without critical assessment of the social sources of anxiety, distraction, anger, and lack of self-care
- lacking in deeper self-reflective practices on individual, cultural, and social levels
- lacking an approach to contemplative education and learning within a critical context

The counsellors, though, were a step ahead of me; having been able to expand their approach along similar lines under a previous administration, they had already planned to take these sessions to the next level, developing an integral, social, emergent mindfulness project for each of these topics. This second-order curriculum builds on the first practices — it is critical and stands for social justice and optimal development for everyone. Following on our earlier analysis of the social, cultural, and developmental qualities of anxiety, anger, and self-care, I now suggest some general activity guidelines for an advanced mindfulness curriculum.

Anxiety

- Investigate and trace the socially conditioned beliefs, tapes, and pressures that run though one's head, see whether or not they are true; look at how these are filtered through experiences of gender, class, race, ethnicity, sexual orientation.
- Question why participants feel anxious and ill, compelled to ace tests, compete for success at school, get into proper colleges, and become financially successful in order to maintain their precarious social and economic status in an economic system that grows more competitive and inequitable (Abeles 2016).
- Learn about and discuss the myth of meritocracy and neoliberal approaches to school, such as high-stakes tests, that induce anxiety and competitiveness. Ask who benefits, and examine why they feel compelled to constantly self-regulate and monitor their social presentation and actions for success in this process.
- Re-evaluate the meaning of their education — imagine and implement less anxiety-laden, more meaningful studying and learning, including contemplative education; develop action plans to resist and challenge unnecessary testing and other policies.
- Explore and face deeper sources of anxiety: the belief that the self is a private, isolated entity that participants must always prop up to feel complete and secure; that they have to prove their worth to themselves and others through achievement or other external standards; that they are never good enough, can never do enough.

Self-Care

- Examine the ideology that each person must be responsible for self-care in a society in which there are inequitable resources for support and conditions that promote trauma, substance abuse, and other emotional and physical problems.

- Investigate bias and inequality around care for self and others in terms of social structure, gender, class, race, ethnicity, sexual orientation.
- Consider various notions of self-care as radical resistance to oppressive conditions.
- Create alternative models of self-care as a social, inclusive, collaborative activity and practise these with each other.

Anger

- Have each participant witness and investigate the socially conditioned thoughts, beliefs and behaviours from their family, from expectations based on gender and other categories, from the media and larger society that lead to feeling angry.
- Discuss the social conditions of why they get angry, who is allowed to get angry, when it is justified, when is it unskilled and unhelpful.
- Explore levels of self-development with respect to anger: what does it look like at different stages? What is grown-up anger?
- Consider righteous anger against social injustices and ways to implement righteous anger with others.
- Engage in skilful, mindful social action that is fuelled by righteous anger.

Stress Revisited

The predominant cultural approach to stress is to naturalize and abstract it away from its social context: it's just an inevitable fact of everyday life for which we each are responsible. The *New York Times* informs us that "stress is unavoidable in modern life" and is a personal matter for which you need to "take control" (Parker-Pope 2017). Stress reduction programs tend to stop at the level of the individual. They teach people coping skills that disregard the broader structural and institutional inequities that contribute to their stress and, by doing so, avoid changing these foundational components (see Becker 2013).

We first experience stress as personal, in one's body and in need of healing. Yet it implicates and is inseparable from the broader social, cultural, political, and economic contexts in which we are literally embodied. For example, a doctor of Eastern medicine, E. Douglas Kihn (2013), traces the link between stress induced by capitalist society and obesity. He argues that the constant pressure in North American society to keep busy, produce, compete, achieve, and sacrifice sleep contributes to overeating and obesity. Obesity, a serious health epidemic, nevertheless serves as a coping device; it slows down all that stressful hurrying since bigger fat cells calm the mind. Stressed out, obese bodies in turn benefit the capitalist economy: they create a more compliant, docile, and tired populace and provide profits to the agribusiness, food processing, medical, diet, and pharmaceutical industries.

Stress that results from the social myth of meritocracy is also a moral problem that raises the question of what it means for all of us to live right; it signals that something is amiss within cultural and social relations themselves and that there is a need for deeper meaning, caring, and connectedness. Science can contribute toward assisting with techniques of stress reduction — and research already shows that our survival and sustainability depends on our global cooperation as interdependent beings — but by itself, science cannot provide the values for a moral, meaningful life.

At a deeper level, much stress arises from the notion of a separate self that feels pressured and closed in by Western concepts of relative time and space. Neoliberal Western life — its loneliness, privatization, competitiveness, income disparities, the need to prove oneself, its racism, prejudice, and divisiveness, as well as the lack of acceptance, community, connection, and caring among people — contributes to increased stress, anxiety, depression, and other unhealthy patterns of experience and behaviour among many children and adults.

Through an emergent mindfulness practice, we can gain deeper insights into the fundamental nature of stress and anxiety of selfhood. It contributes to the moral — and scientific — awareness that we are inseparable from each other in the absolute sense, which fuels the drive to work for the welfare of all. Conscious meditation can help dismantle ego- and sociocentric (group) attachments and lead to more evolved states and stages of consciousness. These states and stages provide glimpses into the fundamental awareness or absolute groundlessness, the inseparability of all beings and things, the realization that things are not inherently solid but are relational and always changing (Marx: "All that is solid melts into air"), and that we ourselves, our natures, can and do change and evolve.

At later, more evolved stages of healthy development, this awareness stabilizes. You become awakened. You then can reflect upon whole belief systems, including contemplative education itself; you de-identify with a particular system and experience yourself in fluid terms as embodying a variety of evolving perspectives arising in different contexts, connected to everyone. Theologian and social activist Thomas Merton's (1966) famous description of his luminous, mystical experience in the middle of a city captures some of this, along with a hint of cosmic laughter:

> In Louisville, at the corner of Fourth and Walnut, in the center of the shopping district, I was suddenly overwhelmed with the realization that I loved all those people, that they were mine and I theirs, that we could not be alien to one another even though we were total strangers. It was like waking from a dream of separateness, of spurious self-isolation in a special world, the world of renunciation and supposed holiness.... This sense of liberation from an illusory difference was such a relief and such a joy to me that I almost laughed out loud.

Breathe and Push

> What does the midwife tell us to do? Breathe. And then? Push. Because if we don't push we will die. If we don't push our nation will die. Tonight we will breathe. Tomorrow we will labor in love through love and your revolutionary love is the magic we will show our children. — Valarie Kaur, a Sikh-American civil rights advocate at a congregation at Metropolitan African Methodist Episcopal Church in Washington on Dec. 31, 2016 (Kaur 2017)

Public education needs a mindfulness that is mindful, or critically conscious, of its own position within education and society. An emergent mindfulness connects unreflective personal experience with an informed awareness of one's actual social relations; it connects private troubles with public issues. It interrogates and challenges individualism, the myth of an unchanging, privatized self, insists on optimal self-development, and points at the evidence, bolstered by science, for our interdependence with all beings and with the Earth itself. It aligns with movements to create schools that are more equitable and just, and for more caring relationships and society.

The goal of an emergent mindfulness should be to enable all students and educators to develop fully our respective unique intellectual, personal, social, and moral capacities. For all of us, mindfulness should be a fiercely compassionate practice in which we uncover, challenge, and transcend how our thoughts, feelings, and actions are conditioned by unhealthy cultural practices and social institutions that (re)produce greed, meanness, and delusion. It is fuelled by a radical prophetic imagination, the task of which is to "bring to public expression those very hopes and yearnings that have been denied so long and suppressed so deeply that we no longer know they are there" (Brueggemann 1989).

An evolving mindfulness in part is a birthing of what exists inside us. At the same time, we grow in unpredictable, creative forms through our relationships — as, for example, with a midwife, with others, with the world. Each is partly true, yet neither is sufficient by itself. We need both personal awakening and caring relationships — your inside is out and your outside is in. Are we not one body/ies being born and coming to know ourselves? In a nascent mindfulness, we can follow Valarie Kaur (above) and take the midwife's advice: breathe and push, be and do. Breathe together as ones who all share the same air and the same universe; push to bring forth a better world together with and through a greater love.

References

1440 Multiversity. 2017. "Using Daily Mindfulness to Enhance Your Brain: An Interview with Daniel Siegel." 1440 Multiversity, August 2. <1440.org/using-daily-mindfulness-enhance-brain-interview-daniel-siegel/>.

Abeles, Vicki. 2016. "Is the Drive for Success Making Our Children Sick?" *New York Times,* January 2. <nytimes.com/2016/01/03/opinion/sunday/is-the-drive-for-success-making-our-children-sick.html>.

Adams, Tristam Vivian. 2016. *The Psychopath Factory: How Capitalism Organizes Empathy*. London: Repeater Books.

Adraque, Honey. 2015. "The Zombie Apocalypse as Mindfulness Manifesto by Ricardo Bessa." *Designideas.pics,* May 19. <designideas.pics/the-zombie-apocalypse-as-mindfulness-manifesto-by-ricardo-bessa/>.

Alexakos, Konstantinos, Leah D. Pride, Arnau Amat, Panagiota Tsetsakos, Kristi J. Lee, Christian Paylor-Smith, et al. 2016. "Mindfulness and Discussing 'Thorny' Issues in the Classroom." *Cultural Studies of Science Education,* 11, 3 (April). <researchgate.net/publication/300371312_Mindfulness_and_discussing_thorny_issues_in_the_classroom>.

Allen, Summer. 2017. "How to Hack Your Brain for Peak Performance." *Greater Good Magazine*, February 17. <greatergood.berkeley.edu/article/item/how_to_hack_your_brain_for_peak_performance>.

Arthington, Phil. 2016. "Mindfulness: A Critical Perspective." *Community Psychology in Global Perspective,* 2, 1. <siba-ese.unisalento.it/index.php/cpgp/article/view/15178/13667>.

Aschoff, Nicole. 2015. *The New Prophets of Capital*. New York: Verso.

Badiou, Alain. 2009. *Second Manifesto for Philosophy*. Cambridge: Polity.

Baer, Ruth A., and Emily L.B. Lykins. 2011. "Mindfulness and Positive Psychological Functioning." In Kennon Sheldon, Todd B. Kashdan, and Michael F. Steger (eds.), *Designing Positive Psychology: Taking Stock and Moving Forward*. New York: Oxford University Press.

Baime, Michael. 2011. "This Is Your Brain on Mindfulness." *Shambhala Sun*, July. <uphs.upenn.edu/pastoral/events/Baime_SHAMBHALA_2011.pdf>.

Baldwin, James. 1961. *Nobody Knows My Name: More Notes of a Native Son*. New York: Dial Press.

Barber, Nicholas. 2014. "Why Are Zombies Still So Popular?" *BBC*, October 21. <bbc.com/culture/story/20131025-zombie-nation>.

Barclay, Eliza. 2017. "Meditation Is Thriving Under Trump: A Former Monk

Explains Why." *Vox,* July 2. <vox.com/science-and-health/2017/6/19/15672864/headspace-puddicombe-trump>.

Barclay, Eliza, and Julia Belluz. 2018. "The Growth of Yoga and Meditation in the US Since 2012 Is Remarkable." *Vox,* November 9. <vox.com/2018/11/8/18073422/yoga-meditation-apps-classes-health-anxiety-cdc>.

Barks, Coleman (translator). 1995. *The Essential Rumi.* New York: HarperCollins.

Bartone, Shaun. 2015. "Neoliberal Buddhism." *Engage!* January 31. <engagedharma.net/2015/01/31/neoliberal-buddhism/>.

Basu, Tanya. 2018. "Mindfulness Is Going Mainstream Because of Science." *Daily Beast,* March 3. <thedailybeast.com/mindfulness-is-going-mainstream-because-of-science>.

Batchelor, Stephen. 1998. *Buddhism Without Beliefs: A Contemporary Guide to Awakening.* New York: Riverhead Books.

Bayda, Ezra. 2010. "Using the Energy of Anger." *Mindful,* August 25. <mindful.org/using-the-energy-of-anger/>.

Bazzano, Manu. 2017. *Zen and Therapy: Heretical Perspectives.* New York: Routledge.

----. 2015. "Guest Editorial Introduction: Before and After Mindfulness." *Self & Society,* 43, 1. <tandfonline.com/doi/full/10.1080/03060497.2015.1018683>.

----. 2013. "In Praise of Stress Induction: Mindfulness Revisited." *European Journal of Psychotherapy and Counselling,* 15, 2. <researchgate.net/publication/262873074_In_praise_of_stress_induction_Mindfulness_revisited>.

Becker, Dana. 2013. *One Nation Under Stress: The Trouble with Stress as an Idea.* New York: Oxford University Press.

Bellah, Robert N., Richard Madsen, William M. Sullivan, Ann Swidler, and Steven M. Tipton. 2007. *Habits of the Heart: Individualism and Commitment in American Life.* Berkeley: University of California Press.

Bennett, Jessica. 2015. "I'm Not Mad, That's Just My RBF." *New York Times,* August 1. <nytimes.com/2015/08/02/fashion/im-not-mad-thats-just-my-resting-b-face.html?_r=0>.

Beres, Derek. n.d. "The Rise of Spiritual Capitalism." *Bigthink.* <bigthink.com/21st-century-spirituality/the-selling-of-spirituality>.

Berila, Beth. 2016. *Integrating Mindfulness into Anti-Oppression Pedagogy: Social Justice in Higher Education.* New York: Routledge.

----. n.d. "Contemplative Practices for Anti-Oppression Pedagogy." <contemplativepracticesforantioppressionpedagogy.com/>.

Binkley, Sam. 2014. *Happiness as Enterprise: An Essay on Neoliberal Life.* Albany: SUNY Press.

Blind Field. 2017. "Against the 'Slow Cancellation of the Future.'" *Blind Field,* January 15. <blindfieldjournal.com/2017/01/15/against-the-slow-cancellation-of-the-future-rip-mark-fisher/>.

Bloom, Sondra. 2013. *Creating Sanctuary: Toward the Evolution of Sane Societies.* New York: Routledge.

Bodhi, Bhikkhu. 2011. "What Does Mindfulness Really Mean? A Canonical Perspective." *Contemporary Buddhism,* 12, 1. < budsas.net/sach/en142.pdf>.

Booth, Robert. 2014. "Mindfulness Therapy Comes at a High Price for Some, Say Experts." *The Guardian,* August 25. <theguardian.com/society/2014/aug/25/mental-health-meditation>.

Boyce, Barry. 2016. "No Blueprint, Just Love." *Mindful,* February 5. <mindful.org/no-blueprint-just-love/>.

-----. 2012. "A Real Education." *Lion's Roar,* May. <lionsroar.com/a-real-education-the-mindful-societymay-2012/>.

Brackett, Marc A., and Susan E. Rivers. 2014. "Transforming Students' Lives with Social and Emotional Learning." <ei.yale.edu/wp-content/uploads/2013/09/Transforming-Students%E2%80%99-Lives-with-Social-and-Emotional-Learning.pdf>.

Brazier, David. 2002. *The New Buddhism.* New York: Palgrave.

Brinkmann, Svend. 2017. *Stand Firm: Resisting the Self-Improvement Craze.* Cambridge: Polity.

Britton, Willoughby. 2012. "Mindful Binge Drinking and Blobology: The Promises and Perils of Contemplative Neuroscience." *Buddhist Geeks,* September 20. <youtube.com/watch?v=RlmqoQVm8nU>.

Brown, Candace Gunther. 2019. *Debating Yoga and Mindfulness in Public Schools: Reforming Secular Education or Reestablishing Religion?* Chapel Hill: University of North Carolina Press.

-----. 2016. "Can 'Secular' Mindfulness Be Separated from Religion?" In Ronald E. Purser, David Forbes, and Adam Burke (eds.), *Handbook of Mindfulness: Culture, Context, and Social Engagement.* New York: Springer.

-----. 2015. "Textual Erasures of Religion: The Power of Books to Redefine Yoga and Mindfulness Meditation as Secular Wellness Practices in North American Public Schools." *Erudit,* 6, 2. <id.erudit.org/iderudit/1032713ar>.

-----. 2014a. "Mindfulness Meditation in Public Schools." *Psychology Today,* December 5. <psychologytoday.com/blog/testing-prayer/201412/mindfulness-meditation-in-public-schools>.

-----. 2014b. "Mindfulness: Stealth Buddhist Strategy for Mainstreaming Meditation?" *Huffington Post,* December 2. <huffingtonpost.com/candy-gunther-brown-phd/mindfulness-stealth-buddh_b_6243036.html>.

Brown, Christopher. 2017. "I've Been in Education for 20 Years, and There's a Disturbing Trend Afoot in Kindergartens Around the US." *Business Insider,* April 17. <businessinsider.com/kindergartens-fail-to-let-kids-play-2017-4>.

Brown, Nicholas J., Tim Lomas, and Francisco Jose Eiroa-Orosa (eds.). 2018. *The Routledge International Handbook of Critical Positive Psychology.* New York: Routledge.

Browning, John Edgar, David Castillo, David Schmid, and David A. Reilly. 2015. *Zombie Masses: Monsters for the Age of Global Capitalism.* New York: Palgrave.

Brueggemann. Walter. 1989. *The Prophetic Imagination.* Minneapolis: Fortress Press.

Bustillos, Maria. 2011. "Inside David Foster Wallace's Private Self-Help Library." *The Awl,* April 5. <theawl.com/2011/04/inside-david-foster-wallaces-private-self-help-library/>.

Cachon, Frances. 2015. "Unsettling the Mind/Body Dualism: Exploring the Transformative Potential of Feminist Pedagogy for Justice-Oriented Citizenship Education." *Citizenship Education Research Journal.* <ojs-o.library.ubc.ca/index.php/CERJ/article/view/12>.

Cahill, Jennifer Fumiko. 2018. "Mindful Bitchface." *Northcoast Journal of Politics, People and Art,* October 18. <www.northcoastjournal.com/humboldt/

mindful-bitchface/Content?oid=11547673>.

Calaprice, Alice. 2005. *The New Quotable Einstein.* Princeton: Princeton University Press.

Cannon, Jennifer. 2016. "Education as the Practice of Freedom: A Social Justice Proposal for Mindfulness Educators." In Ronald E. Purser, David Forbes, and Adam Burke (eds.), *Handbook of Mindfulness: Culture, Context, and Social Engagement.* New York: Springer. <academia.edu/30238675/Education_as_the_Practice_of_Freedom_A_Social_Justice_Proposal_for_Mindfulness_Educators>.

Carrette, Jeremy, and Richard King, 2005. *Selling Spirituality: The Silent Takeover of Religion.* New York: Routledge.

CASEL. 2018a. "Core SEL Competencies." <casel.org/core-competencies/>.

----. 2018b. "What Is SEL." <casel.org/what-is-sel/>.

Cazdyn, Eric. 2012. *The Already Dead: The New Time of Politics, Culture, and Illness.* Durham: Duke University Press.

Cederström, Carl, and André Spicer. 2017. *Desperately Seeking Self-Improvement: A Year Inside the Optimization Movement.* New York: OR Books/Counterpoint.

----. 2015. *The Wellness Syndrome.* London: Polity.

Change.org. n.d. "A Manifesto for a Revolution in Public Education." Reclaiming the Conversation on Education Conference, Barnard College, May 4, 2013. <change.org/p/citizens-who-care-about-public-teachers-students-parents-and-teacher-educators-a-manifesto-for-a-revolution-in-public-education>.

Changing Minds at Concord High School. n.d. <changingmindsprogram.com/the-program/>.

Coates, Ta-Nehisi. 2015. *Between the World and Me.* New York: Spiegel & Grau.

Coconuts Bangkok. 2012. "Big complaint: Ronald McDonald Buddha image!" April 20. <coconuts.co/bangkok/news/random-big-complaint-ronald-mcdonald-buddha-image/>.

Cohen, Elliot. 2010. "From the Bodhi tree, to the analyst's couch, then into the MRI scanner: The Psychologisation of Buddhism." *Annual Review of Critical Psychology,* 8. <thediscourseunit.files.wordpress.com/2016/05/arcp8cohen.pdf>.

Confino, Jo. 2014. "Thich Nhat Hanh: Is Mindfulness Being Corrupted by Business and Finance?" *The Guardian,* March 28. <theguardian.com/sustainable-business/thich-nhat-hanh-mindfulness-google-tech>.

"The Congressman: Brainwave." 2013. Rubin Museum, April 20. <rubinmuseum.org/events/event/the-congressman>.

Cook-Greuter, Susanne R. 2013. "Nine Levels of Increasing Embrace in Ego Development: A Full-Spectrum Theory of Vertical Growth and Meaning Making." <cook-greuter.com/Cook-Greuter%209%20levels%20paper%20new%201.1'14%2097p%5B1%5D.pdf>.

----. 2005. "Ego Development: Nine Levels of Increasing Embrace." <newpossibilitiesassociates.com/uploads/9_levels_of_increasing_embrace_update_1_07.pdf>.

Corcoran, Nina. 2017. "The Rise and Fall of McDonald's Happy Meals." January 16. <consequenceofsound.net/2017/01/the-history-of-mcdonalds-happy-meals/>.

Costandi, Moheb. 2015. "Bold Assumptions: Why Brain Scans Are Not Always What They Seem." *Brain Decoder*, April 1. <behdad.org/mirror/www.braindecoder.com/bold-assumptions-why-brain-scans-are-not-always-what-they-seem-1069949099.

html>.

Cottone, R. Rocco. 2013. "A Paradigm Shift in Counseling Philosophy." *Counseling Today*, September 1. <ct.counseling.org/2013/09/a-paradigm-shift-in-counseling-philosophy/>.

Counseling and Values. 2007. Special Issue: "Integral Theory in Counseling." *Counseling and Values,* 51, 3 (April).

Coyne, James C. 2013. "Positive Psychology Is Mainly for Rich White People." *Mind the Brain,* August 21. <mindthebrain.blog/2013/08/21/positive-psychology-is-mainly-for-rich-white-people/>.

Cozolino, Louis. 2017. *The Neuroscience of Psychotherapy: Healing the Social Brain.* New York: Norton.

Dargis, Manhola. 2016. "Review, 'I Saw the Light,' A Hank Williams Biopic." *New York Times,* March 25. <nytimes.com/2016/03/25/movies/i-saw-the-light-review-hank-williams.html>.

Davidson, Miri. 2015. "Badiou's Happiness Lesson." *Verso Blog,* August 28. <versobooks.com/blogs/2192-badiou-s-happiness-lesson>.

Davies, William. 2015. *The Happiness Industry: How the Government and Big Business Sold Us Well-Being.* New York: Verso.

Davis, Angela Y. 2013. "Recognizing Racism in the Era of Neoliberalism." *Truthout,* May 6. <truth-out.org/opinion/item/16188-recognizing-racism-in-the-era-of-neoliberalism>.

Davis, Lauren Cassani. 2015. "When Mindfulness Meets the Classroom." *Atlantic,* August 31. <theatlantic.com/education/archive/2015/08/mindfulness-education-schools-meditation/402469/>.

de Lemus, Soledad, Russell Spears, and Miguel Moya. 2012. "The Power of a Smile to Move You: Complementary Submissiveness in Women's Posture as a Function of Gender Salience and Facial Expression." *Personality and Social Psychology Bulletin,* 38, 12 (August 31). <journals.sagepub.com/doi/pdf/10.1177/0146167212454178>.

Democracy Now. 2012. "Dr. Gabor Maté on the Stress-Disease Connection, Addiction and the Destruction of American Childhood." *Democracy Now,* December 25. <democracynow.org/2012/12/25/dr_gabor_mat_on_the_stress>.

DeMott, Robert. n.d. "Sample Text for *The Grapes of Wrath* / John Steinbeck; Introduction and Notes by Robert DeMott." <catdir.loc.gov/catdir/enhancements/fy1505/2005058182-s.html>.

Denby, David. 2016a. "Stop Humiliating Teachers." *New Yorker,* February 11. <newyorker.com/culture/cultural-comment/stop-humiliating-teachers>.

----. 2016b. "The Limits of 'Grit.'" *New Yorker,* June 21. <newyorker.com/culture/culture-desk/the-limits-of-grit>.

Denizet-Lewis, Benoit. 2017. "Why Are More American Teenagers Than Ever Suffering from Severe Anxiety?" *New York Times,* October 11. <nytimes.com/2017/10/11/magazine/why-are-more-american-teenagers-than-ever-suffering-from-severe-anxiety.html?hp&action=click&pgtype=Homepage&clickSource=story-heading&module=second-column-region&region=top-news&WT.nav=top-news>.

deVos, Corey. 2011. "Responding to the Death of Osama bin Laden." *Integral Life,* May 4. <integrallife.com/responding-death-osama-bin-laden/>.

Digges, Jason. n.d. "Why Isn't Integral More Popular?" *Beams and Struts.*

<beamsandstruts.com/articles/item/694-jargonless-integral>.

Dockett, Lauren, and Rich Simon. 2017. "The Addict in All of Us: Dr. Gabor Maté on the Problem We All Live With." *Alternet*, October 20. <alternet.org/drugs/addict-all-us-dr-gabor-mate-problem-we-all-live?akid=16247.2685856.50RdX0&rd=1&src=newsletter1084142&t=10>.

Doran, Peter. 2018a. "McMindfulness: Buddhism as Sold to You by Neoliberals." *The Conversation,* February 23. <theconversation.com/mcmindfulness-buddhism-as-sold-to-you-by-neoliberals-88338>.

----. 2018b. "Towards a Mindful Cultural Commons." *Culture Matters,* February 27. <culturematters.org.uk/index.php/culture/religion/item/2743-towards-a-mindful-commons>.

Douglass, Ryan. 2017. "More Men Should Learn the Difference Between Masculinity and Toxic Masculinity." *Everyday Feminism,* August 27. <everydayfeminism.com/2017/08/masculinity-vs-toxic-masculinity/?utm_source=feedburner&utm_medium=feed&utm_campaign=Feed%3A+EverydayFeminism+%28Everyday+Feminism%29&mc_cid=ab018316f5&mc_eid=37260c1942>.

Drummond, Katie. 2012. "A Man's Smile Can Make Women Act Subordinate." *Prevention,* November 26. <nbcnews.com/id/49544363/ns/health-mens_health/t/mans-smile-can-make-women-act-subordinate/#.WLxpc_IwAzE>.

Durbin, Jonathan. 2017. "Kurt Andersen's Beautiful Dark Twisted Fantasy." *Village Voice,* September 5. <villagevoice.com/2017/09/05/kurt-andersens-beautiful-dark-twisted-fantasy/>.

Dyson, Michael Eric. 2017. *Tears We Cannot Stop: A Sermon to White America*. New York: St. Martin's.

Ecclestone, Kathryn. 2011. "Emotionally Vulnerable Subjects and New Inequalities: The Educational Implications of an 'Epistemology of the Emotions.'" *International Studies in Sociology of Education,* 21, 2.

Education Trust. 2009. "The New Vision for School Counselors: Scope of the Work." January 1. <edtrust.org/resource/the-new-vision-for-school-counselors-scope-of-the-work/>.

Egginton, William. 2015. "What Are We Talking About When We Talk About Zombies?" *The Philosophical Salon: Los Angeles Review of Books,* July 6. <thephilosophicalsalon.com/what-are-we-talking-about-when-we-talk-about-zombies/>.

Ehrenreich, Barbara. 2015. "Mind Your Own Business." *The Baffler,* March. <thebaffler.com/salvos/mind-your-business>.

----. 2010. *Bright-Sided: How Positive Thinking Is Undermining America*. New York: Picador.

Eisner, Hannah Wolff. 2017. "Into the Middle of Things: Traumatic Redemption and the Politics of Form." April. <wesscholar.wesleyan.edu/cgi/viewcontent.cgi?article=2847&context=etd_hon_theses>.

Elias, Maurice J. 2012. "Leading the Way in Social, Emotional, and Character Development Standards." *Edutopia,* May 14. <edutopia.org/blog/secd-standards-kansas-maurice-elias>.

Emdin, Christopher. 2014. "5 New Approaches to Teaching and Learning: The Next Frontier." *Huffington Post,* April 2. <huffingtonpost.com/christopher-emdin/5-new-approaches-to-teaching-strategies_b_4697731.html>.

Enck-Wanzer, Darrel. 2011. "Barack Obama, the Tea Party, and the Threat of Race:

On Racial Neoliberalism and Born Again Racism." *Communication, Culture and Critique*, 4, 1 (March 1). <darrel.wanzerserrano.com/wp-content/uploads/Enck-Wanzer_Tea_Party_Essay.pdf>.

Epstein, Mark. 2014. *The Trauma of Everyday Life*. New York: Penguin

Ergas, Oren. 2017. "Reclaiming 'Self' in Teachers' Images of 'Education' Through Mindfulness as Contemplative Inquiry." *Journal of Curriculum and Pedagogy*, 14, 3.

Eriksen, Karen P., and Garrett J. McAuliffe. 2006. "Constructive Development and Counselor Competence." *Counselor Education and Supervision*, 45, 3 (March). <pdfs.semanticscholar.org/e323/0ee687fbc0a03d353d49a81acdffe7f0840f.pdf>.

Farias, Miguel, and Catherine Wikholm. 2015. *The Buddha Pill: Can Meditation Change You?* London: Watkins Publishing.

Faulkner, Nicholas. 2013. "Guilt, Anger, and Compassionate Helping." In Michael Ure and Mervyn Frost (eds.), *The Politics of Compassion*. New York: Routledge.

Felver, Joshua C., Cintly E. Celis-de Hoyos, Katherine M. Tezanos, and Nirbay N. Singh. 2015. "A Systematic Review of Mindfulness-Based Interventions for Youth in School Settings." *Mindfulness*, 7, 1 (February). <researchgate.net/publication/273349460_A_Systematic_Review_of_Mindfulness-Based_Interventions_for_Youth_in_School_Settings>.

Fisher, Danny. 2010. "Mindfulness and the Cessation of Suffering: An Exclusive New Interview with Mindfulness Pioneer Jon Kabat-Zinn." *Lion's Roar*, October 7. <lionsroar.com/mindfulness-and-the-cessation-of-suffering-an-exclusive-new-interview-with-mindfulness-pioneer-jon-kabat-zinn/>.

Fisher, Kathleen M. 2017. "Look Before You Leap: Reconsidering Contemplative Pedagogy." *Teaching, Theology, and Religion*, 20, 1 (January 12). <onlinelibrary.wiley.com/doi/10.1111/teth.12361/full>.

Fisher, Lawrence M. 2008. "Tea and Empathy with Daniel Goleman." *Strategy + Business*, August 26. <strategy-business.com/article/08308?gko=b3d2e>.

Fisher, Mark. 2009. *Capitalist Realism: Is There No Alternative?* London: Zero.

Flores, Natalie. 2016. "A Critical and Comprehensive Review of Mindfulness in the Early Years." In Ronald E. Purser, David Forbes, and Adam Burke (eds.), *Handbook of Mindfulness: Culture, Context, and Social Engagement*. New York: Springer.

Fong, Benjamin Y. 2013. "Bursting the Neuro-Utopian Bubble." *New York Times*, August 11. <opinionator.blogs.nytimes.com/2013/08/11/bursting-the-neuro-utopian-bubble/>.

Forbes, David. 2016a. "Critical Integral Contemplative Education." In Ronald E. Purser, David Forbes, and Adam Burke (eds.), *Handbook of Mindfulness: Culture, Context, and Social Engagement*. New York: Springer. <academicworks.cuny.edu/bc_pubs/100/>.

----. 2016b. "Modes of Mindfulness: Prophetic Critique and Integral Emergence." *Mindfulness*, 7, 6. <academicworks.cuny.edu/cgi/viewcontent.cgi?article=1102&context=bc_pubs>. ___. 2012. "Occupy Mindfulness." *Beams and Struts*. <beamsandstruts.com/articles/item/982-occupy-mindfulness>.

----. 2004. *Boyz 2 Buddhas: Counseling Urban High School Male Athletes in the Zone*. New York: Peter Lang.

----. 1987. "Clinical Notes on 'The Case of the Little Prince.'" In Glenn C. Ellenbogen (ed.), *Oral Sadism and the Vegetarian Personality: Readings from the Journal of Polymorphous Perversity*. New York: Ballantine.

Forman, Mark D. 2010. *A Guide to Integral Psychotherapy: Complexity, Integration, and Spirituality in Practice*: Albany: SUNY Press.

Fortin, Jacey. 2019. "Traditional Masculinity Can Hurt Boys, Say New A.P.A. Guidelines." *New York Times,* January 10. <www.nytimes.com/2019/01/10/science/apa-traditional-masculinity-harmful.html?action=click&module=RelatedLinks&pgtype=Article>.

Foucault, Michel. 1991. "Governmentality." In Graham Burchell, Colin Gordon, and Peter Miller (eds.), *The Foucault Effect: Studies in Governmentality.* Chicago: University of Chicago Press.

----. 1988. "Technologies of the Self." In Luther H. Martin, Huck Gutman, and Patrick H. Hutton (eds.), *Technologies of the Self: A Seminar with Michel Foucault.* Amherst: University of Massachusetts Press.

Fowler, James W. 1995. *Stages of Faith: The Psychology of Human Development and the Quest for Meaning.* New York: HarperOne.

Fraga, Juli. 2016. "How Mindfulness and Storytelling Helps Kids Heal and Learn." KQED *Mind/Shift*, September 26. <ww2.kqed.org/mindshift/2016/09/26/how-mindfulness-and-storytelling-help-kids-heal-and-learn/>.

Fromm, Erich. 2010. *The Pathology of Normalcy*. Herndon VA: Lantern Press.

Gap. 2017. "GapKids Celebrates the Back to School Season with the Launch of the 'Forward With' Campaign and Partnership with Lionsgate for the Upcoming Feature Film 'Wonder.'" *PR Newsletter*, August 9. <prnewswire.com/news-releases/gapkids-celebrates-the-back-to-school-season-with-the-launch-of-the-forward-with-campaign-and-partnership-with-lionsgate-for-the-upcoming-feature-film-wonder-300501947.html>.

GapKids Back to School — Meditation. 2017. *Gap*, July 25. <youtube.com/watch?v=ZZF_uMfpmyg>.

Garbarino, James. 2000. *Lost Boys: Why Our Sons Turn Violent and How We Can Save Them.* New York: Anchor.

Garcia Lorca, Federico. 1955. *Poet in New York*. New York: Grove Press.

Gelles, David. 2017. "How to Be Mindful on the Subway." *New York Times*, March 8. <nytimes.com/2017/03/08/well/mind/how-to-be-mindful-on-the-subway.html>.

Gerrans, Phillip, and Chris Letheby. 2017. "Model Hallucinations." *Aeon,* August 8. <aeon.co/essays/psychedelics-work-by-violating-our-models-of-self-and-the-world>.

Gerszberg, Caren Osten. 2017. "The Future of Education: Mindful Classrooms." *Mindful.org*. <mindful.org/future-education-mindful-classrooms/>.

Giroux, Henry A. 2017. "Why the Democratic Party Can't Save Us from Trump's Authoritarianism." *Truthout*, August 21. <truth-out.org/news/item/41672-why-the-democratic-party-can-t-save-us-from-trump-s-authoritarianism>.

----. 2014a. "Barbarians at the Gates: Authoritarianism and the Assault on Public Education." *Truthout,* December 30. <truth-out.org/articles/barbarians-at-the-gates-authoritarianism-and-the-assault-on-public-education/>.

----. 2014b. *Zombie Politics and Culture in the Age of Casino Capitalism*. New York: Peter Lang.

Goldberg, Michelle. 2015. "The Long Marriage of Mindfulness and Money." *New Yorker,* April 18. <www.newyorker.com/business/currency/the-long-marriage-of-mindfulness-and-money>.

Goldhill, Olivia. 2017. "'Positive Thinking' Has Turned Happiness into a Duty and a Burden, Says a Danish Psychologist." *Quartz,* March 4. <qz.com/924103/ happiness-hasbecome-an-emotional-burden-says-a-danish-psychologist-svend-brinkmann/?utm_source=qzfb>.

Goldstein, Elisha. 2011. "Osama Bin Laden Dead: A Mindful Response." *Huffington Post,* November 17. <huffingtonpost.com/elisha-goldstein-phd/osama-bin-laden-dead_b_856706.html>.

Goleman, Daniel. 2007a. "Emotional Intelligence, Social Intelligence." *Daniel Goleman,* June 12. <danielgoleman.info/three-kinds-of-empathy-cognitive-emotional-compassionate/>.

----. 2007b. *Social Intelligence: The New Science of Human Relationships.* New York: Bantam.

----. 2005. *Emotional Intelligence: Why It Can Matter More Than IQ.* New York: Bantam.

Goodman, Trudy A., and Susan Kaiser Greenland. 2009. "Mindfulness with Children: Working with Difficult Emotions." In Fabrizio Didonna (ed.), *Clinical Handbook of Mindfulness.* New York: Springer.

Goto-Jones, Chris. 2013. "Zombie Apocalypse as Mindfulness Manifesto (After Žižek)." *Postmodern Culture,* 24, 1 (September). <mentalpraxis.com/ uploads/4/2/5/4/42542199/goto-jones_zombie_mindfulness_manifesto.pdf>.

Graham, David A. 2017. "'Alternative Facts': The Needless Lies of the Trump Administration." *Atlantic,* January 22. <theatlantic.com/politics/archive/2017/01/ the-pointless-needless-lies-of-the-trump-administration/514061/>.

Grant, Adam. 2014. "The Dark Side of Emotional Intelligence." *The Atlantic,* January 2. <theatlantic.com/health/archive/2014/01/the-dark-side-of-emotional-intelligence/282720/?utm_source=atlfb>.

Green, Gerald. 1956. *The Last Angry Man.* New York: Charles Scribner's Sons.

Greenland, Susan Kaiser. 2011. "Ready for School? Executive Function = Success." *Huffington Post,* October 31. <huffingtonpost.com/susan-kaiser-greenland/ready-for-school-executiv_b_942743.html>.

----. 2010. *The Mindful Child: How to Help Your Kid Manage Stress and Become Happier, Kinder, and More Compassionate.* New York: Atria.

Griffin, Annaliese. 2017. "Women Are Flocking to Wellness Because Modern Medicine Still Doesn't Take Them Seriously." *Quartz,* June 15. <qz.com/1006387/ women-are-flocking-to-wellness-because-traditional-medicine-still-doesnt-take-them-seriously/>.

Gross, Rita. 1993. *Buddhism after Patriarchy.* Albany: SUNY Press.

Grossman, Paul, and Nicholas T. Van Dam. 2011. "Mindfulness, by Any Other Name … : Trials and Tribulations of *Sati* in Western Psychology and Science." *Contemporary Buddhism,* 12, 1. <albany.edu/~me888931/Grossman%20&%20 Van%20Dam%202011%20Contemporary%20Buddhism.pdf>.

Grosz, Elizabeth, and Vikki Bell. 2017. "Interview with Elizabeth Grosz." *Theory Culture & Society,* May 22. <theoryculturesociety.org/interview-elizabeth-grosz/>.

Gunnlaugson, Olen. 2009. "Establishing Second-Person Forms of Contemplative Education: An Inquiry into Four Conceptions of Intersubjectivity." *Integral Review,* 5, 1 (June). <integral-review.org/issues/vol_5_no_1_gunnlaugson_establishing_second_person_forms_of_contemplative_education.pdf>.

Gunnlaugson, Olen, and Michael Brabant (eds.). 2016. *Cohering the Integral We*

Space: Engaging Collective Emergence, Wisdom and Healing in Groups. Tucson AZ: Integral Publishing.

Gunnlaugson, Olen, Charles Scott, Hesoon Bai, and Edward W. Sarath (eds.). 2017. *The Intersubjective Turn: Theoretical Approaches to Contemplative Learning and Inquiry Across Disciplines.* Albany: suny Press.

Hackman, Michelle, and Eric Morath. 2018. "Teachers Quit Jobs at Highest Rate on Record." *Wall Street Journal,* December 28. <wsj.com/articles/teachers-quit-jobs-at-highest-rate-on-record-11545993052?mod=e2fb>.

Haney, Dawn. 2016. "Growing the Ranks of White Buddhists Against White Supremacy." *Buddhist Peace Fellowship*, May 20. <buddhistpeacefellowship.org/growing-ranks-white-buddhists-white-supremacy/>.

Hanley, Adam W., Neil Abell, Debra S. Osborn, Alysia D. Roehrig, and Angela I. Canto. 2016. "Mind the Gaps: Are Conclusions About Mindfulness Entirely Conclusive?" *Journal of Counseling & Development,* 94 (January). <researchgate.net/publication/289244761_Mind_the_Gaps_Are_Conclusions_About_Mindfulness_Entirely_Conclusive>.

Haque, Umair. 2016. "The Myth of Positivity." *Uplift*, October 8. <upliftconnect.com/the-myth-of-positivity/>.

Hari, Johann. 2017. "The Likely Cause of Addiction Has Been Discovered, and It Is Not What You Think." *Huffington Post,* April 18. <https://www.huffingtonpost.com/johann-hari/the-real-cause-of-addicti_b_6506936.html>.

Hattery, Angela J., and Earl Smith. 2017. *Policing Black Bodies: How Black Lives Are Surveilled and How to Work for Change.* Lanham: Rowman and Littlefield.

Hawn, Goldie. 2011. *10 Mindful Minutes: Giving Our Children — and Ourselves — the Social and Emotional Skills to Reduce Stress and Anxiety for Healthier, Happy Lives.* New York: Perigee.

Healey, Kevin. 2016. "Dreaming the Virtual: Why Lucid Dreamers Should Steer the Digital Economy." *Huffington Post,* April 27. <huffingtonpost.com/kevin-healey2/dreaming-the-virtual-why_b_9791298.html>.

----. 2013. "Searching for Integrity: The Politics of Mindfulness in the Digital Economy." *Nomos Journal,* August 5. <nomosjournal.org/2013/08/searching-for-integrity/>.

Hedges, Chris. 2015. "The Great Unravelling." *Truthdig,* August 30. <truthdig.com/report/item/the_great_unraveling_20150830>.

----. 2009. *Empire of Illusion: The End of Literacy and the Triumph of Spectacle.* New York: Nation Books.

Heffernan, Virginia. 2015. "The Muddied Meaning of 'Mindfulness.'" *New York Times,* April 14. <nytimes.com/2015/04/19/magazine/the-muddied-meaning-of-mindfulness.html>.

Heschel, Abraham Joshua. 1975. *The Prophets: Volume II.* New York: Harper.

Hickel, Jason, and Martin Kirk. 2017. "Don't Be Scared About the End of Capitalism — Be Excited to Build What Comes Next." *Fast Company*, September 11. <fastcompany.com/40454254/dont-be-scared-about-the-end-of-capitalism-be-excited-to-build-what-comes-next>.

Hochschild, Arlie. 2016. *Strangers in Their Own Land: Anger and Mourning on the American Right.* New York: New Press.

----. 2012. *The Managed Heart: Commercialization of Human Feeling,* Berkeley: University of California Press.

Holloway, Kali. 2017. "The Damage We Do to Boys and Men that Explains the Trump Presidency." *Alternet,* August 14. <alternet.org/election-2016/damage-we-do-boys-and-men-explains-trump-presidency?akid=15978.2685856.OJDtWr&rd=1&src=newsletter1081099&t=6>.

----. 2015. "Why We're Sick and Tired of Wellness." *Alternet,* August 11. <alternet.org/personal-health/why-were-sick-and-tired-wellness>.

Holm, Marie. 2016. "Partner's Perspective: Casting a (Not-So) Critical Eye on Mindfulness Research." *The Mindful Globe,* August 17. <themindfulglobe.org/blog/2016/08/17/partners-perspective-casting-a-not-so-critical-eye-on-mindfulness-research-%E2%80%A2-by-marie-holm/>.

Holmes, Jack. 2016. "A Trump Surrogate Drops the Mic: 'There's No Such Thing as Facts.'" *Esquire,* December 1. <esquire.com/news-politics/videos/a51152/trump-surrogate-no-such-thing-as-facts/>.

Honey, Larisa. 2014. "Self-Help Groups in Post-Soviet Moscow: Neoliberal Discourses of the Self and Their Social Critique." *Laboratorium.* <soclabo.org/index.php/laboratorium/article/view/330/1028>.

Horgan, John. 2015. "Meta-Meditation: A Skeptic Meditates on Meditation." *Scientific American,* July 8. <blogs.scientificamerican.com/cross-check/meta-meditation-a-skeptic-meditates-on-meditation/>.

Horowitz, Daniel. 2017. *Happier? The History of a Cultural Movement That Aspired to Transform America.* New York: Oxford University Press.

Hsu, Funie. 2017. "We've Been Here All Along." *Lion's Roar*, May 17. <lionsroar.com/weve-been-here-all-along>.

----. 2016. "What Is the Sound of One Invisible Hand Clapping? Neoliberalism, the Invisibility of Asian and Asian American Buddhists, and Secular Mindfulness in Education." In Ronald E. Purser, David Forbes, and Adam Burke (eds.), *Handbook of Mindfulness: Culture, Context, and Social Engagement.* New York: Springer. <academia.edu/30684271/What_Is_the_Sound_of_One_Invisible_Hand_Clapping_Neoliberalism_the_Invisibility_of_Asian_and_Asian_American_Buddhists_and_Secular_Mindfulness_in_Education>.

----. 2013. "The Heart of Mindfulness: A Response to the New York Times." *Buddhist Peace Fellowship*, November 4. <buddhistpeacefellowship.org/the-heart-of-mindfulness-a-response-to-the-new-york-times/>.

Hyland, Terry. 2017. "McDonaldizing Spirituality: Mindfulness, Education and Consumerism." *Journal of Transformative Education,* 15, 4 (March). <researchgate.net/publication/315109433_McDonaldizing_Spirituality_Mindfulness_Education_and_Consumerism>.

----. 2015. "On the Contemporary Applications of Mindfulness: Some Implications for Education." *Journal of Philosophy of Education,* 49, 2 (May). <researchgate.net/publication/277019680_On_the_Contemporary_Applications_of_Mindfulness_Some_Implications_for_Education>.

Illouz, Eva. 2008. *Saving the Modern Soul: Therapy, Emotions, and the Culture of Self-Help.* Berkeley: University of California Press.

Impedovo, M.A., and Sufiana Khatoon Malik. 2015. "Contemplative Practice for Beginning Teachers: Should It Be Included in the Teacher Education Curriculum?" *Teachers College Record,* December 11. <researchgate.net/publication/312580352_Contemplative_Practice_for_Teacher_Students_Should_

It_Be_Included_in_Teaching_Training_Curriculum>.

Ingersoll, R. Elliott, and David M. Zeitler. 2010. *Integral Psychotherapy: Inside Out/ Outside In*. Albany: SUNY Press.

Ivey, Allen, Mary Bradford Ivey, Carlos Zalaquett, and Kathryn Quirk. 2009. "Counseling and Neuroscience: The Cutting Edge of the Coming Decade." *Counseling Today,* December 3. <ct.counseling.org/2009/12/reader-viewpoint-counseling-and-neuroscience-the-cutting-edge-of-the-coming-decade/>.

Jamison, Leslie. 2018. "I Used to Insist I Didn't Get Angry. Not Anymore." *New York Times,* January 17. <nytimes.com/2018/01/17/magazine/i-used-to-insist-i-didnt-get-angry-not-anymore.html>.

Jennings, Patricia A. 2015. *Mindfulness for Teachers: Simple Skills for Peace and Productivity in the Classroom*. New York: Norton.

Johnson, Kurt, and David Robert Ord. 2013. *The Coming Interspiritual Age*. Vancouver: Namaste Publishing.

Joiner, Thomas. 2017a. "Mindfulness Would Be Good for You. If It Weren't So Selfish." *Washington Post*, August 25. <washingtonpost.com/outlook/mindfulness-would-be-good-for-you-if-it-werent-all-just-hype/2017/08/24/b97d0220-76e2-11e7-9eac-d56bd5568db8_story.html?utm_term=.6ff1b54e84b9#comments>.

----. 2017b. *Mindlessness: The Corruption of Mindfulness in a Culture of Narcissism*. New York: Oxford University Press.

K–12 Education. n.d. "Education: Knowledge and Skills for the Jobs of the Future." *Obama White House*. <obamawhitehouse.archives.gov/issues/education/k-12>.

Kabat-Zinn, Jon. 2011. "Some Reflections on the Origins of MBSR, Skillful Means, and the Trouble with Maps." *Contemporary Buddhism,* 12, 1 (May).

----. 2006. *Coming to Our Senses: Healing Ourselves and the World Through Mindfulness*. New York: Hatchette.

Kamenetz, Anya. 2016. "Why Teachers Say Practicing Mindfulness Is Transforming the Work." *KQED News: Mind/Shift*, August 19. <ww2.kqed.org/mindshift/2016/08/19/why-teachers-say-practicing-mindfulness-is-transforming-the-work/>.

Kapleau, Roshi Philip. 1989. *The Three Pillars of Zen*. New York: Anchor.

Kaufman, Peter. 2017. "Critical Contemplative Pedagogy." *Radical Pedagogy,* 14, 1. <academia.edu/31097956/Critical_Contemplative_Pedagogy>.

Kaur, Valarie. 2017. "'Breathe! Push!' Watch This Sikh Activist's Powerful Prayer for America." *Washington Post*, March 6. <washingtonpost.com/news/acts-of-faith/wp/2017/03/06/breathe-push-watch-this-sikh-activists-powerful-prayer-for-america/?utm_term=.d3cc4bbad970>.

Kegan, Robert. 1994. *In Over Our Heads: The Mental Demands of Modern Life*. Cambridge: Harvard University Press.

Kelly, Maura. 2012. "Trickle Down Distress: How America's Broken Meritocracy Drives Our National Anxiety Epidemic." *Atlantic*, July 3. <theatlantic.com/health/archive/2012/07/trickle-down-distress-how-americas-broken-meritocracy-drives-our-national-anxiety-epidemic/259383/>.

Keohane, Joe. 2015. "In Praise of Meaningless Work: Mindfulness Mantras Are the Latest Tool of Corporate Control." *New Republic*, March 2. <newrepublic.com/article/121171/praise-meaningless-work>.

Kihn, E. Douglas. 2013. "The Political Roots of American Obesity." *Truthout,* May 4.

<truthout.org/articles/the-political-roots-of-american-obesity/>.

Kim, Jennifer. 2015. "Why Mindfulness Matters in Marketing to Women." *AdAge*, June 18. <adage.com/article/agency-viewpoint/mindfulness-matters-marketing-women/299087/>.

King, Jason H. 2010. "Are Professional Counselors Becoming Social Workers?" *Counseling Today*, 52, 12 (June).

Kirp, David L. 2017. "Don't Suspend Students. Empathize." *New York Times*, September 2. <nytimes.com/2017/09/02/opinion/sunday/dont-suspend-students-empathize.html?emc=eta1>.

Kisner, Jordan. 2017. "The Politics of Conspicuous Displays of Self-Care." *New Yorker*, March 14. <newyorker.com/culture/culture-desk/the-politics-of-selfcare>.

Krauze, Lauren. 2017. "The Untold Story of America's Mindfulness Movement." *Tricycle*, September 26. <tricycle.org/trikedaily/untold-story-america-mindfulness-movement/>.

Kreitner, Richard. 2017. "'Trump Is Just Tearing Off the Mask': An Interview with Eric Foner." *The Nation*, April 18. <thenation.com/article/trump-is-just-tearing-off-the-mask-an-interview-with-eric-foner/>.

Kreplin, Ute, Miguel Farias, and Inti A. Brazil. 2018. "The Limited Prosocial Effects of Meditation: A Systematic Review and Meta-Analysis." *Scientific Reports*, 8 (February 5). <nature.com/articles/s41598-018-20299-z>.

Krupka, Zoë. 2015. "Mindfulness Is an Ideal Tool to Induce Compliance." *Science*, 2.0, September 23. <science20.com/the_conversation/mindfulness_is_an_ideal_tool_to_induce_compliance-157249>.

Kucinskas, Jaime. 2018. *The Mindful Elite: Mobilizing from the Inside Out*. New York: Oxford.

Kushner, Aviya. 2018. Why We Must Pay Attention to What 'Pay Attention' Means. *Forward*, October 25. <forward.com/culture/412551/why-we-must-pay-attention-to-what-pay-attention-means/?utm_content=culture_Newsletter_MainList_Title_Position-1&utm_source=Sailthru&utm_medium=email&utm_campaign=Automated%20Culture%202018-10-26&utm_term=Arts>.

Lakoff, George. 2010. *Moral Politics: How Liberals and Conservatives Think*. Chicago: University of Chicago Press.

Lantieri, Linda, and Vicki Zakrzewski. 2015. "How SEL and Mindfulness Can Work Together." *Greater Good Magazine*, April 7. <greatergood.berkeley.edu/article/item/how_social_emotional_learning_and_mindfulness_can_work_together>.

Larocca, Amy. 2017. "The Wellness Epidemic." *The Cut*, June 27. <thecut.com/2017/06/how-wellness-became-an-epidemic.html?utm_source=fb&utm_medium=s3&utm_campaign=sharebutton-t>.

Larsen, Steen Nepper. 2014. "Compulsory Creativity: A Critique of Cognitive Capitalism." *Culture Unbound*, 6. <cultureunbound.ep.liu.se/v6/a09/cu14v6a09.pdf>.

Lauro, Sarah Juliet. 2013. "What I've Learned: Zombie Scholar." *Esquire*, June 17. <esquire.com/news-politics/news/a23099/zombie-scholar-quotes/>.

Lee, Frances. 2017. "Why I've Started to Fear My Fellow Social Justice Advocates." *Yes Magazine*, October 13. <yesmagazine.org/people-power/why-ive-started-to-fear-my-fellow-social-justice-activists-20171013/>.

Lee, Trymaine. 2014. "Preschool to Prison: No Child Too Young for Zero-Tolerance." *MSNBC*, March 21. <msnbc.com/msnbc/preschool-prison-no-child-too-young>.

Levine, Bruce E. 2013. "Why Life in America Can Literally Drive You Insane." *AlterNet*, July 30. <alternet.org/personal-health/whats-behind-dramatic-rise-mental-illness>.

Lile, Jesse. 2018. Personal Correspondence. November 13.

Lind, Michael. 2012. "Education Reform's Central Myths." *Salon,* August 1. <salon.com/2012/08/01/school_choice_vs_reality/>.

Lindhal, Jared. R. 2014. "Why Right Mindfulness Might Not Be Right for Mindfulness." *Mindfulness.* <link.springer.com/article/10.1007/s12671-014-0380-5>.

Lopez, Donald. 2012. "The Scientific Buddha." *Tricycle*, Winter. <tricycle.org/magazine/scientific-buddha/>.

Lopez, German. 2017. "Research Says There Are Ways to Reduce Racial Bias. Calling People Racist Isn't One of Them." *Vox,* August 14. <vox.com/identities/2016/11/15/13595508/racism-trump-research-study>.

Lorde, Audre. 1997. "The Uses of Anger." *Women's Studies Quarterly,* 25, 1–2. <scribd.com/doc/157368878/Audre-Lorde-The-Uses-of-Anger>.

Love, Shayla. 2018. "Meditation Is a Powerful Mental Tool — and for Some People It Goes Terribly Wrong." *Tonic,* November 14. <tonic.vice.com/en_us/article/vbaedd/meditation-is-a-powerful-mental-tool-and-for-some-it-goes-terribly-wrong>.

Loy, David. 2015. *A New Buddhist Path: Enlightenment Evolution and Ethics in the Modern World.* Boston: Wisdom.

----. 2013. "Why Buddhism and the West Need Each Other: On the Interdependence of Personal and Social Transformation." *Journal of Buddhist Ethics,* 20. <blogs.dickinson.edu/buddhistethics/files/2013/09/Loy-Why-Buddhism-final.pdf>.

----. 2010. *The World Is Made of Stories.* Boston: Wisdom.

----. 2005. "Lack and Liberation in Self and Society: An Interview with David Loy." *Center for Sacred Sciences.* <centerforsacredsciences.org/index.php/Holos/holos-david-loy.html>.

----. 2002. *A Buddhist History of the West: Studies in Lack.* Albany: SUNY Press.

Magee, Rhonda V. 2016. "The Way of ColorInsight: Understanding Race and Law Effectively Through Mindfulness-Based ColorInsight Practices." <mindandlife.org/wp-content/uploads/2016/01/Magee-Revised-The-Way-of-ColorInsight-Dec_21_-2016.pdf>.

----. 2015. "How Mindfulness Can Defeat Racial Bias." *Greater Good Magazine,* May 14. <greatergood.berkeley.edu/article/item/how_mindfulness_can_defeat_racial_bias>.

Malabou, Catherine. 2008. *What Should We Do with Our Brain?* New York: Fordham University Press. <asounder.org/resources/malabou_brain.pdf>.

Marbley, Aretha, Janeé Steele, and Garrett J. McAuliffe. 2011. "Teaching Social and Cultural Issues, in Counseling." In Garrett J. McAuliffe and Karen Eriksen (eds.), *Handbook of Counselor Preparation: Constructivist, Developmental, and Experiential Approaches.* Thousand Oaks: Sage.

Marche, Stephen. 2013. "Why Zombies Are Everywhere Now." *Esquire,* June 19. <esquire.com/entertainment/movies/a23139/why-zombies-are-everywhere/>.

Marx, Karl. 1967. *Capital,* Volume 1. New York: International Publishers.

Masters, Robert Augustus. n.d. "Spiritual Bypassing: Avoidance in Holy Drag." <robertmasters.com/writings/spiritual-bypassing/>.

Maté, Gabor. 2010. *In the Realm of Hungry Ghosts: Close Encounters with Addiction*. Berkeley: North Atlantic Books.

Mathiowetz, Dean. 2016. "'Meditation Is Good for Nothing': Leisure as a Democratic Practice." *New Political Science*. <escholarship.org/uc/item/3gn282xf>.

Matthews, Gerald, Moshe Zeidner, and Richard D. Roberts. 2004. *Emotional Intelligence: Science and Myth*. Cambridge: MIT Press.

Max, D.T. 2009. "The Unfinished: David Foster Wallace's Struggle to Surpass 'Infinite Jest.'" *New Yorker*, March 9. <newyorker.com/magazine/2009/03/09/the-unfinished>.

May, Cindi. 2017. "Mindfulness Training for Teens Fails Important Test." *Scientific American*, October 31. <scientificamerican.com/article/mindfulness-training-for-teens-fails-important-test/?wt.mc=SA_Facebook-Share>.

McAdams, Dan P., and Brady K. Jones. 2017. "Making Meaning in the Wake of Trauma: Resilience and Redemption." In Elizabeth M. Altmaier (ed.), *Reconstructing Meaning After Trauma: Theory, Research, and Practice*. Cambridge: Elsevier. <scholars.northwestern.edu/en/publications/making-meaning-in-the-wake-of-trauma-resilience-and-redemption>.

McAuliffe, Garrett J., and Karen Eriksen. 2011. *Handbook of Counselor Preparation: Constructivist, Developmental, and Experiential Approaches*. Thousand Oaks: Sage.

McGuigan, Jim. 2014. "The Neoliberal Self." *Culture Unbound*, 6 (February). <www.cultureunbound.ep.liu.se/v6/a13/cu14v6a13.pdf>.

McIntosh, Steve. 2012. *Evolution's Purpose: An Integral Interpretation of the Scientific Story of Our Origins*. New York: Select Books.

McMahan, David. 2016. "Neural Maps and Enlightenment Machines: Implicit Anthropologies and Epistemologies in the Scientific Approach to Mindfulness." Paper presented at the conference, "Beyond the Hype: Buddhism and Neuroscience in a New Key," November 11, Columbia University, New York.

McNamee, Sheila. 1996. "Psychotherapy as a Social Construction." In Hugh Rosen and Kevin T. Kuchlwein (eds.), *Constructing Realities: Meaning-Making Perspectives for Psychotherapists*. San Francisco: Jossey-Bass.

McWeeny, Jen. 2010. "Liberating Anger, Embodying Knowledge: A Comparative Study of Maria Lugones and Zen Master Hakuin." *Hypatia*, 25, 2.

Merton, Thomas. 1966. *Conjectures of a Guilty Bystander*. New York: Doubleday.

Millward-Hopkins, Joel. 2017. "Neoliberal Psychology." *Open Democracy*, May 8. <www.opendemocracy.net/transformation/joel-millward-hopkins/neoliberal-psychology>.

Mindful Moment Program. n.d. "Holistic Life Foundation." <hlfinc.org/services/mindful-moment-program/>.

Mindful Nation UK. 2015. "Mindfulness All-Party Parliamentary Group (MAPPG)." October. <themindfulnessinitiative.org.uk/images/reports/Mindfulness-APPG-Report_Mindful-Nation-UK_Oct2015.pdf>.

Mindful Schools. n.d. "Healthy Habits of Mind Film." <mindfulschools.org/resources/healthy-habits-of-mind/>.

Mindful Teachers. 2014. "Restorative, Not Punitive, Responses to Youthful Wrongdoing (Interview with Dr. Fania E. Davis)." August 17. <mindfulteachers.org/2014/08/restorative-not-punitive-responses-to-youthful-wrongdoing.html>.

Mindfulnet.org. n.d. "What Is Mindfulness?" <mindfulnet.org/page2.htm>.

MindUP. n.d. <mindup.org/>.

Mirk, Sarah. 2016. "Audre Lorde Thought of Self-Care as an 'Act of Political Warfare.'" *Bitchmedia,* February 18. <bitchmedia.org/article/audre-lorde-thought-self-care-act-political-warfare>.

Mitchell, Scott A. 2014. "The Tranquil Meditator: Representing Buddhism and Buddhists in US Popular Media." *Religion Compass,* 8, 3.

Mohn, Tanya. 2017. "Reading This While Walking? In Honolulu It Could Cost You." *New York Times,* October 23. <nytimes.com/2017/10/23/business/honolulu-walking-and-texting-fine.html?smid=tw-nytimes&smtyp=cur&ncid=newsltus hpmgnews__TheMorningEmail__102417&mtrref=undefined>.

Moloney, Paul. 2016. "Mindfulness: The Bottled Water of the Therapy Industry." In Ronald E. Purser, David Forbes, and Adam Burke (eds.), *Handbook of Mindfulness: Culture, Context, and Social Engagement.* New York: Springer.

----. 2013. *The Therapy Industry: The Irresistible Rise of the Talking Cure, and Why It Doesn't Work.* London: Pluto Press.

Monbiot, George. 2016a. "Neoliberalism — the Ideology at the Root of All Our Problems." *Guardian,* April 15. <theguardian.com/books/2016/apr/15/neoliberalism-ideology-problem-george-monbiot>.

----. 2016b. "The Zombie Doctrine." *George Monbiot,* April 15. <monbiot.com/2016/04/15/the-zombie-doctrine/>.

----. 2016c. "Neoliberalism Is Creating Loneliness. That's What's Wrenching Society Apart." *The Guardian,* October 12. <theguardian.com/commentisfree/2016/oct/12/neoliberalism-creating-loneliness-wrenching-society-apart>.

Morgan, Patricia Fay. 2014. "A Brief History of the Current Reemergence of Contemplative Education." *Journal of Transformative Education,* 13, 3 (December 30). <thecontemplativeacademy.com/uploads/8/6/6/4/8664369/brief_history.pdf>.

Moulier-Boutang, Yann. 2012. *Cognitive Capitalism.* Oxford: Polity Press.

Moyers, Bill. 2017. "The Dangerous Case of Donald Trump: Robert Jay Lifton and Bill Moyers on 'A Duty to Warn.'" *Bill Moyers.com,* September 14. <billmoyers.com/story/dangerous-case-donald-trump-robert-jay-lifton-bill-moyers-duty-warn/>.

Murphy, Stacy Notaris. 2012. "What's On the Radar of Today's Counselor?" *Counseling Today,* July 1. <ct.counseling.org/2012/07/whats-on-the-radar-of-todays-counselor/>.

Murray, Tom. 2009. "What Is the Integral in Integral Education? From Progressive Pedagogy to Integral Pedagogy." *Integral Review,* 5, 1 (June). <integral-review.org/backissue/vol-5-no-1-jun-2009/>.

Nathan, Linda. 2017. "Grit Isn't Enough to Help Students Overcome Poverty — and It's Time to Stop Pretending That It Is." *Alternet,* October 19. <alternet.org/grit-isnt-enough-help-students-overcome-poverty?akid=16242.2685856.0cehaO&rd=1&src=newsletter1084099&t=22>.

National Association of State Boards of Education. 2013. "From Practice to Policy: Social-Emotional Learning." October. <casel.org/wp-content/uploads/2016/06/FPP-Social-Emotional-Learning.pdf>.

National Center for Law and Policy. 2016. "Legal & Practical Concerns Regarding the District's Calmer Choice Mindfulness Curriculum." February 2. <capecodtimes.com/assets/pdf/CC190322.PDF>.

Network for Public Education. 2017. "Charters and Consequences: An Investigative Series." November 18. <right-to-education.org/sites/right-to-education.org/files/resource-attachments/NPE_Report_Charters_and_Consequences_2017_en.pdf>.

News from Brown. 2017. "Study Documents Range of Challenging Meditation Experiences." *News from Brown*, May 24. <news.brown.edu/articles/2017/05/experiences>.

Ng, Edwin. 2017. "Fuck Your Right Speech (Are You Listening?)." *Buddhist Peace Fellowship*, September 4. <buddhistpeacefellowship.org/fuck-right-speech-listening/>.

----. 2015. "Mindfulness and Justice: Planting the Seeds of a More Compassionate Future." *Religion and Ethic*, June 29. <abc.net.au/religion/articles/2015/06/29/4264094.htm>.

Ng, Edwin, and Ronald Purser. 2016. "Mindfulness and Self-Care: Why Should I Care?" *Patheos: American Buddhist Perspectives*, April 4. <patheos.com/blogs/americanbuddhist/2016/04/mindfulness-and-self-care-why-should-i-care.html>.

Nhat Hanh, Thich. 2002. *Anger: Wisdom for Cooling the Flames*. New York: Riverhead.

----. 1992. *Peace Is Every Step*. New York: Bantam.

Nhat Hanh, Thich, and Katherine Weare. 2017. *Happy Teachers Change the World: A Guide for Cultivating Mindfulness in Education*. Berkeley: Parallax Press.

Nixon, Dan. 2018. "The Battle for Our Attention: The Defining Problem of Our Time?" *Perspectiva*, August 6. <perspectivainsideout.com/2018/08/06/the-battle-for-our-attention-the-defining-problem-of-our-time/>.

Nowogrodski, Anna. 2016. "Power of Positive Thinking Skews Mindfulness Studies." *Scientific American*, April 21. <scientificamerican.com/article/power-of-positive-thinking-skews-mindfulness-studies/>.

Nussbaum, Martha. 2003. *Upheavals of Thought: The Intelligence of Emotions*. Chicago: University of Chicago Press.

Odets, Clifford. 1979. "Awake and Sing!" In *Six Plays of Clifford Odets*. New York: Grove Press.

O'Donnell, Aislinn. 2016. "Contemplative Pedagogy and Mindfulness: Developing Creative Attention in an Age of Distraction." In Oren Ergas and Sharon Todd (eds.), *Philosophy East/West: Exploring Intersections Between Educational and Contemplative Practices*. Malden: Wiley Blackwell.

O'Faolan, Anna. 2017. "Mindfulness: When Not to Use It." *Uplift*, August 3. <upliftconnect.com/mindfulness-when-not-to-use-it/>.

Oliver, Kelly. 2017. "Education in the Age of Outrage." *New York Times*, October 16. <nytimes.com/2017/10/16/opinion/education-outrage-morality-shaming.html?action=click&pgtype=Homepage&clickSource=story-heading&module=opinion-c-col-left-region&region=opinion-c-col-left-region&WT.nav=opinion-c-col-left-region&_r=0>.

Olson, Gary. 2013. "Education, Neoliberal Culture, and the Brain." *Dissident Voice*, July 6. <dissidentvoice.org/2013/07/education-neoliberal-culture-and-the-brain/>.

O'Rourke, Meghan. 2012. *The Long Goodbye: A Memoir*. New York: Riverhead.

Orr, Deborah. 2014. "In a Mindful, Moral Voice: Mindful Compassion, the Ethic of Care and Education." *Paideusis*, 21, 2. <journals.sfu.ca/pie/index.php/pie/article/view/374/201>.

----. 2002. "The Uses of Mindfulness in Anti-Oppressive Technologies: Philosophy and Praxis." *Canadian Journal of Education,* 27, 4. <files.eric.ed.gov/fulltext/ EJ728316.pdf>.

Palmer, Parker J., and Arthur Zajonc. 2010. *The Heart of Higher Education: A Call to Renewal.* San Francisco: Jossey-Bass.

Parker, Ian. 1999. "Critical Psychology: Critical Links." *Radical Psychology,* 1, 1. <radpsynet.org/journal/vol1-1/Parker.html>.

Parker-Pope, Tara. 2017. "How to Be Better at Stress." *New York Times,* July 24. <nytimes.com/guides/well/how-to-deal-with-stress?mc=aud_dev&mcid=fb-nytimes&mccr=MarLLAPP&mcdt=2018-03&subid=MarLLAPP&ad-keywords=AudDevGate>.

Paterson, Jim. 2016. "Mind Matters." *ASCA School Counselor,* 54, 1 (September/ October).

Patten, Terry. 2018a. "What It Really Means to Be 'Woke': Radical Activism Is Spiritual as Well as Political." *Alternet,* March 8. <alternet.org/activism/now-time-woke-radical-evolutionary-activism-spiritual-political?akid=16819.2685856.FMJLJd& rd=1&src=newsletter1089746&t=16>.

----. 2018b. *A New Republic of the Heart: An Ethos for Revolutionaries — A Guide to Inner Work for Holistic Change.* Berkeley: North Atlantic Books.

Patten, Terry, and Marco V. Morelli. n.d. "Occupy Integral!" <beamsandstruts.com/ articles/item/814-occupy-integral>.

Payne, Richard K. 2017. "Death of the Mindfulness Fad?" *Richard K. Payne,* January 12. <rkpayne.wordpress.com/2017/01/12/death-of-the-mindfulness-fad/>.

Penny, Laurie. 2016. "Life-Hacks of the Poor and Aimless." *The Baffler,* July 8. <thebaffler.com/blog/laurie-penny-self-care>.

Perrotta, Anthony. 2015. "Q: What Does the Quote at the End of 'Mad Max: Fury Road' Mean?" *Screenprism,* June 15. <screenprism.com/insights/article/ what-does-the-quote-at-the-end-of-mad-max-fury-road-mean>.

Petty, Sheryl (ed.). 2017. "Social Justice, Inner Work & Contemplative Practice: Lessons & Directions for Multiple Fields." *ICEA Journal,* 1, 1 (July). <contemplativemind. org/files/ICEA_vol1_2017.pdf>.

Pinar, William, and Madeline R. Grumet (eds.). 2014. *Toward a Poor Curriculum.* Kingston: Educator's International Press.

Poole, Steven. 2012. "Your Brain on Pseudoscience: The Rise of Popular Neurobollocks." *NewStatesman,* September 6. <newstatesman.com/culture/ books/2012/09/your-brain-pseudoscience-rise-popular-neurobollocks>.

Preza, Elizabeth. 2017. "Americans 'Enduring a Death Toll Equal to 9-11 Every Three Weeks' From Opioid Crisis: Report." *Rawstory,* July 31. <rawstory.com/2017/07/ americans-enduring-a-death-toll-equal-to-9-11-every-three-weeks-from-opioid-crisis-report/>.

Purpel, David. 2010. "Education in a Prophetic Voice." *Encounter: Education for Meaning and Social Justice,* Autumn. <great-ideas.org/Encounter/Purpel23(3). pdf>.

Purser, Ronald. 2015. "The Myth of the Present Moment." *Mindfulness,* 6, 3 (June). <researchgate.net/publication/272039382_The_Myth_of_the_Present_Moment>.

Purser, Ronald, and David Forbes. 2017. "How to Be Mindful of McMindfulness." *Alternet,* May 30. <alternet.org/culture/hollow-mindful-overkill-david-gelles>.

----. 2014. "Search Outside Yourself: Google Misses a Lesson in Wisdom 101." *Huffington Post,* May 5. <huffingtonpost.com/ron-purser/google-misses-a-lesson_b_4900285.html>.

Purser, Ronald, and David Loy. 2013. "Beyond McMindfulness." *Huffington Post,* July 1. <huffingtonpost.com/ron-purser/beyond-mcmindfulness_b_3519289.html>.

Purser, Ronald, and Edwin Ng. 2017. "Cutting Through the Corporate Mindfulness Hype." *Huffington Post,* December 6. <huffingtonpost.com/ron-purser/cutting-through-the-corporate-mindfulness-hype_b_9512998.html>.

----. 2015. "Corporate Mindfulness Is Bullsh*t: Zen or No Zen, You're Working Harder and Being Paid Less." *Salon,* September 27. <salon.com/2015/09/27/corporate_mindfulness_is_bullsht_zen_or_no_zen_youre_working_harder_and_being_paid_less/>.

Pyles, Loretta. 2018. *Healing Justice: Holistic Self-Care for Change Makers.* New York: Oxford University Press.

Quart, Alissa. 2017. "Faking 'Wokeness': How Advertising Targets Millennial Liberals for Profit." *The Guardian,* June 6. <theguardian.com/us-news/2017/jun/06/progressive-advertising-fake-woke>.

Rakow, Katja. 2013. "Therapeutic Culture and Religion in America." *Religion Compass,* 7, 11. <academia.edu/6467041/Therapeutic_Culture_and_Religion_in_America>.

Ravitch, Diane. 2014. *Reign of Error: The Hoax of the Privatization Movement and the Danger to America's Public Schools.* New York: Vintage.

Real, Terrence. 2017. "The Long Shadow of Trump Trauma: How it Is Threatening Our Interpersonal Relationships." *Alternet,* September 25. <alternet.org/trump-trauma/couples-therapy-age-trump?akid=16123.2685856.S2TYgE&rd=1&src=newsletter1082988&t=4>.

Ream, Amanda. 2014. "Why I Disrupted the Wisdom 2.0 Conference." *Tricycle,* February 19. <tricycle.org/blog/2014/02/19/why-i-disrupted-wisdom-20-conference/>.

Rechtschaffen, Daniel. 2014. *The Way of Mindful Education: Cultivating Well-Being in Teachers and Students.* New York: Norton

Renshaw, Tyler L., and Clayton R. Cook. 2017. "Introduction to the Special Issue: Mindfulness in the Schools — Historical Roots, Current Status, and Future Directions." *Psychology in the Schools,* 54, 1. <onlinelibrary.wiley.com/doi/10.1002/pits.21978/pdf>.

Resnick, Brian. 2017. "Is Mindfulness Meditation Good for Kids? Here's What the Science Actually Says." *Vox,* October 19. <vox.com/science-and-health/2017/5/22/13768406/mindfulness-meditation-good-for-kids-evidence>.

Reveley, James. 2016. "Neoliberal Meditations: How Mindfulness Training Medicalizes Education and Responsibilizes Young People." *Policy Futures in Education,* 14, 4 (March). <researchgate.net/publication/298795751_Neoliberal_meditations_How_mindfulness_training_medicalizes_education_and_responsibilizes_young_people>.

----. 2015. "Foucauldian Critique of Positive Education and Related Self-Technologies: Some Problems and New Directions." *Open Review of Educational Research,* 2, 1 (January 27). <tandfonline.com/doi/pdf/10.1080/23265507.2014.996768>.

Riding, Laura. 1993. *Four Unposted Letters to Catherine.* New York: Persea Books.

Rilke, Rainer Maria. 2011. "A Year with Rilke." January 6. <yearwithrilke.blogspot.com/2010/12/our-closest-friend.html>.

Robbins, Christopher G. 2004. "Racism and the Authority of Neoliberalism: A Review of Three New Books on the Persistence of Racial Inequality in a Color-blind Era." *Journal for Critical Education Policy Studies*, 2, 2.<jceps.com/wp-content/uploads/PDFs/02-2-09.pdf>.

Rodriguez, Ashley. 2016. "US Employers Are Officially Barred from Requiring Service Workers to Be Happy on the Job." *Quartz*, May 10. <https://qz.com/680243/us-employers-are-officially-barred-from-requiring-service-workers-to-be-happy-on-the-job/>.

Roeser, Robert W., David R. Vago, Cristi Pinela, Laurel S. Morris, Cynthia Taylor, and Jessica Harrison. 2014. "Contemplative Education: Cultivating Ethical Development Through Mindfulness Training." In Larry Nucci, Darcia Narvaez, and Tobias Krettenauer (eds.), *Handbook of Moral and Character Education*. New York: Routledge.

Rollins, Jonathan. 2010. "Making a Definitive Progress." *Counseling Today*, 52, 12 (June).

Rosch, Eleanor. 2008. "Beginner's Mind: Paths to the Wisdom that Is Not Learned." In Michel Ferrari and Georges Potworowski (eds.), *Teaching for Wisdom: Cross-Cultural Perspectives on Fostering Wisdom*. Hillsdale: Erlbaum. <academia.edu/24474400/Beginner_s_Mind_Paths_to_the_Wisdom_that_is_Not_Learned>.

Rose, Nikolas. 1998. *Inventing Our Selves: Psychology, Power, and Personhood*. Cambridge: University of Cambridge Press.

Rowe, James K. 2016. "Micropolitics and Collective Liberation: Mind/Body Practice and Left Social Movements." *New Political Science*, 38, 2. <cloudfront.escholarship.org/dist/prd/content/qt46n2q8mg/qt46n2q8mg.pdf>.

----. 2015. "Zen and the Art of Social Maintenance Movements." *Waging Nonviolence*, March 21. <wagingnonviolence.org/feature/mindfulness-and-the-art-of-social-movement-maintenance/>.

Rozsa, Matthew. 2018. "A Traumatic Vision of Masculinity Lies at the Root of a Resentful 'Incel' Movement." *Alternet*, November 19. <alternet.org/traumatic-vision-masculinity-lies-root-resentful-incel-movement?src=newsletter1098031>.

Ryan, Edward. 2017. "The Agony of Enlightenment." *Cushion and Couch, Institute for Meditation and Psychotherapy*, Summer. <myemail.constantcontact.com/Cushion-and-Couch--Summer-2017-.html?soid=1108653809093&aid=8wsWDTBPeAc#Ryan>.

Saari, Antti. 2017. "Emotionalities of Rule in Pedagogical Mindfulness Literature." *Journal of Management, Spirituality and Religion*, 15, 2 (August 2).

Saari, Antti, and Jani Pulkki. 2012. "'Just a Swinging Door' — Examining the Egocentric Misconception of Meditation." *Paideusis*, 20, 2. <academia.edu/4718048/Saari_A._and_Pulkki_J._2012_Just_a_Swinging_Door_Examining_the_Egocentric_Misconception_of_Meditation._Paideiusis_Vol._20_No._2_pp._15-24>.

Safran, Jeremy D. 2014. "McMindfulness: The Marketing of Well-Being." *Psychology Today*, June 13. <psychologytoday.com/blog/straight-talk/201406/mcmindfulness>.

Salinger, J.D. 1961. *Franny and Zooey*. Boston: Little Brown.

Santorelli, Saki F. 2016. "Does Mindfulness Belong in Public Schools? Two Views: Yes — Mindfulness Is a Secular Practice that Benefits Students." *Tricycle*, Spring.

<tricycle.org/magazine/does-mindfulness-belong-public-schools/>.

Satel, Sally, and Scott O. Lilienfeld. 2015. *Brainwashed: The Seductive Appeal of Mindless Neuroscience*. New York: Basic Books.

Sawyer, Keith. 2013. "Brain Imaging: What Good Is It?" *Psychology Today*, October 21. <psychologytoday.com/us/blog/zig-zag/201310/brain-imaging-what-good-is-it>.

Schnall, Marianne. 2011. "Goldie Hawn Talks 'MindUP' and Her Mission to Bring Children Happiness." *Huffington Post*, April 20. <huffingtonpost.com/marianne-schnall/goldie-hawn-mindup_b_850226.html>.

Schoenert-Reichl, Kim and Vicki Zakrzewski. 2014. "How to Close the Social-Emotional Gap in Teacher Training." *Greater Good Magazine*, January 8. <greatergood.berkeley. edu/article/item/how_to_close_the_social_emotional_gap_in_teacher_training>.

Schulson, Michael. 2016. "Put Your Money Where Your Mind Is: A For-Profit Meditation Studio Opens in New York." *Religion Dispatches*, January 21. <religiondispatches.org/put-your-money-where-your-mind-is-a-for-profit-meditation-studio-opens-in-new-york/>.

Schwartz, Katrina. 2014. "Low-Income Schools See Big Benefits in Teaching Mindfulness." *KQED Mind/Shift*, January 17. <ww2.kqed.org/mindshift/2014/01/17/low-income-schools-see-big-benefits-in-teaching-mindfulness/>.

Scofield, Be. 2012, July 7. "Why Eckhart Tolle's Evolutionary Activism Won't Save Us." *Tikkun*. <tikkun.org/tikkundaily/2012/07/07/why-eckhart-tolles-evolutionary-activism-wont-save-us/>.

Shaw, Tamsin. 2016. "The Psychologists Take Power." *New York Review of Books,* February 25. <politique-actu.com/dossier/psychologists-take-power-tamsin-shaw/1584533/>.

Sheridan, Kate. 2017. "'Mindfulness' is a Meaningless Word with Shoddy Science Behind It." *Newsweek*, October 11. <newsweek.com/mindfulness-meaningless-word-shoddy-science-behind-it-682008>.

Sherrell, Carla, and Judith Simmer-Brown. 2017. "Spiritual Bypassing in the Contemporary Mindfulness Movement." *Initiative for Contemplation Equity and Action Journal*, 1, 1 (July). <contemplativemind.org/files/ICEA_vol1_2017.pdf>.

Shonin, Edo. 2015. "'This Is Not McMindfulness by Any Stretch of the Imagination.'" Interview with Jon Kabat-Zinn. *The Psychologist: The British Psychological Society,* May 18. <thepsychologist.bps.org.uk/not-mcmindfulness-any-stretch-imagination>.

Shore, Cris, and Susan Wright. 2000. "Coercive Accountability: The Rise of Audit Culture in Higher Education." In Marilyn Strathern (ed.), *Audit Cultures: Anthropological Studies in Accountability, Ethics and the Academy*. London: Routledge. <researchgate. net/profile/Cris_Shore/publication/245682716_Coercive_accountability_the_rise_of_audit_culture_in_higher_education/links/557ed48d08aeea18b7795367/Coercive-accountability-the-rise-of-audit-culture-in-higher-education>.

Shriver, Timothy P., and John M.Bridgeland. 2015. "Social-Emotional Learning Pays Off." *Education Week*, February 26. <edweek.org/ew/articles/2015/02/26/social-emotional-learning-pays-off.html>.

Simmer-Brown, Judith. 1987. "Pratītyasamutpāda: Seeing the Dependent Origination of Suffering as the Key to Liberation." *Journal of Contemplative Psychotherapy*, 4. <windhorseguild.org/pdf/jcp/vol_4/Pratityasamutpada,%20Vol%204.pdf>.

Simpson, Daniel. 2017. "From Me to We: Revolutionising Mindfulness in Schools." *Contemporary Buddhism*, March 13. <danielsimpson.info/archive/

mindfulness-in-schools-constructive-critique>.

Singer, Natasha. 2017. "Silicon Valley Courts Brand-Name Teachers, Raising Ethics Issues." *New York Times*, September 2. <nytimes.com/2017/09/02/technology/silicon-valley-teachers-tech.html>.

Slaby, Jan. 2010. "The Brain Is What We Do With It. Review of C. Malabou 'What Should We Do With Our Brain?'" *Journal of Consciousness Studies,* 17. <janslaby.com/downloads/malabou_review_slaby2.pdf>.

Slaten, Christopher D., Decoteau J. Irby, Kevin Tate, and Roberto Rivera. 2015. "Towards a Critically Conscious Approach to Social and Emotional Learning in Urban Alternative Education: School Staff Members' Perspectives." *Journal for Social Action in Counseling and Psychology,* 7, 1. <researchgate.net/publication/281783350_Towards_a_Critically_Conscious_Approach_to_Social_and_Emotional_Learning_in_Urban_Alternative_Education_School_Staff_Members%27_Perspectives>.

Smail, David. 2012. *Power, Interest and Psychology: Elements of a Social Materialist Understanding of Distress.* Ross-on-Wye: PCCS Books.

Smith, David Geoffrey. 2014. *Teaching as the Practice of Wisdom.* New York: Bloomsbury.

Solnit, Rebecca. 2018. "All the Rage: What a Literature that Embraces Female Anger Can Achieve." *The New Republic*, September 24. <newrepublic.com/article/151100/rebecca-solnit-book-review-women-rage>.

Spirit Rock Meditation Center. 2015. Angela Davis & Jon Kabat-Zinn. Video. April 21. <eventbrite.com/e/video-of-angela-davis-jon-kabat-zinn-east-bay-meditation-center-benefit-tickets-16355428527#>.

Stanley, Elizabeth A. 2014. "Mindfulness-Based Mind Fitness Training (MMFT): An Approach for Enhancing Performance and Building Resilience in High Stress Contexts." In Amanda Ie, Christelle T. Ngnoumen, and Ellen J. Langer (eds.), *The Wiley-Blackwell Handbook of Mindfulness.* London: Wiley-Blackwell.

Stanley, Steven. 2012. "Mindfulness: Towards a Critical Relational Perspective." *Social and Personality Psychology Compass,* 6 (September 5).

Stanley, Steven, Meg Barker, Victoria Edwards, and Emma McEwen. 2014. "Swimming Against the Stream? Mindfulness as a Psychosocial Research Methodology." *Qualitative Research in Psychology.* <orca.cf.ac.uk/68206/1/Stanley%20Barker%20Edwards%20McEwen%20accepted%20manuscript%20for%20ORCA.pdf>.

Stanley, Steven, Victoria Edwards, Barbara Ibinarriaga-Soltero, and Grace Krause. 2018. "Awakening Psychology: Investigating Everyday Life with Social Mindfulness." *Sage Research Methods Cases.* <dx.doi.org/10.4135/9781526440853>.

Stanley, Steven, and Charlotte Longden. 2016. "Constructing the Mindful Subject: Reformulating Experience Through Affective-Discursive Practice in Mindfulness-Based Stress Reduction." In Ronald E. Purser, David Forbes, and Adam Burke (eds.), *Handbook of Mindfulness: Culture, Context, and Social Engagement.* New York: Springer.

Stein, Sadie. 2012. "Singular, Difficult, Shadowed, Brilliant." *The Paris Review*, October 20. <theparisreview.org/blog/2012/10/30/singular-difficult-shadowed-brilliant/>.

Steinbeck, John. 2002. *East of Eden.* New York: Penguin.

----. 1977. *The Grapes of Wrath.* New York: Penguin.

Steinmetz-Jenkins, Daniel. 2017. "Is Atheism the Reason for Ta-Nehisi Coates'

Pessimism on Race Relations?" *The Guardian,* October 22. <theguardian.com/ commentisfree/2017/oct/22/atheism-ta-nehisi-coates-pessimism-race-relations>.

Stephens, Jordan. 2017. "Toxic Masculinity Is Everywhere. It's Up to Us Men to Fix This." *The Guardian,* October 23. <www.theguardian.com/commentisfree/2017/ oct/23/toxic-masculinity-men-privilege-emotions-rizzle-kicks>.

Stergiopoulos, Erene. 2017. "The New Chronic." *Hazlitt,* February 10. <hazlitt.net/ feature/new-chronic>.

Stetsenko, Anna. 2015. "Theory for and as Social Practice of Realizing the Future: Implications from a Transformative Activist Stance." In Jack Martin, Jeff Sugarman, and Kathleen L. Slaney (eds.), *The Wiley Handbook of Theoretical and Philosophical Psychology: Methods, Approaches, and New Directions.* New York: John Wiley and Sons. <academia.edu/28983426/Theory_for_and_as_Social_Practice_of_ Realizing_the_Future_Implications_from_a_Transformative_Activist_Stance>.

Strain, Charles R. 2018. "Borrowing a Prophetic Voice, Actualizing the Prophetic Dimension: Rita Gross and Engaged Buddhism." *Journal of Buddhist Ethics,* 25. <blogs.dickinson.edu/buddhistethics/files/2018/11/Strain-prophetic-voice-final. pdf>.

Szalavitz, Maia. 2012. "Q&A: Jon Kabat-Zinn Talks About Bringing Mindfulness Meditation to Medicine." *Time,* January 11. <healthland.time.com/2012/01/11/ mind-reading-jon-kabat-zinn-talks-about-bringing-mindfulness-meditation-to-medicine/>.

Tabaka, Marla. 2017. "Here's What's Possibly Causing Your Smartphone Separation Anxiety." *Inc.,* April 12. <inc.com/marla-tabaka/brain-hacking-why-you-have-smartphone-separation-anxiety.html>.

Tadlock-Marlo, Rebecca L. 2011. "Making Minds Matter: Infusing Mindfulness and School Counseling." *Faculty Research & Creative Activity,* 29. <thekeep.eiu.edu/ cgi/viewcontent.cgi?article=1028&context=csd_fac>.

Taffel, Ron. 2014. "Are Therapists Seeing a New Kind of Attachment?" *AlterNet,* November 6. <alternet.org/how-modern-life-making-us-addicted-and-insane?>.

Tang, Yi-Yuan, Britta K. Hölzel, and Michael I. Posner. 2015. "The Neuroscience of Mindfulness Meditation." *Nature Reviews Neuroscience,* 16, 4 (March 18). <researchgate.net/publication/273774412_The_neuroscience_of_ mindfulness_meditation>.

Taubman, Peter. 2009. *Teaching by Numbers: Deconstructing the Discourse of Standards and Accountability in Education.* New York: Routledge.

Thompson, Evan. 2016. "iscs Closing Keynote: What Is Mindfulness? An Embodied Cognitive Science Perspective." *Mind and Life Institute,* December 6. <youtube. com/watch?v=Q17_A0CYa8s>.

----. 2001. "Empathy and Consciousness." *Journal of Consciousness Studies,* 8, 5–7. <evanthompsondotme.files.wordpress.com/2012/11/jcs-empathy.pdf>.

Tillich, Paul. 1967. *My Search for Absolutes.* New York: Simon & Schuster.

Time for Me. 2019. Catalogue. <timeformecatalog.com/search.html?brand= Mindful%20Minerals&hawka=1>.

Tlalka, Stephany. 2016. "The Trouble with Mindfulness Apps." *Mindful,* August 10. <mindful.org/trouble-mindfulness-apps/>.

Tricycle. 2012. "Aren't We Right to Be Angry?" *Tricycle,* Summer. <tricycle.org/magazine/ arent-we-right-be-angry/?utm_source=Tricycle&utm_campaign=4ab1d91848-

Daily_Dharma_01_23_2017&utm_medium=email&utm_term=0_1641abe55e-4ab1d91848-307825233>.

Tveten, Julianne. 2018. "First Silicon Valley Sold You Social Media — Now It's Trying to Sell You the Antidote." *Alternet,* March 8. <alternet.org/news-amp-politics/silicon-valley-controlling-your-media?akid=16819.2685856.FMJLJd&rd=1&src=newsletter1089746&t=30>.

Tweedy, Rod. 2017. *The Political Self: Understanding the Context for Mental Illness.* London: Karnac.

Twenge, Jean M. 2017. "Have Smartphones Destroyed a Generation?" *Atlantic,* September. <theatlantic.com/magazine/archive/2017/09/has-the-smartphone-destroyed-a-generation/534198/?utm_source=atlfb)>.

Ueda, Noriyuki. 2013. "The (Justifiably) Angry Marxist: An Interview with the Dalai Lama." *Tricycle,* August 29. <tricycle.org/trikedaily/justifiably-angry-marxist-interview-dalai-lama/?utm_source=Tricycle&utm_campaign=173cb8cac3-D>.

Van Dam, Nicholas T. and Nick Haslam. 2017. "What Is Mindfulness? Nobody Really Knows, and That's a Problem." *The Conversation,* October 10. <theconversation.com/what-is-mindfulness-nobody-really-knows-and-thats-a-problem-83295?utm_source=facebook&utm_medium=facebookbutton>.

Van Dam, Nicholas T., Marieke K. van Vugt, David R. Vago, Laura Schmalzl, Clifford D. Saron, Andrew Olendzki, et al. 2017. "Mind the Hype: A Critical Evaluation and Prescriptive Agenda for Research on Mindfulness and Meditation." *Perspectives on Psychological Science,* October 10. <journals.sagepub.com/doi/10.1177/1745691617709589>.

Van Gordon, William, and Mark D. Griffiths. 2015. "For Mindful Teaching of Mindfulness: A Letter in Response to Our Exclusive Online Interview with Jon Kabat-Zinn." *The Psychologist: The British Psychological Society,* July. <thepsychologist.bps.org.uk/volume-28/july-2015/mindful-teaching-mindfulness>.

Varela, Francisco. J. 1999. *Ethical Know-How: Action, Wisdom, and Cognition.* Palo Alto: Stanford University Press.

Vaznis, James. 2016. "In Mass. Schools, a Focus on Well-Being." *Boston Globe,* January 5. <bostonglobe.com/metro/2016/01/05/mass-schools-focus-well-being/m4d2GADYQEor4qApNf8JQM/story.html>.

Veroufakis, Yanis. 2017. "A New Deal for the 21st Century." *New York Times,* July 6. <nytimes.com/2017/07/06/opinion/yanis-varoufakis-a-new-deal-for-the-21st-century.html?action=click&pgtype=Homepage&clickSource=story-heading&module=opinion-c-col-right-region&region=opinion-c-col-right-region&WT.nav=opinion-c-col-right-region&_r=0>.

Von Stamwitz, Alicia. 2012. "If Only We Would Listen: Parker J. Palmer on What We Could Learn about Politics, Faith, and Each Other." *The Sun,* November. <thesunmagazine.org/issues/443/if-only-we-would-listen>.

Wallace, David Foster. 2005. "Transcription of the Kenyon Commencement Address." <web.ics.purdue.edu/~drkelly/DFWKenyonAddress2005.pdf>.

Wallis, Glenn. 2014. "Mineful Response and the Rise of Corporatist Spirituality." *Speculative Non-Buddhism,* February 17. <speculativenonbuddhism.com/2014/02/17/mineful-response-and-the-rise-of-corporatist-spirituality/>.

Walton, Alice G. 2016. "The Many Benefits of Meditation for Children." *Forbes,* October 18. <forbes.com/sites/alicegwalton/2016/10/18/the-many-

benefits-of-meditation-for-children/#627c8dfdbe33>.

Waters, Lea, Adam Barsky, Amanda Ridd, and Kelly Allen. 2015. "Contemplative Education: A Systematic, Evidence-Based Review of the Effect of Meditation Interventions in Schools." *Educational Psychology Review, 27,* 1 (March). <link. springer.com/article/10.1007/s10648-014-9258-2>.

Way, Katie. 2017. "G20 Protesters Overtake Hamburg as 'Zombies.'" *Inverse,* July 6. <inverse.com/article/33803-zombie-art-collective-protest-g20-summit?utm_source=facebook.com&utm_medium=on_site&utm_campaign=desktop_article-top>.

Welwood, John. 2011. "Human Nature, Buddha Nature: On Spiritual Bypassing, Relationship, and the Dharma. An interview with John Welwood by Tina Fossella." Spring. <johnwelwood.com/articlesandinterviews.htm>.

Whippman, Ruth 2017. *America the Anxious: Why Our Search for Happiness Is Driving Us Crazy and How to Find It for Real.* New York: St. Martin's Griffin.

----. 2016. "Actually, Let's Not Be in the Moment." *New York Times,* November 26. <nytimes.com/2016/11/26/opinion/sunday/actually-lets-not-be-in-the-moment. html?_r=0>.

Wickelgren, Ingrid. 2012. "How Social and Emotional Learning Could Harm Our Kids." *Scientific American,* November 27. <blogs.scientificamerican. com/streams-of-consciousness/how-social-emotional-learning-could-harm-our-kids/>.

Wieczner, Jen. 2016. "Meditation Has Become a Billion-Dollar Business." *Fortune,* March 12. <fortune.com/2016/03/12/meditation-mindfulness-apps/>.

Wilber, Ken. 2016. *Integral Meditation: Mindfulness as a Path to Grow Up, Wake Up, and Show Up in Your Life.* Boston: Shambhala.

----. 2007. "Sidebar E: The Genius Descartes Gets a Postmodern Drubbing." *Kenwilber. com.* <kenwilber.com/Writings/PDF/E-Descartes.pdf>.

----. 2006. *Integral Spirituality: A Startling New Role for Religion in the Modern and Postmodern World.* Boston: Shambhala.

----. 2005. "Integral Spirituality in Real Life." *Beliefnet.* <beliefnet.com/inspiration/angels/2005/05/integral-spirituality-in-real-life.aspx>.

----. 2000. *Integral Psychology: Consciousness, Spirit, Psychology, Therapy.* Boston: Shambhala.

----. 1999. *One Taste: The Journals of Ken Wilber.* Boston: Shambhala.

----. 1998. *The Marriage of Sense and Soul: Integrating Science and Religion.* New York: Random House.

Williams, Camille. 2017. "When Spiritual Bypassing Meets Racism Meets Gaslighting." October 17. <camillewilliams.net/2017/10/17/when-spiritual-bypassing-meets-racism-meets-gaslighting/>.

Williams, Monica T. 2013. "Can Racism Cause PTSD? Implications for DSM-5." *Psychology Today,* May 20. <psychologytoday.com/blog/culturally-speaking/201305/can-racism-cause-ptsd-implications-dsm-5>.

Wilson, Jeff. 2014. *Mindful America: The Mutual Transformation of Buddhist Meditation and American Culture.* New York: Oxford University Press.

Winn, Patrick. 2015. "The Slave Labor Behind Your Favorite Clothing Brands: Gap, H&M and More Exposed." *Salon,* March 22. <salon.com/2015/03/22/the_slave_labor_behind_your_favorite_clothing_brands_gap_hm_and_more_exposed_partner/>.

Witt, Keith. 2017. "The (Positive) Power of Shadow." February 13. <drkeithwitt.com/positive-power-shadow/>.

----. 2014. *Integral Mindfulness: Clueless to Dialed in — How Integral Mindful Living Makes Everything Better.* Tucson, AZ: Integral Publishers.

Wittgenstein, Ludwig. 1980. *Culture and Value.* Translated by Peter Winch. Chicago: University of Chicago Press.

Woods, Jr., Robert H., and Kevin Healey (eds.). 2013. *Prophetic Critique and Popular Media: Theoretical Foundations and Practical Applications.* New York: Peter Lang.

Woolf, Virginia. 1985. *Moments of Being.* New York: Harcourt.

Wootson Jr., Cleve R. 2017. "Rev. William Barber Builds a Moral Movement." *Washington Post*, June 29. <washingtonpost.com/news/acts-of-faith/wp/2017/06/29/woe-unto-those-who-legislate-evil-rev-william-barber-builds-a-moral-movement/?utm_term=.d45df6b5cae7>.

Worthen, Molly. 2018. "The Misguided Drive to Measure 'Learning Outcomes.'" *New York Times*, February 23. <nytimes.com/2018/02/23/opinion/sunday/colleges-measure-learning-outcomes.html?action=click&pgtype=Homepage&clickSource=story-heading&module=opinion-c-col-right-region&region=opinion-c-col-right-region&WT.nav=opinion-c-col-right-region>.

Wortman, Camille. 2011. "Positive Emotions: Do They Have a Role in the Grieving Process?" *This Emotional Life.* <thisemotionallife.org/blogs/positive-emotions-do-they-have-role-grieving-process>.

Wray, Amanda, and Ameena Batada. 2017. "Contemplative Pedagogy: Equipping Students for Everyday Social Activism." *The Arrow*, 4, 2 (April). <arrow-journal.org/wp-content/uploads/2017/05/A.Wray-A.Batada-Contemplative-Pedagogy-Vol.4.2.pdf>.

Wright, Megh. 2017. "RIP Dick Gregory." *Vulture*, August 21. <vulture.com/2017/08/rip-dick-gregory.html>.

Wright, Robert. 2016. "American Foreign Policy Has an Empathy Problem." *The Nation*, December 21. <thenation.com/article/american-foreign-policy-has-an-empathy-problem/>.

Yahm, Sarah. 2018. "Prescribing Mindfulness Allows Doctors to Ignore Legitimate Female Pain." *Slate,* February 5. <slate.com/technology/2018/02/doctors-are-increasingly-pushing-mindfulness-on-chronic-pain-patients.html>.

Yosso, T.J. 2005. "Whose Culture Has Capital?" *Race, Ethnicity and Education,* 8, 1 (March). <artslb.org/wp-content/uploads/2017/05/Whose-culture-has-capital-A-critical-race-theory-discussion-of-community-cultural-wealth-Tara-Yosso.pdf>.

Zakrzewski, Vicki. 2016. "Why Don't Students Take Social-Emotional Learning Home?" *Greater Good Magazine*, March 31. <greatergood.berkeley.edu/article/item/why_dont_students_take_social_emotional_learning_home>.

----. 2015. "Social-Emotional Learning: Why Now?" *Greater Good Magazine,* January 7. <greatergood.berkeley.edu/article/item/social_emotional_learning_why_now>.

----. 2014. "A Paradigm Shift in Education: Social-Emotional Learning." *SEEN Magazine,* November 23. <seenmagazine.us/Articles/Article-Detail/ArticleId/4397/A-Paradigm-Shift-in-Education>.

Index

academic success, focus on, 92–94, 101, 144, 148, 150, 190

"acting up," 199

activism, political, 6, 73–74, 98, 115, 124, 189, 194, 197–99

Adams, Tristam Vivian, 163

addiction, 127, 130–33, 142, 163
  alcoholism, 123, 127, 130–31
  opioids, prescription, 128, 131
  social media, 16, 128, 133, 176
  substance abuse, 73, 110, 123, 130–31, 185, 191, 202

African-Americans, 6, 151, 157, 186
  anger and stress, 73, 128, 161, 189
  racism, 122, 124, 126, 149, 200

agape (union with absolute), 48–49, 205

alcoholism, *see* addiction

alienation, societal, 4, 16, 64–65, 119, 139
  individualism, 12, 112
  school, 18, 132, 148, 188, 191

Allah, 115

Already Dead, The (Cazdyn), 140

"alternative facts," 46

America the Anxious (Whippman), 39

American culture, 53, 82–83, 89, 99, 141, 168, 193, 204

American Dream, thwarted, 73, 123–24, 127–28

Ancient One, the, 42

Andersen, Kurt, 99

anger, 99, 165, 185–86, 203
  ego attachment, 72–73, 84
  as healthy, 65, 68–69, 72, 74
  individualized, 68–69, 147, 163, 184
  judgment of, 74–77
  justified, 12, 68–72, 74, 124, 150, 197, 203
  management, 40, 69–71, 94, 148, 155, 201

anti-racism, 2, 124–25, 200

anti-war movement, 3

anxiety, 39, 102, 132
  isolation, 127, 142, 163, 184
  neoliberalism, 120–23, 134–35, 138–39, 173
  social media, 133, 176
  in youth, 16, 95, 147, 185, 189, 193, 201–4

Aristotle, 38

Assad, Bashar al-, 162–63

assessment, outcomes, 32, 95, 120, 157, 201

Association for Contemplative Mind in Higher Education, 171

atheism, 115–16

attention, 172, 201
  choice, 79–86
  economy, 16–18, 132, 135, 141, 173, 193
  individualism, 27, 94
  interiority, 100, 151–52
  paying, 4, 16, 19–21, 31, 50, 52, 89, 92, 183
  regulation of, 17–18, 26, 94, 122, 143–44, 148
  training, 158–59, 164–65, 175, 189–90, 199
  unwanted, 63, 129

audit culture, 120–22, 145, 148

austerity culture, 26–27, 120–21

authenticity,
  lack of, 75
  struggle for, 3, 64, 70, 85

Awake and Sing!, 5–6